LEARNING IN INFANTS AND YOUNG CHILDREN

MICHAEL HOWE

Lecturer in Psychology, University of Exeter

M

First published 1975 by
THE MACMILLAN PRESS LTD
London and Basingstoke
Associated companies in New York Dublin Melbourne Johannesburg and Madras

SBN 333 18783 0 (hard cover)
333 18784 9 (paper cover)

Printed in Great Britain by
THE ANCHOR PRESS LTD
Tiptree, Essex

LEARNING IN INFANTS AND YOUNG CHILDREN

for Sylvia, Nicholas and Lucy

Contents

Preface

It has been remarked that each generation is only twenty years removed from barbarism, the implication being that the maintenance of civilisation is heavily dependent on what each of us learns during our childhood. In recent years attempts to understand the nature of human learning processes have been aided by the increasing use of scientific methods and procedures, and a body of knowledge concerning the processes and mechanisms of learning in the human species is steadily accumulating.

This book is about learning in infants and young children. It is aimed at all those who have an interest in how the young are influenced by the world they experience. Teachers, psychologists and others who are professionally or personally involved with the growth, development and social welfare of the young may benefit from the knowledge of early learning that research has made available.

The book tries to show how learning processes are closely involved in the events that lead to human development and a child's acquisition of crucial abilities. I have made an effort to place the findings of empirical investigations of learning squarely into the context of the developing child. At the same time I have kept in mind the importance of seeing each child as an individual and I have attempted to show how early variations in learning contribute to individual differences that influence later life.

The book begins with an Introduction, which first indicates the centrality and importance of learning in human life, and mentions a number of frequently raised practical questions. It discusses the plasticity of man, pointing out inadequacies in the notion that man has a fixed, innate 'human nature'. The fact that early learning is determined both by individual characteristics of the learner and by attributes of his environment is illustrated, and there is a brief description of alternative approaches to understanding learning in infants and young children.

Chapter 1 describes how learning in young infants is influenced by the characteristics of the child at birth. Right from the beginning, what the infant acquires through experience is limited as much by the existing capacities of the learner as by the stimulation provided by the environment in which he is placed. Learning is partly determined by mechanisms such as the sensory receptors, which are largely formed before birth, and in which post-natal development is relatively stable in the face of environmental differences. Further pre-formed influences on learning are suggested by the presence of some apparently endogenous patterns and rhythms observed in young infants. Certain signalling responses which appear to have important functions for the infant are described. Chapter 1 also examines some forms of learning in the very young, showing the earliest effects of experience as a modifier of human performance.

Chapter 2 surveys the evidence produced by experimental investigations of learning in infants. It describes the research methods that have been used and the major forms of learning that have been studied, classical conditioning, operant conditioning and habituation. The concept of reinforcement is introduced, and phenomena such as extinction and certain experimental artefacts are discussed. Chapter 2 also considers some remarks about the assumption of the equivalence of associability, and extends discussion about different kinds of approaches to the understanding of human learning.

Chapter 3 considers some theoretical issues that are important in psychology, and it may be omitted by readers whose main concern is for knowledge of direct practical value. This chapter examines in greater detail the concept of reinforcement, and surveys the impact of early learning on the infant. A discussion concerning the representativeness of the kinds of learning that have been examined in experimental research leads to the topic of perceptual learning. A range and variety of reinforcing events is surveyed, and different ways of classifying reinforcers are considered. Knowledge about the reinforcing qualities of various events is used by some psychologists as a basis for making inferences about the kinds of mechanisms that may underlie observed behaviour; a contrasting behaviourist approach to the classification of reinforcing events is also introduced.

The mother's important role in early social learning is considered in chapter 4. It is explained that the infant first has to learn to recognise its mother. Subsequent separation causes distress and in some circumstances, it has been claimed, long-lasting ill-effects. Observational studies are described. These have been undertaken in order to acquire a detailed knowledge of patterns of interaction between mother and child. The mother contributes to a variety of the child's needs, some of which depend on regular and close interaction with an adult. It is suggested that data from the observational studies of mother–infant interaction, through which bonds of attachment are formed, may help explain the ill-effects observed in studies of the effects of maternal deprivation.

Chapter 5 draws attention to the role of language in young children's learning. In a brief discussion of the contribution of learning to the child's acquisition of language it is suggested that learning is clearly essential but that unlearned mechanisms are also involved. The function of language for learning is seen to alter as the child becomes older. At first, precise linguistic control over behaviour is noticeably absent. However, language comes to have a useful labelling function. Later on, increasingly sophisticated mediating processes become available, so that, by using language as a basis of reasoning, a child's capacity for acquiring information and solving problems is remarkably increased

Chapter 6 extends the description of social learning commenced in chapter 4. It considers the dependence of much learning on an individual's ability to observe other people, and the frequent involvement of imitation. The concept of identification is used to describe, and sometimes to explain, certain social learning phenomena, and it is emphasised that most kinds of learning, especially those involving observation, require the learner to have developed efficient strategies of attending to significant events. Reinforcement is another important factor in social learning, and this is illustrated by descriptions of the application of behaviour-modification techniques to practical problems that concern social behaviour. Finally, there is some discussion of the role of social learning in the acquisition of aggressive behaviour. It is suggested that such behaviour is typically preceded by an abundance of opportunities to learn to act aggressively.

Chapter 7 is concerned with differences between individuals in human learning. Following a discussion of the manner in which learning contributes cumulatively to the young human, evidence on individual differences from three sources is considered. The first source is research on mental retardation, which has given rise to a number of hypotheses about underlying differences in what individuals acquire through learning. The second source of evidence is research on social class, and in the research that is surveyed there is considerable emphasis on the importance of linguistic factors in learning. There is some discussion of

Bernstein's suggestions concerning the possible importance of class-related language differences. Cross-cultural research provides the third source of evidence about the factors underlying individual differences in performance. There is some discussion of changing ideas about the relationships between thought and culture, and learning is compared in literate and non-literate societies.

The final chapter discusses attempts that have been made to apply knowledge about learning to the acceleration of rates at which knowledge and skills are acquired. Individuals with extraordinary learning abilities are often found to have benefited from unusually stimulating early environments. Information about such individuals is introduced in discussing the issues concerned with the acceleration of learning in normal children. There has also been interest in the possibility of providing compensatory educational experience for children who have been deprived of some of the opportunities for early learning that appear to be necessary for success at school, and after a broad discussion of human plasticity, a number of such compensatory programmes are described, and the findings of their effects are summarised. Two fairly recent innovations are mentioned. One, the use of teaching machines, has had rather limited success, but it is suggested that the future impact of a second innovation, computer-assisted instruction, may be considerably larger.

I am very grateful to Dr Harry Kay, who read a version of the manuscript and made numerous helpful suggestions. I would also like to thank Professor Brian Foss, who gave valued encouragement, and Mrs Margaret Topham, who cheerfully drew upon her considerable typing skills.

Introduction

We are all aware of the importance of learning to man. Psychologists seek to understand the ways in which a person's nature is influenced by his interactions with his environment. It is the intention of this book to show how scientific methods have been used to investigate learning in infants and young children.

Learning is as basic an activity for humans as are breathing and walking. Many people possess a good deal of commonsense knowledge about how children learn, since at one time or another most of us are involved not only in our own learning but in helping others acquire knowledge and skills, and humans are constantly learning from each other. It is by no means only those of us who are formally dubbed 'teachers' that have a role in such interactions. In fact, most people learn considerably more from their mothers than from anyone else.

Society makes numerous demands for knowledge about human learning. Various practical questions have been raised. For instance : how can skills and knowledge most easily be acquired? To what extent is it possible to accelerate normal rates of learning? Can we compensate for early environmental impoverishment? It is reasonable to suppose that findings of psychological research will contribute towards answers to these questions, but scientific knowledge cannot solve some of the most important problems that concern human learning. Experimental research can no more decide 'What is worth learning?' than can biological knowledge answer questions about the meaning of life.

In some instances the value of scientific research into human learning lies in extending and clarifying established knowledge. For example, much was known about the effects of reward and punishment on human behaviour before any systematic investigation was undertaken. Such research has confirmed some widespread beliefs about reward and punishment, has contradicted others, and has encouraged the consistent application of simple principles that have led to the valuable practical gains associated with procedures such as 'behaviour modification'.

In other instances the findings of research into human learning have been strongly at variance with existing beliefs and practices. Thus, for several generations infants have been placed in institutional care on the assumption that the fulfilment of physical needs would ensure their well-being. However, the results of systematic enquiries indicate that this is not so. It appears that for normal development young children need to live in environments where they can take part in frequent, regular interactions with individual adults.

1.1 THE PLASTICITY OF MAN

A broad concern about human learning is expressed in questions about the adaptability, or 'plasticity', of man. To what extent is there a fixed 'human nature' that emerges irrespective of the particular events and environmental forces that an individual experiences? The future survival of mankind may depend on the willingness of people to inhibit aggressive and violent forms of behaviour. Yet it has been claimed that human aggression and violence are inevitable, since they form part of a fixed, innate, 'human nature'. If this is correct, the increasing potency that technology gives to aggressive forces may soon have disastrous consequences.

Fortunately evidence suggests that human nature is not a fixed innate quantity but the product of complex biological and environmental factors, among which learning is of considerable importance. But, as Eisenberg (1972) points out, human behaviour can be strongly influenced by our own beliefs about human nature: what we choose to believe about the nature of man has important social consequences. Eisenberg emphasises the danger of 'myth and pseudoknowledge', by which man's nature is regarded as having innately self-destructive components. He quotes statements by Freud and Konrad Lorenz to the effect that human aggression is inborn, and notes that the so-called evidence they provide for this view ignores important differences and misrepresents analogy for homology. He points out that the mere observation that aggressive behaviour in man is similar in some respects to innately mediated behaviour in other species justifies no conclusions about the mechanisms underlying human behaviour.

Eisenberg states that beliefs about human nature can act as self-fulfilling prophecies. As an illustration, he points out that when the 'nature' of insanity was thought to be violent and inmates in asylums were chained and beaten they did indeed behave violently. With changing conceptions of insanity, treatment was altered and violent symptoms decreased considerably. Later, when the insane were seen as socially incompetent by nature and were 'protected' from the outside world, they developed various symptoms of institutionalisation, such as compliance, dependence, and an inability to make decisions. There is ample evidence to show that the appearance of aggressive behaviour is preceded by an abundance of opportunities for learning. Eisenberg notes that the ubiquity of violence – and violence that is seen to be successful – in Western society guarantees opportunities for children to learn it. And if learning cannot account for all instances of human aggression, the social forces leading to its acquisition 'are so evident that preoccupation with hypothesised biological factors is almost quixotic' (Eisenberg, 1972, p. 127). This appears to be true for many kinds of complex human behaviour. It is in the nature of members of the human species to walk, to see, to breathe, and so on, as long as certain naturally occurring conditions are met, but the acquisition of most of the more specifically 'human' aspects of human behaviour is highly dependent on the availability of opportunities for learning.

1.2 LEARNING AND THE LEARNER

A number of generalisations can be made about learning, for example the principle of reinforcement: that certain kinds of environmental enrichment can bring about increases in the rate of learning. It would be possible for a list of such generalisations or principles to form the basis of a book about learning, but this would be inadequate for communicating an understanding of the nature and function of learning in infants and young children. A major reason is that learning in humans must be seen as a cumulative process, bringing about progressive changes in the learner. To be able to make any statements or practical suggestions concerning how something is to be learned, we have to know a certain amount about the nature of the learner.

The inadequacy of making generalisations from simple principles as a basis for an approach to understanding human learning is illustrated by the following example, taken from research into learning in young infants. The points it illustrates could be drawn from investigations studying children of any age. B. L. White and his colleagues at Harvard University have carried out a body of experiments investigating the acquisition by infants of the skills involved in 'prehension', that is, the ability to reach for objects and to grasp and hold them (White, 1971). In particular, they have examined visually guided reaching, and have observed steps involved in the infant's acquisition of the ability to integrate visual perception and motor behaviour, so that he becomes able to reach out and grasp something he sees. Visually guided reaching is extremely important for man, since manipulation of his environment is largely dependent on the ability to control the movements of objects. Reaching for and holding objects is essential for tool-using and tool-making, and these activities were as important to man's evolution as they are to his present functioning.

At birth, infants are completely lacking in prehensile abilities, yet by about six months most children are able to pick up a wooden cube placed in front of them. To do so involves more than a few simple responses. Try to imagine building a machine to perform the same functions: to detect an object and using this information to make contact, grasp and hold it. In children this ability is acquired through learning, although certain maturational processes place a limit on the rate of acquisition. The acquisition of the necessary skills involves the progressive modification of initially simple 'reflex' motor patterns, and the increasing integration of originally separate actions. Activities thus become more highly organised, and increasingly selective in operation, so that the infant acquires both an increasing range of skills and increasing control over his existing repertoire.

One of White's concerns has been whether it is possible to accelerate infants' acquisition of visually guided reaching abilities. In a series of experiments infants have been provided with opportunities for increased practice in some of the component skills that are known to be involved in guided reaching. Prominent among these underlying skills is visual attention. Infants have to acquire the ability to give prolonged attention to objects in the environment: they cannot do this at birth. Accordingly, White provided attractive visual stimuli, and these were successful in that infants exposed to them made longer visual fixations than infants not exposed to them. However, infants who received this 'visual enrichment' treatment were actually slower than the others in achieving a fixed standard of performance in the task of visually guided reaching. Paradoxically, then, practice in an important sub-skill appeared to delay rather than accelerate progress in the acquisition of reaching skills.

However, the situation is only paradoxical under the assumption that the acquisition of a compound skill is simply a matter of adding together its components, just as one mixes together milk, eggs and flour to make a cake. In fact, in the learning of complex human abilities circumstances are, generally speaking, very different. The *sequencing* of events is also crucial. It is important not only that the individual is exposed to environmental stimulation, but that particular kinds of stimulation occur at appropriate times. The cumulative nature of learning makes this necessary. In the case of sophisticated skills, such as those encountered in mathematics, it is taken for granted that the understanding of certain concepts is only possible if certain simpler concepts have previously been mastered, and mathematical instruction is accordingly sequenced to ensure that learners are prepared by previous knowledge for the new material they encounter. Appropriate sequencing of what is to be learned is also necessary in the case of simpler learned skills such as those involved in visually guided reaching.

In short, the research findings make it clear that not only must the infant receive appropriate experiences, but that they must also be made available at appropriate times, to fit in with the cumulative acquisition of more advanced abilities. This raises the possibility that the practical failure of White's 'enriching' stimuli was due to faulty timing. The visual stimulation provided may have been inappropriate for the stage that had been reached in the acquisition of skills leading to directed reaching. In other words, the right stimulation may have been provided at the wrong time. To investigate this possibility it would be useful to have a detailed account of the development of the behaviour of young infants towards the point at which they are able to reach out and pick up physical objects. Such an account would show the normal sequence of changes in behaviour. Fortunately, there is a fairly extensive body of reported observations of the progressive changes in behaviour involved in prehension, starting with observations by H. M. Halverson in the 1930s (Kessen *et al.*, 1970). One finding of the observational sturies is that young infants spend a great amount of time simply looking at their hands, particularly during the third month of life (White, 1971).

This raises an interesting possibility. The fact that an infant spends a considerable time regarding his hands suggests that this activity may have a role in his learning to deal with the environment. It is possible that the visual stimuli provided by White may have distracted the infants' attention from their hands, thus interfering with an activity that is important for normal development. The findings of a later experiment provide empirical support for this suggestion. White argued that if the negative effects of visual stimuli were due to decreased hand regard, what was needed was a way of providing opportunities for increased visual attention that did not interfere with looking at the hands. The problem was ingeniously solved by devising brightly coloured and patterned mittens, which directed visual attention towards the hands, rather than away from them. In the condition in which these were worn, not only was the amount of visual attention increased, but the acquisition of visually guided reaching was accelerated.

This rather lengthy illustration clarifies certain aspects of the nature of learning in young children that partly determine the structure and contents of this book. It shows that scientific knowledge about learning can have clear practical value; and the more detailed the knowledge, the higher the likelihood of success in attempts to improve the efficiency or the ease of learning. In the above example, the results of trying to put into practice a little knowledge in the form of a simple generalisation about enrichment were entirely negative. In order to make an intervention of clear practical value, it was necessary to have knowledge beyond an understanding of basic principles of learning, which included an awareness of the characteristics of the learner. Rather than simply studying learning as such, it is necessary to investigate learning *by the learner*. This may appear self-evident, but the above example serves to emphasise the extent to which the course of learning depends on the detailed nature of the learner, even though this may be largely determined by the cumulative effects of previous learning. The acquisition of abilities through learning typically requires circumstances whereby events in the environment are sequenced so as to provide stimulation that effectively matches the learner's existing capacities.

The above considerations have influenced the form of the account of learning in children that is provided in this book. It is customary to discuss human learning and child development as if they were entirely separate areas of concern. Learning theorists are therefore apt to write as if the nature of the learner were of relatively minor concern, and developmental psychologists, who are quite properly concerned with the changing nature of the child, do not always give much attention to the important role of learning in these changes. This book will be more concerned than is customary in accounts of learning with the progressive changes in children growing in age and experience. The process of learning is largely cumulative, and previous learning is an important factor determining what the child can learn in the present and in the future. However, this book makes no attempt to catalogue acquired skills and abilities or to provide the detailed description of the nature of infant and child that would be appropriate in an introduction to child development. The emphasis is on not what is learned but on how it is learned, that is to say on learning processes rather than the learned content. It is influenced primarily by the fact that the impact of learning is cumulative. To understand human learning we have to start at the beginning and follow the child's progress, and as the above illustration makes clear, in order to make practical interventions, we often need to know not only what the individual has already achieved, but also how he got there. This is often true in problems of applied psychology.

1.3 DIFFERING APPROACHES TO HUMAN LEARNING

Research into learning in young humans is a comparatively recent phenomenon – most studies cited in this book have been carried out since the Second World War – and in the circumstances it is not surprising that there is still considerable ignorance about some important aspects of human learning. Neither is it surprising that there have been some false starts in the growth of a body of theory and experiments, nor that some of the research has proceeded in ways that will later prove to have been less than fruitful, nor that some of the assumptions made about the forms of explanation to be sought will prove to have been inappropriate. It is necessary to know something about the guiding principles underlying various kinds of research in child psychology, if we are to bring together the findings of researchers who have held differing points of view and have adopted differing procedures, and at this point it will be sufficient to make a simple division between two approaches. First are vantage points that can be described as 'cognitive' or 'structuralist'. The work of the eminent scientist Jean Piaget forms the best-known instance, and a major aim of this approach is to discover something about the nature of, and the changes that can take place in, the systems of mechanisms underlying behaviour. Observed human activities form a basis for inferences about the underlying cognitive structures. Researchers of the second kind favour approaches that can be broadly described as 'behaviourist', and are generally reluctant to make such inferences. They certainly place greater restrictions on the kind of inferences they are willing to make, being conscious of the fact that unchecked inferential reasoning in an absence of hard data can easily degenerate into simple guesswork and speculation. For this reason, the second category of researchers prefer to restrict their efforts to the enumeration of laws and relationships that are reasonably closely based on directly observed data.

One source of possible confusion is that the term 'behaviourist' has three different meanings. First, the word has been used somewhat loosely to describe approaches to psychological science in which there is insistence on objective methods of observation and measurement, and effectively controlled experimentation. Such an emphasis on objectivity is common to most modern psychological approaches and theories, including those of a structural or cognitive nature. A second, somewhat tighter use of the term is as a label for approaches based on, or strongly influenced by, those traditional theories of learning (sometimes called 'S–R theories') in which there is emphasis on plotting regularities and observing relationships between observable events ('stimuli') and subsequent activities ('responses'). (In fact S–R theories often depart from directly observable data, and various kinds of hypothetical S–R chains are postulated.) The third and narrowest common use of the term 'behaviourist' in research on learning refers to approaches that owe their origin to the work of B. F. Skinner. Researchers who follow Skinner's ideas aim to build a science of behaviour that is squarely based on observable data, and they differ strikingly from cognitive theorists in being extremely reluctant to attach importance to discussion of hypothesised processes underlying the activities that can be observed and measured. Whereas this third meaning of the term 'behaviourist' can be seen as contrasting with structural approaches such as Piaget's, the distinction is less clear when the alternative meanings are implied. In the following pages the word will refer, broadly speaking, to the second and third of these definitions, except when qualified to give a more explicit meaning.

It is conceivable that until recently research on human learning has been too strongly influenced by those investigators who prefer to attempt building a science of behaviour that gives relatively little consideration to the active and independent role of the learner. Such a bias, encountered in most approaches to which the second and third meanings of the word 'behaviourist' are applicable, has a great deal to recommend itself as a basis for scientific enterprise in the study of learning in animals. When rigorously applied to the study of learning in human infants and children, some of the advantages of behaviourist over alternative strategies for acquiring scientific knowledge are diminished. Humans are very active beings and their behaviour enjoys a good deal of autonomy. It is by no means strictly controlled by environmental events. Having said this, it must be admitted that in some areas of research on learning in young children, for example that which concerns the acquisition of aggressive patterns of behaviour, a behaviourist approach has been extremely fruitful in providing an understanding of causes and quantified knowledge of great practical value. Research based on alternative approaches has not yet produced findings of comparable practical use.

REFERENCES

Eisenberg, L. (1972). The human nature of human nature. *Science, N.Y.* clxxvi, 123–8

Kessen, W., Haith, M. M., and Salapatek, P. H. (1970). Human infancy: a bibliography and guide. In P. H. Mussen (ed.), *Carmichael's Manual of Child Psychology,* 3rd edn, vol. 1, Wiley, New York

White, B. L. (1971). *Human Infants: Experience and Psychological Development*, Prentice-Hall, Englewood Cliffs, New Jersey

I

The Beginnings of Infant Learning

The newborn child does not immediately strike the observer as being a very competent individual. He is helpless, apparently inattentive, and lacking manifest abilities beyond crying and sucking. He appears to exist in a void of 'buzzing confusion', to use William James's expression.

Yet the infant's mind is by no means a blank sheet of wax, a 'tabula rasa' shaped after birth in a manner depending entirely on the nature of the stimuli provided by the environment. In 1890 James criticised this view, which regards the infant as 'absolutely passive clay' on which 'experience rains down' to impress the clay most strongly where the drops fall thickest, 'and so the final shape of mind is moulded'. James pointed out that were this account correct a species of dogs bred for generations in the Vatican, always surrounded by numerous examples of fine sculpture, would, in time, become accomplished connoisseurs of sculpture. 'Anyone', he concludes, 'may judge of the probability of this consummation.'

Certainly, the behavioural repertoire of the newborn child is limited. However, the capacities for action that emerge after birth are not formed entirely by the environment, but also depend on a number of unlearned functions, some of which are apparent at birth, some of which develop shortly afterwards, and on others which, while not maturing until considerably later, are not greatly affected in their development by vagaries in the child's environment, within normally encountered limits. In short, various unlearned elements in the young infant contribute to his future capacities, and this fact distinguishes him from a mere tabula rasa or 'absolutely passive clay'.

By way of illustration, the sensory receptors provide instances of mechanisms whose nature strongly influences human learning, but which themselves develop in a manner that is largely independent of learning. The form of the sensory receptors is a factor determining which of the various kinds of energy transmission in the environment, that is, which potential stimuli, are to be received, coded and transmitted as data for learning. For the human learner, the effective environment consists only of what has been 'selected' by his receptors, and hence the extent to which the human organism can be modified by contact with the external world is subject to one stringent limitation. The effective range of environmental events that can influence the learner includes only those stimuli for which the individual possesses perceptive mechanisms that ensure detection.

1.1 SENSORY CAPACITIES OF THE NEWBORN

1.1.1 *Hearing and taste*

At the time of birth, there are ample signs that an infant's apparatus for receiving information from the environment has advanced a long way towards completion. It was once believed that all children at birth are deaf, but research carried out in the U.S.S.R. by A. I. Bronshtein and his colleagues shows that this is incorrect. If an auditory tone is presented while a newborn infant is sucking, the sucking temporarily ceases, indicating some degree of sensitivity to the noise. Stratton and Connolly (1973) have found that newborn infants are able to discriminate in each of three auditory dimensions: time, pitch and intensity. Bronshtein also obtained evidence that the receptors for taste can discriminate at birth. He carried out an experiment in which when babies sucked they were given either sugar solution or salt solution. It was found that providing sugar led to increased sucking, whereas when sucking led to salt solution, it declined. This finding indicates the newborn has some sensitivity to taste.

1.1.2 *Vision*

Some visual capacities are also present at birth. The functioning of vision at this stage is quite rudimentary; and until the age of about one month the infant remains unable to focus at will, the visual system being locked at a focal distance of around 18 centimetres (White, 1971). The newborn baby can gaze at clearly outlined stationary targets (Fantz, 1963), though the response of blinking when an item suddenly approaches does not emerge until the second month. Some evidence obtained by Haith (1966) suggests that infants at five days of age may be sensitive to visual movement. He used a visual stimulus consisting of a line of closely spaced lamps, which were illuminated and turned off in succession to give the appearance of movement. To provide a measure of the infants' sensitivity to this stimulus Haith measured the extent to which presentation of it suppressed ongoing sucking movements, and he found that suppression of sucking was greater with the apparently moving visual stimulus that when a stationary light was presented.

1.1.3 *Pattern discrimination*

During the first two weeks of life some ability to discriminate between visual patterns is present. Fantz (1967) observed that infants stared at a visual target in the form of a bull's eye longer than at a blank circle. However, as Bronson (1969) has pointed out, this discrimination between patterns does not necessarily indicate that the processes required in adult pattern perception are present. In adults, differential reactions to novel and familiar stimuli imply that there is some kind of recognition of familiar items, and this capacity necessitates the encoding and retention of information about the patterns. The individual must possess some representation of the pattern, against which he can match newly perceived items as being familiar or unfamiliar. This kind of ability appears to be absent in infants less than two months of age. The visual preferences in the newborn may be due to the manner in which cells are organised in the retina, and might involve feedback from visual input to the muscles of the eye at a subcortical level (Salapatek, 1968; Cunningham, 1972). Incidentally, it is also conceivable that young infants' eyes have important functions additional to that of seeing the external environment. Jeffrey (1969) reports an unpublished study by M. Haith using infrared light sources to record infants' activities in complete darkness. Eye movements were observed, apparently having a searching or exploring function, perhaps indicating some form of continuous monitoring.

In general, the evidence available indicates that some sensory mechanisms, including the visual system, can operate in a rudimentary way at birth. In the succeeding weeks the ability to discriminate increases, and some important functions such as accommodation begin to emerge.

1.2 THE NEWBORN CHILD'S ACTIVITIES

The newborn child's capacities for action are very limited. Many of the earliest actions take the form of reflexes, some of which are later modified by exercise, and form the points of departure for subsequent learned patterns of behaviour. Some reflexes, such as the knee-jerk, remain substantially unchanged, and others appear to drop out and atrophy (Piaget and Inhelder, 1969). The infant is capable of sucking, and the suppression of sucking was in fact used in some of the experiments mentioned above, as a *measure* of the perceptual capabilities of the infant, suppression of sucking providing an indication of the infant's sensitivity to an event in the environment.

1.2.1 *Sucking in the newborn*

Sucking is one of the important human behaviours involving contact with the external world that are present from the first few hours of life. Wolff (1969) has shown that sucking occurs in constant rhythms or patterns that are apparently endogenous, that is to say, unlearned, since they can be observed from the earliest days. During sleep there are bursts of spontaneous sucking-like movements involving the lips and tongue. The rate of this non-nutritive sucking varies around two sucks per second. The pattern of the bursts differs greatly between individuals, but within any individual infant there is considerable constancy in their form. It is not clear exactly what is the significance of these patterns, but two pieces of evidence suggest that the parts of the brain that are important for learning and higher mental operations are involved (Schaffer, 1971). Firstly, the patterns appear to be independent of motor feedback, since babies for whom this would be reduced or altered because of congenital oral defects such as cleft palate are unaffected. Secondly, children who suffer from brain damage do exhibit disturbances in their patterns of sucking movements.

Since sucking is one of the few observable and measurable forms of continuous organised behaviour in the young infant it has received considerable attention in studies of early learning, and it has probably been the most frequently measured response in studies of behaviour in young infants. The modification of sucking has been attempted in a number of investigations. Sucking is one of the few forms of behaviour for which there has been considerable research examining the continuity between the earliest reflex-like responses and more flexible later forms. In common with some other forms of behaviour that are present at or soon after birth, sucking and the related patterns of searching movements by the mouth known as 'rooting' first appear as relatively stereotyped reflex-like activities, and subsequently become increasingly adaptive to variations in the individual's circumstances.

1.2.2 *Signalling responses: crying and smiling*

Another category of organised behaviour patterns manifest early in life takes the form of 'signalling' responses, the function of which is to communicate information about the infant's needs to his caretakers, notably the mother. The crying response is present at birth, and remains important throughout infancy. A second behaviour that has the function of attracting the mother's attention is smiling. The initial onset of smiling does not appear to depend on specific experiences, and it is found in infants of all human cultures, including babies born blind. In most children, smiling does not occur reliably until around the second month, whereas normal infants can cry at any time following birth. However, smiling provides a good illustration of some of the ways in which experience can contribute to the modification of behaviour. In the case of smiling the major changes are not in the form of the responses but in the circumstances that can elicit smiles.

Crying, the signalling response present at birth, has in common with sucking the characteristic of occurring in bursts or patterns, there being characteristic durations of cries and the intervals between them for each infant, but great variability occurs between individuals (Prechtl *et al.*, 1969). In common with the sucking patterns it appears that the differences in patterns of crying are related to unlearned brain functioning, since infants who have suffered neurological damage do not show the regularity in patterns of crying behaviour found in normal babies (Schaffer, 1971). Interestingly, Schaffer found that babies later diagnosed as 'autistic', having a form of infantile psychosis characterised by impairment or absence of speech, ritualistic or stereotyped responses and a range of inappropriate behaviours, are often found to lack the ability to cry in instances where crying in normal infants would have a signalling function. Since there is some evidence that constitutional differences rather than environmental events alone underlie behaviour described as autistic, the suggestion that there is a relationship between autism and crying behaviour is consistent with the view that the mechanisms underlying crying in the young infant and resulting in individual differences in crying are largely preformed at birth. The evidence on autism consists largely of findings that family characteristics are markedly different among autistic and other abnormal children. For instance, in a large percentage of subnormal children, one or both of the parents are of low intelligence, and there is mental illness or subnormality in siblings, whereas these abnormalities rarely occur among the families of children diagnosed as autistic (Hermelin and O'Connor, 1970).

In summary, the first section of this chapter has looked into some behaviours and sensory capacities that are present in the child at birth and influence the manner in which he interacts with the world, and thus learns, in the future. Despite its apparent helplessness the neonate is by no means unformed, and subsequent learning will not take the form of the moulding of a tabula rasa by the environment, but of the impinging of selected environmental events on existing organised structures. The fact that both sucking and crying behaviours occur in apparently endogenously organised patterns of activity provides supporting evidence for unlearned organised brain activity that influences learning and behaviour. In addition, the acquisition of some responses not present at birth appears to depend largely on physiological maturation, and specific learning does not seem to be crucial. For instance, the fact that blind babies are able to smile suggests that this activity in its early form does not depend on any learning that involves rewards or visual observation: maturation appears to be the major factor.

1.3 MATURATION AND LEARNING

Indeed, maturational factors are probably involved in many of the activities that emerge during the first months of an infant's life. Behaviour is determined by the interaction of both physiological determinants and experience, and it is not possible to apportion the contributions of each as if they are added together. In any case, maturation and learning are not simple distinct entities: Schneirla (1966) defines maturational influences as the contributions to development of growth and tissue differentiation, and experience is described as the contribution of stimulation from all available sources. Both maturation and experience are augmented by trace effects surviving from earlier development. Only the briefest mention of maturational processes can be included here. As it is not possible to obtain direct physiological evidence on the functional development of the nervous system, it is necessary to rely on anatomical analyses, in the form of 'histological' investigations, which use microscopic techniques to examine the fine-tissue structures in the neocortex at various ages. Few anatomical changes can be observed during the first month, but there is marked development in the two following months, and psychological trends in visual developments provide a neat match to these structural changes. Perceptual abilities develop markedly after the first month of life.

1.3.1 *Myelinisation*

In humans, in common with other species, a very large proportion of the physiological formation of the brain occurs before birth, but in some respects maturation of the structures involved in higher mental functions lags behind the rest. In order that information can be transmitted in the brain with maximum efficiency, a process known as 'myelinisation' must occur. This consists of covering parts of the nerves with a fatty tissue that markedly increases the capacity of nerves to conduct impulses, and thus transmit information. At the time of birth the process of myelinisation is complete in all cranial nerves except those involved in optic and olfactor functions, but only a small proportion of the cerebral neurons required for advanced learning are myelinised. However, by two years of age myelinisation is virtually complete, and by the age of six a child's brain size is almost identical to that of an adult.

An additional body of evidence illustrating the importance of maturational processes is available from studies of smiling in premature infants (Bronson, 1969). It is found that premature infants smile up to ten weeks later than normal infants of the same post-natal age. This strongly suggests that the development of smiling is at least as dependent on neocortical maturation as it is on an infant's visual experience during the months following birth.

1.4 EXPERIENCES AND EARLY CHANGES

The foregoing pages have provided an outline of some of the infant's capacities at birth, and the next step is to examine some of the modifications in these capacities that take place soon after birth. Firstly, it is necessary to consider the effect of his environment; and it would be reasonable to expect to discover some broad trends in the nature of the changes, some general patterns or themes in the kinds of change that occur through learning. Secondly, we shall examine a specific instance of learning in the young human. Following this, in chapter 2, there is a more systematic discussion of the forms of infant learning that have been investigated by experimental psychologists, and some enquiry into the nature of those experience-dependent changes in human characteristics that are known as human learning.

The term 'experience' is generally synonymous with 'exposure to the environment', and it is usually inferred that learning has taken place when changes in behaviour occur as a result of experience, practice or training. Changes resulting from physical growth, genetic causes or temporary states of fatigue or arousal are not regarded as learning (Reese and Lipsitt, 1970). It should also be noted that 'experience', defined rather more broadly, can affect the organism in ways that do not involve learning. For instance Bayley (1970) cites evidence that nutritive deficiencies can affect human intelligence, and and findings of a study in Latin America indicate that prolonged malnutrition reduces intellectual competence in children of school age. Certain drugs may have equally profound effects. Richards and Bernal (1971) found that the administration of Pethilorfan to women during labour not only changed infants' behaviour during the first ten days of their lives, but consequently influenced mother–child interaction. The authors suggest that the characteristic style of interaction between mother and infant is determined at this early period in life and, taking this as so, the drug clearly exerts a large, albeit indirect, impact on the child.

1.5 THE EFFECTS OF EXPERIENCE ON THE INFANT

In what ways does experience alter the characteristics of the young learner? What broad statements can be made about the kinds of modifications that early learning brings about? It has been shown that one reflex activity, sucking, can be modified by experiences at an early age; generally speaking it is true that much early learning consists in modifications to what initially appear as automatic responses to simple physical stimuli. Bruner (1969) notes that the acquisition of voluntary responses in young children typically involves modification of earlier involuntary reflex behaviour. For example, an analysis of the various steps in the emergence of visually guided reaching behaviour, as described in the Introduction, reveals that between birth and two months of age there is a simple traction response involving flexion of the arm and hand, elicited by simple external proprioceptive stimuli from stretching. The response cannot be induced by visual stimuli at this stage. At around four weeks a primitive grasping reflex appears, in which catching and holding movements are produced by contact with an object.

There follows gradual integration and modification of actions, through which changes take place in the manner by which responses are elicited. Actions come to be increasingly under voluntary internal control, rather than being 'triggered off' by specific external sensory stimuli as happens with the reflex activities that are present at or soon after birth.

The main themes or trends in the changes that take place within the young child through learning can be categorised under two main headings. Each contains a range of phenomena, and each is dependent on and interweaves with the other. These major categories of change take the forms of, first, increasing selectivity of behaviour, and second, the shift from reactions to physical stimuli towards responses to objects.

1.5.1 *Selectivity*

The increasing selectivity of behaviour has been studied in the case of sucking by Piaget (1952). Between birth and one month of age there is little change in the movements involved in the response, but there are modifications in the range of environmental conditions that trigger off sucking. It is as if the infant is becoming increasingly able to make a distinction between objects that simply provide something to suck, and objects that are suckable and nourishing. Instead of sucking taking place as if for the sake of sucking, it becomes the means to an end. When hungry, the infant becomes increasingly abrupt in ejecting objects that are suckable but do not provide nourishment. In addition, as mentioned earlier, from an early age the rate of sucking can be modified by the taste of the solution offered.

1.5.2 *Increasing selectivity of smiling responses*

Unfortunately, as Kessen *et al.* (1970) point out, there has been rather little research designed to investigate continuity in the normal child between the reflex behaviour of the young infant and the more mature forms of cognitive and social behaviour in the older child, except in the case of sucking. Apart from sucking, one of the few forms of behaviour in which changes have been systematically investigated is smiling.

The increasing selectivity of responses has been extensively studied in connection with smiling. Although smiles do not occur in newborns, precursors of smiling can be detected during the early weeks, in the form of spontaneous discharge patterns. By the second month smiling can often be observed in alert infants following auditory signals such as a high-pitched voice (Wolff, 1963) or by the visual presentation of two or more dots. The infant appears to be smiling as a reaction to specific stimuli, visual or auditory, but with increasing age the human face comes to be the most effective cue for eliciting smiling in the infant. At this stage (Schaffer, 1966) the child first smiles at all people, but from around three months the child ceases to smile on seeing strangers, and smiles only on seeing his mother and other familiar human figures.

This increasing selectivity in the conditions that bring about smiling demonstrates increasing powers of recognition. The fact that a specific person can be recognised implies that the infant has acquired some kind of internal representation or scheme comprising features that make it possible to discriminate between different visual events. In chapter 4 we shall enquire more closely into the manner by which infants are able to build up internalised information about environmental events, enabling discrimination between familiar and unfamiliar objects.

1.5.3 *Recognition of the mother*

The acquisition of internalised structures that enable the infant to recognise familiar items is a process that undergoes progressive refinement. The fact that the presentation of two dots can initially elicit a smile as effectively as a full human face indicates that the infant at this stage has only the rudiments of the inner representation required to distinguish effectively between a face and a non-face. By one month of age infants show greater responsiveness to faces than to some other patterns (Schaffer, 1971), and the next step is to distinguish between the mother's face and the faces of strangers. Findings summarised by Schaffer indicate that this becomes possible around the third month. One team of investigators observed differences in responses to mothers and strangers at six weeks, and another (Wahler, 1967) found that infants aged three months responded differently to their mothers and to strangers when the adults talked, smiled at the infants, or touched them.

The ability to recognise the familiar is something that as adults we take for granted, and it requires some imagination to appreciate the considerable amount of learning that occurs in the three months between birth and the stage at which visual recognition of the mother is possible. The infant's internal representation is sufficiently precise to enable faces to be matched with this representation and classified correctly as 'mother' or 'not mother'. Even when the mother's face is presented repeatedly, the image on the retina of the eye alters with variation in the angle of visual direction and distance. Considerable perceptual learning is required in order for a single item presented on successive occasions to be understood as equivalent despite the changes in input to the eye.

To recapitulate, changes occurring through learning in infancy allow increased selectivity in the child's behaviour. In particular, there is increased ability to respond differentially according to whether objects are recognised as 'familiar' or not. For this to be possible the learner must be able to construct representations of items against which new objects can be matched. These representations must be stored in the infants' memory in a manner that permits their retrieval whenever necessary.

1.5.4 *Responding to objects*

The second major trend in the changes that accompany learning in the infant is in the movement away from reactions to physical stimuli and towards responsiveness to objects. What is the difference between reacting to a stimulus and responding to an object? Essentially the difference lies in the individual who reacts, and not in the 'objects' or 'stimuli' whose presence leads to his response. To respond to a particular physical stimulus typically requires only a simple mechanism that can detect the presence of that event. Thus it is fairly easy to construct devices that are sensitive to, for instance, differences in temperature, sound or light; the human body can detect events at this level without the involvement of those 'higher' parts of the brain that are heavily involved in learning. Similarly, it would be relatively easy to design a mechanism that could be triggered off when a number of dots are presented, reproducing an aspect of the situation in which smiling is initially elicited in the human infant.

1.5.5 *Imprinting*

This has something in common with the phenomena of 'imprinting' observed in other species. In imprinting, responses that are not entirely dependent on learning can initially be elicited by any stimulus that has certain physical characteristics. This usually occurs early in life (Sluckin, 1966). For instance, in certain varieties of geese, 'attachment' behaviour, which takes the form of following, is normally elicited initially by the sight of the mother. However, if an alternative object, such as a human, is present at the time when the behaviour is initially elicited, the imprinted behaviour is subsequently directed to the human. All that is necessary is that the alternative object possesses certain broad defining physical characterisitics that are normally first provided by the presence of the mother.

In order to respond discriminately to a relatively narrow range of objects it is essential for an organism to have processing capacities that are much more complex than the detecting mechanisms necessary for responding to simple physical characteristics. Some idea of the difficulty of object recognition can be gained by trying to imagine how one might devise an instrument that would discriminate visually between objects. For example, how could we build a machine that would make a simple response when placed near, say, a chair, but which would not respond to any other objects? Obviously a rather complex device is required. How might such a device be designed? Presumably it would need to store some information about the nature of chairs, in order to test whether each object brought near to it matches the requirements for a chair. Simple physical dimensions would not be adequate, since chairs vary in shape, size and weight. A start might be to specify something like 'four vertical or near-vertical structures, surmounted by one horizontal or near-horizontal surface'. This information, incorporated perhaps in the form of a computer programme, might provide a good start towards discriminating chairs from non-chairs: a telephone or a typewriter would fail the test for 'chairness' provided by these specifications. However, a table or a desk might get through the net, so one would need further specifications to enable successful discrimination between chairs and objects such as these. It is clear that to be able to respond to objects rather than to other similar stimuli the responder has to possess considerable information about the possible characteristics of objects, and he has to be able to use this information in making decisions about the presence or absence of the objects, that is to say, to recognise them.

While it is true that the increasing ability to respond to objects rather than to simple stimuli provides one of the main themes underlying the modifications taking place in the infant through learning, the clear distinction between simple physical stimuli on the one hand and objects on the other represents something of an oversimplification. It is probably more accurate to think of variations in the level of analysis involved. Thus the young infant's smile is initially evoked by items (two or more visual dots) that are simple in the sense that they require a relatively small amount of information to enable correct classification of events into items to be smiled at or items not to be smiled at. (Note that the decision is not necessarily a conscious one, involving the infant's awareness.) However, the infant at four months old smiles on seeing his mother's face, but he does not smile at a stranger's face, and in this case correct detection requires in the infant a considerably more complex body of information about the particular dimensions of the mother's face.

1.5.6 *The mother as a collection of stimuli*

The human infant does not at first respond to its mother in the adult sense, but to simple attributes present in her. In other words, she happens to provide some of the stimuli that successfully elicit a response in the infant. The fact that two dots – normally the mother's eyes – elicit smiling in young infants is explicable on the assumption that smiling has the biologically useful function of maintaining or helping to maintain the mother's presence. This would have been especially helpful for primitive human groups when predators were near; infants who smile engage their mothers' attention, and are therefore unlikely to be snatched away by lurking beasts. Hence it is possible that smiling evolved at a time when it had considerable biological significance, increasing the chances of survival. Generally speaking, in the majority of occasions when two dots are placed in close proximity to the eyes of a young infant, they take the form of the mother's eyes. Schaffer (1971) suggests that infants may be inherently structured in such a way that they are maximally sensitive to the mother's eyes. Such inborn organisation would provide one means of ensuring that infants will respond to objects they are likely to encounter, and seems to be involved in imprinting.

The tendency for young infants to respond not to individuals as such but to certain simplified attributes that happen to be fairly reliably associated with individuals has also been investigated in non-human organisms. Well-known research by H. Harlow, for example, has shown that the tactile quality of their mothers is particulary important in the growth of infant monkeys; infant monkeys deprived of their real mothers cling to furry models even though these are stationary, unresponsive, and are not involved in supplying the physical needs of the infants (Harlow, 1958). Ploog (1969) has carried out a programme of research showing that when infant squirrel monkeys interact with their mothers they are frequently responding not to their mother as a whole, but to simple attributes or stimuli that are present as parts of the mother's body. Ploog finds that actions such as grasping the fur, searching for and sucking the nipples are guided by simple cues such as angles, curvatures and tactile stimuli. These form 'cornerstones' to which the infant monkey responds with 'behaviour fractions', forming an initial base from which the total behaviour of the mature organism is built up through learning. In brief, the mother is not initially perceived by the infant as a social being or even as a single unitary object, but simply as an aggregate of stimuli that trigger off certain behaviour patterns (which appear to be largely innate in the squirrel monkey). Her function is to provide a composite of objects that the infant can cling to, including fur, nipples, angles, curvatures and warmth.

The situation for the newborn human infant is not entirely dissimilar. It is difficult to conceive of the cuddly human baby as primarily a non-social being, whose responses are largely unco-ordinated and who reacts impersonally not to a beloved mother but to a number of separate stimuli that she happens to provide, but this is indeed the nature of the newborn infant. Up until the third quarter of the first year the child has limited appreciation of the permanence of objects, or of their continuous existence independent of his experiencing them (Piaget, 1954). At first the sensations that will eventually be abstracted and organised as a world of objects are simply unconnected and unintegrated sequences of sensations. The young child behaves as if an object ceases to exist when it leaves his sensory field. Piaget has carried out a series of experiments demonstrating the child's growing awareness of the continuous existence of objects as independent entities. To the newborn, everything is conceived solely in relation to his actions, as if he were the centre of the world, although he is completely unaware of this fact (Inhelder, 1971). Even at six months, if a toy in the visual field is taken away or lowered into a cloth, the child seems to forget it immediately, as if it ceases to exist when it can no longer be seen. However, a clearer understanding of the permanency of objects is gradually acquired, and consequently by the end of the first year children begin to search for objects that have left the perceptual field (Piaget, 1968).

Following increased contact with the environment the infant comes to build up in himself information providing representations of the environment that enable him to deal with combinations of stimuli, so he is no longer limited to reacting to one simple stimulus at a time.

Accompanying this progress there is growth in the infant's ability to integrate his own actions, as illustrated in the reaching for seen objects described in the Introduction.

As the child changes from being an organism that reacts to stimuli to being an individual who responds selectively to patterns of events he classifies as objects, there is a concurrent development of awareness of himself. The growth of self-awareness has been studied by Piaget, and Vygotskii (1962) has carried out important research that emphasises the role of language in development of higher levels of awareness.

Having provided an outline of some of the major changes that learning brings about, we can proceed in the next chapter, to focus on the forms that learning takes in the young child. Before doing so it will be useful to provide an illustration of the kind of experiment that has been used to study the early effects of experience in young infants.

1.6 AN ILLUSTRATION OF INFANT LEARNING

Learning can be demonstrated in a human infant either by a change in the manner in which he responds to an event, or by a change in the range of stimuli that elicit a particular response. Of course, such changes may also occur for any of a number of reasons other than learning, and this consideration makes it essential to use certain careful experimental controls in studies of child learning. To study a change in a response, it is useful to have a response that can easily be observed and reliably measured, and as we have mentioned this is one reason why sucking has received a good deal of attention in studies of early learning. However, in this investigation the activity measured was not sucking, but turning the head. One purpose of the study was to compare learning in the newborn with learning in infants up to six months in age, and certain naturally occurring changes in sucking that accompany child development would have complicated the interpretation of differences in sucking performance between infants of different ages.

Turning the head is something that newborns can do, and it is relatively easy to construct a measuring apparatus consisting of a light head cradle lined with foam, which is fixed to the head and automatically and reliably records head movements. In a study by the Czech researcher Hanus Papousek (Papousek, 1967; Papousek and Bernstein, 1969) the youngest group of infants averaged three days of age. All were healthy, not premature, and each was tested in the late morning. First, measures were taken of the amount of head-turning that occurred naturally. On a number of occasions a bell was sounded behind the midline of the infant's head, and it was established that this sound by itself did not elicit head-turning. In the next stage of the experiment the bell was sounded for ten seconds, and if the infant turned his head to left during this period he was given milk through a rubber nipple connected to a bottle. If the baby did not turn his head to the left during this period a nurse who assisted in the experiment tried to elicit a head turn by touching the left corner of his mouth with the nipple. If this did not lead to a head turn, the nurse turned the infant's head to the left and placed the nipple in the mouth, later turning the head back to the middle. Each session lasted about twelve minutes, and included ten such trials. If there were five positive responses (that is, if the infant turned his head at least thirty degrees without prompting, on presentation of the bell) during the ten trials of one daily session, learning (conditioning) was said to have occurred.

In short, we have a situation in which the hungry infant rotates his head, and he then receives milk. The sooner he turns his head, the sooner he is fed. Under these conditions, can the infant learn to turn his head to obtain milk? Papousek's findings shows that newborn infants can do this, but only after a very large number of trials. In most of the fourteen newborns tested there was initially no rotation of the head at all, and in most cases about twenty trials were necessary before stimulating the mouth with the nipple was successful in producing head-turning. To achieve the criterion for successful learning, that is spontaneous head-turning on five trials out of ten in one daily session, took, on average, 177 trials. Since there were only ten trials each day, the average infant took about eighteen days to achieve the required standard of performance; and in fact there were large individual differences between the infant learners. The fastest took only seven days, but the slowest babies needed over a month.

Papousek measured a number of other aspects of the infants' performance, and he also tested groups of older infants, averaging three months and five months of age. It was found that the 'latency' of response, that is the time interval between the presentation of the bell and the baby's response, was lower for the older infants. In addition, the number of trials needed to achieve the learning criterion was less for the older babies. Whereas the newborns on average required 177 trials, the three- and five-month-old groups needed only forty-two and twenty-eight trials, respectively. Another difference between the newborn and older babies lies in stability, or resistance to decay, of learned behaviours.

The older infants were much more likely than the newborns to exhibit groups of correct responses on successive trials, whereas in the newborns, although the frequency of correct responses gradually increased, the correct responses tended to be isolated. In addition, the number of trials required for 'extinction' of the conditioned responses, that is to say the cessation of head-turning in a situation where the bell was presented but head-turning was not followed by a nipple, was much less for the newborn than for the other groups.

These results provide a clear demonstration that learning can occur in the newborn, although by the time the criterion for successful learning is met most infants in his study were about three weeks of age, and no longer newborn in the strictest sense. However, learning in the youngest infants was much slower and less stable than in older babies.

The demonstration that infants can learn at a very early stage in life does not by itself prove that learning plays a large part in the early changes in the infants' capacities that occur naturally. Nor is it necessarily true that any learning that does occur is similar in form to the phenomena studied by Papousek. These problems are among those considered in the next chapter.

REFERENCES

Bayley, N. (1970). Development of mental abilities. In P. H. Mussen (ed.), *Carmichael's Manual of Child Psychology*, 3rd edn, vol. 1, Wiley, New York

Bronson, G. (1969). Vision in infancy: structure–function relationships. In R. J. Robinson (ed.), *Brain and Early Behavior: Development in Fetus and Infant*, Academic Press, New York

Bruner, J. S. (1969). Processes of growth in infancy. In J. A. Ambrose (ed.), *Stimulation in Early Infancy*, Academic Press, New York

Cunningham, M. (1972). *Intelligence: its Organization and Development*. Academic Press, New York

Fantz, R. L. (1963). Pattern vision in newborn infants. *Science, N.Y.* cxl, 296–7

Fantz, R. L. (1967). Visual perception and experience in early infancy: a look at the hidden side of behavior development. In H. W. Stevenson, E. H. Hess and H. L. Rheingold (eds), *Early Behavior: Comparative and Developmental Approaches*, Wiley, New York

Haith, M. M. (1966). The response of the human newborn to visual movement. *J. exp. Child Psychol.* iii, 235–43

Harlow, H. F. (1958). The nature of love. *Am. Psychol.* xiii, 673–85

Hermelin, B., and O'Connor, N. (1970). *Psychological Experiments with Autistic Children*, Pergamon, Oxford

Inhelder, B. (1971). The sensory-motor origins of knowledge. In D. N. Walcher and D. L. Peters (eds), *Early Childhood: the Development of Self-Regulatory Mechanisms*, Academic Press, New York

Jeffrey, W. E. (1969). Early stimulation and cognitive development. In J. P. Hill (ed.), *Minnesota Symposia on Child Psychology*, University of Minnesota Press, Minneapolis, Minnesota

Kessen, W., Haith, M. M., and Salapatek, P. H. (1970). Human infancy: a bibliography and guide. In P. H. Mussen (ed.), *Carmichael's Manual of Child Psychology*, 3rd edn, vol. 1, Wiley, New York

Papousek, H. (1967). Experimental studies of appetitional behavior in human newborns and infants. In H. W. Stevenson, E. H. Hess and H. L. Rheingold (eds), *Early Behavior: Comparative and Developmental Approaches*, Wiley, New York

Papousek, H., and Bernstein, P. (1969). The functions of conditioning and stimulation in human neonates and infants. In J. A. Ambrose (ed.), *Stimulation in Early Infancy*, Academic Press, New York

Piaget, J. (1952). *The Origins of Intelligence in Children*, International Universities Press, New York

Piaget, J. (1954). *The Construction of Reality in the Child*, Basic Books, New York

Piaget, J. (1968). *Six Psychological Studies*, University of London Press, London

Piaget, J., and Inhelder, B. (1969). *The Psychology of the Child*. Routledge & Kegan Paul, London

Ploog, D. (1969). Early communication processes in squirrel monkeys. In R. J. Robinson (ed.), *Brain and Early Behavior: Development in the Fetus and Infant*, Academic Press, New York

Prechtl, H. F. R., Theorell, K., Grausbergen, A., and Lind, J. (1969). A statistical analysis of cry patterns in normal and abnormal newborn infants. *Dev. Med. Child Neurol.* xi, 142–52

Reese, H. W., and Lipsitt, L. P. (1970). *Experimental Child Psychology*, Academic Press, New York

Richards, M. P. M., and Bernal, J. F. (1971). Social interaction in the first few days of life. In H. R. Schaffer (ed.), *The Origins of Human Social Relations*, Academic Press, New York

Salapatek, P. (1968). Visual scanning of geometric figures by the human newborn. *J. comp. physiol. Psychol.* lxvi, 247–58

Schaffer, H. R. (1966). The onset of fear of strangers and the incongruity hypothesis. *J. Child Psychol. Psychiat.* vii, 95–106

Schaffer, H. R. (1971). *The Growth of Sociability*, Penguin, New York

Schneirla, T. C. (1966). Behavioral development and comparative psychology. *Q. Rev. Biol.* xli, 283–302

Sluckin, W. (1966). Early experience. In B. M. Foss (ed.), *New Directions in Psychology*, Penguin, Harmondsworth

Stratton, P. M., and Connolly, K. (1973). Discrimination by newborns of the intensity, frequency and temporal characteristics of auditory stimuli. *B. J. Psychol.* lxiv, 219–32

Vygotskii, L. S. (1962). *Thought and Language*. M.I.T. Press, Cambridge, Massachusetts

Wahler, R. G. (1967). Infant social attachments : a reinforcement theory interpretation and investigation. *Child Dev.* xxxviii, 1079–88

White, B. L. (1971). *Human Infants: Experience and Psychological Development*, Prentice-Hall, Englewood Cliffs, New Jersey

Wolff, P. H. (1963). Observations on the early development of smiling. In B. M. Foss (ed.), *Determinants of Infant Behaviour*, vol. 2. Wiley, Chichester

Wolff, P. H. (1969). The natural history of crying and other vocalizations in early infancy. In B. M. Foss (ed.), *Determinants of Infant Behavior*, vol. 4, Methuen, London

2

Varieties of Learning in the Infant

Having gained some knowledge of the initial characteristics of the human infant, and of the broad kinds of change that learning brings about, we are in a position to make a more systematic examination of those aspects of human learning that have been studied by experimental psychologists. In this chapter we shall make some broad comments about the nature of learning as a means of adapting to human environments, and about some of the limitations to what can be learned. We shall then examine some empirical research on learning in young humans.

It is necessary to introduce and define some of the basic concepts and terminology that together form part of the language of experimental research, and have influenced both the direction of enquiries and the manner in which problems have been attacked. Most experimental investigations of the specific effects of experience on infants' behaviour fall into one of three categories. These are two forms of simple learning known as 'classical conditioning' and 'operant conditioning', and a third kind of change that depends on experience, 'habituation'. The three categories refer to the kinds of modifications that learning brings about, and to the experimental circumstances in which learning takes place. It is open to question whether there are any fundamental differences in the nature of the underlying learning process. The essential concepts introduced in this chapter form a somewhat mixed bag, and the most important of them are 'reinforcement' and 'extinction'.

A prime function of learning is to enable the individual to adapt his activities so that he can cope with the tasks of living in his environment. In humans, this coping often takes the form of modifying the environment itself, as happens when men build houses and install central heating in them. Sometimes it takes the form of travelling from one physical environment to a distant place that caters more effectively for the individual's needs.

2.1 LEARNED AND UNLEARNED BEHAVIOUR

The most complex instances of human behaviour are known to be the consequences of considerable learning. Among other species, however, observers have found many examples of complicated behaviour in which the role of learning is a minor one. Complex behaviour patterns that are largely innate or 'built-in' may be adequate for the survival of a species in cases where this does not depend on a large proportion of the individual members surviving to maturity, and where the environment in certain important respects is predictable. However, the survival of mammals, and especially man, is dependent on a degree of flexibility in behaviour that is only possible when it is learned.

2.1.1 *An illustration of complex unlearned behaviour*

One example of organised but largely unlearned patterns of behaviour in an insect will serve to illustrate both the impressive complexity that is possible with built-in behavioural repertoires and a major limitation. Observers of a solitary species of wasp known as *sphex* have found that the female insect builds a burrow for the purpose of enclosing and protecting her eggs. When the burrow is completed she finds a cricket, and she then stings it. The sting has the result of paralysing but not killing the cricket, which the wasp then drags into her burrow. She lays her eggs beside the paralysed but still living cricket. The wasp *sphex* seals her burrow, and flies away, never returning to it. When the eggs hatch the wasp grubs have food readily available in the form of the paralysed cricket, which having been preserved alive has remained intact.

This is certainly a remarkable sequence of activities, and it is little wonder that observers noting behaviour of similar degrees of complexity have claimed that highly intelligent socially organised insect behaviour occurs, for instance among the so-called armies of ants. However, a simple experimental intervention serves to demonstrate that striking through this kind of activity may be, it differs in one very important manner from intelligent human behaviour. The difference concerns the individual's ability to adapt behaviour to the requirements of a changing environment, and it consequently influences the chances of survival in the individual member of a species.

At one stage in the sequence of activities followed by the wasp *sphex,* she brings the paralysed cricket to the burrow and, leaving it outside for a brief period, goes in as if to ensure that all is well. She then emerges and drags the cricket in. Whilst the wasp is in the burrow an observer can intervene by moving the paralysed cricket a few inches away, and then note the effect on the wasp's activities of this disruption of the normal sequence. The wasp reacts by bringing the cricket back to its position just outside the burrow, and then she goes into it again. Then the observer once more moves the cricket a few inches away from the burrow. The wasp's response is to repeat the previous sequence yet again, dragging the cricket back to the burrow, and then re-entering it. However many times the cricket is moved away from the burrow, the wasp *sphex* goes on repeating her original action sequence. It appears to be performing a fixed sub-routine of behaviours that cannot be modified to adapt to the environmental changes introduced by human intervention.

In short, the wasp's behaviour, although impressive in its apparent degree of organisation and complexity, is stereotyped and rigid in a manner that harshly restricts the individual's power to adapt to alterations in environmental circumstances. Although the actions of the wasp at first sight resemble organised serial activities in humans, closer inspection reveals a sequence of fixed responses to specific stimuli. In the *sphex* this kind of mechanism is adequate to ensure the survival of the species. Among humans, however, the limited number of offspring that can be produced makes it essential that a high proportion of individual members reach maturity, and therefore greater modifiability of behaviour is necessary.

The distinction between learned and unlearned behaviour is one of degree, and is not absolute. In insects and other lower species some learning is often involved in largely inborn behaviour patterns. Correspondingly, modified innate reflex actions are present in some human activities that are in large part the outcome of learning. Generally speaking, the higher the species, the greater the contribution of learning to behaviour.

The forms of infant learning observed in experimental research are typically simple, and some of the complicating factors encountered in much human learning are absent. Complex forms of learning clearly involve processes not included in the classical and operant-conditioning phenomena that have been investigated in much of the research. In addition, there may be other kinds of learning that require fundamentally different principles. Certainly, a number of questions arise concerning the representativeness for real life of the kinds of learning to be encountered in the present chapter. However, the research that we shall describe does provide useful evidence concerning children's growing capacity to learn, and it demonstrates some of the ways in which learning serves the young human as a means of adapting to his environment.

Having made these qualifications we shall now describe some of the research that has been carried out on learning in human infants. The first categories, classical conditioning and operant conditioning, represent two kinds of learning observed in rather different circumstances. In both forms of learning the individual acquires some kind of association between events that were unrelated in his previous experience. In studies of classical conditioning there is emphasis on changes in the circumstances that elicit a response in the learner. Investigations of operant conditioning, on the other hand, typically measure changes in the responses that a learner makes.

2.2 CLASSICAL CONDITIONING

Classical conditioning is a form of learning in which it is possible to observe in a relatively simple form the establishment of an association whereby an external event, or stimulus, comes to elicit an action, or response, by the organism. The response that is chosen to be measured is one that already occurs in the learner, but which is initially not in any way connected with the stimulus. The most familiar demonstration of classical conditioning is a study by the Russian scientist Pavlov, involving salivation in dogs. Salivation is a response that occurs naturally in dogs when food (a stimulus) is presented. Pavlov showed that the response of salivating, which normally follows the stimulus of food, can be induced by an entirely different stimulus (known as a conditioned stimulus) if presentation of the new stimulus is paired with presentation of the original (unconditioned) food stimulus. A dog can learn to make the response of salivating following the stimulus of a buzzer, where there was initially no connection at all, as far as the dog was concerned, between the sound of the buzzer and the salivating response. Pavlov's procedure was to pair the buzzer with the presentation of food. The dog would then salivate, as a natural response to the food. Eventually, the buzzer sounded alone, in the absence of food, and Pavlov observed that a salivation response occurred. What is learned by the dog in these circumstances takes the form of some kind of association between the food and the sound of the buzzer, two originally unconnected events. An initially neutral stimulus comes to elicit a response previously induced by the event with which that stimulus was paired.

There has been a considerable amount of research on classical conditioning in infants and young children. In some early Russian studies of this form of learning salivation was the response observed, following Pavlov's research on dogs. However, salivation is not an ideal response to observe and measure in young humans, especially since the salivary glands are not fully functional in newborns.

2.2.1 *Classical conditioning in newborn human infants*

Sucking and related mouth movements have been among the most frequently measured responses in studies of classical learning in infants. In an early experiment undertaken by D. P. Marquis in 1931 (Reese and Lipsitt, 1970), infants were observed over the first nine days of their lives. Conditioning sessions took place at every feeding time. To measure sucking responses a balloon was fastened under each infant's chin, and connected to a recording device. The feeding bottle, which naturally elicits sucking by infants, formed the unconditioned stimulus, and the to-be-conditioned or neutral stimulus was the sound of a buzzer. In the experimental sessions, the buzzer sounded for five seconds, following which the bottle was made available, and during each feeding there were between two and five such pairings of the two stimuli. Marquis obtained complete data on eight infants, and she reported that seven of them gave evidence of conditioning, as demonstrated by the occurrence of sucking and mouth opening movements when the buzzer sounded. In addition to these anticipatory responses, the sound of the buzzer led to a decrease in crying and general activity.

Marquis's findings provide fairly convincing evidence that learning in the form of classical conditioning can occur in newborns. Recent studies, notably by Lipsitt and Kaye (1964) and Kaye (1967), using more refined experimental control procedures to prevent the possibilities of confusion between true learning and the effects of other factors (artefacts), have substantially confirmed Marquis's original results. Lipsitt and Kaye examined the possibility that the changes in sucking observed by Marquis were simply due to the infants' becoming increasingly sensitive to the sound of the buzzer. To check on this possibility, they ran a control group of infants to whom the buzzer was sounded, but not paired with the bottle. These infants did slightly increase their rate of sucking, but the increase was much smaller than in the main experimental group, indicating that the changes were largely the result of genuine learning.

2.2.2 *Reward and aversive conditioning*

There are different forms of classical conditioning. One important distinction is between 'reward conditioning' and 'aversive conditioning'. The example given above is an instance of reward conditioning, and the evidence is that it can take place from the earliest days of life, although conditioning is somewhat unstable in the youngest infants. Aversive classical conditioning, on the other hand, has not been demonstrated to occur reliably at birth. An early study by Watson and Raynor (Seligman, 1970) in which a nine-month-old infant, Albert, learned to respond fearfully to a white rabbit after its presence had been paired with a startling noise, has been cited as an example of classical aversive conditioning in a young child. After pairing the white rabbit with the unpleasant noise, the response of crying, which initially occurred as a reaction to the noise, came to be elicited by the rabbit as well, and by white furry objects. As it happens, it is questionable whether this experiment really provides an instance of straightforward classical conditioning, as the procedure used was in certain respects closer to that of operant conditioning. Aversive conditioning is demonstrated when a response such as eyelid movement or foot withdrawal, which naturally follows an unpleasant or irritating event, for instance electric shock or a puff of air to the eye, is found to occur on the presentation of a neutral event (typically a noise) after this has been paired on a number of occasions with the noxious stimulus. As in appetitive classical conditioning, what is learned takes the form of some association between initially unconnected events.

A study by Lintz *et al.* (1967) provides an illustration of aversive conditioning in babies. The subjects were infants aged one to four months, and the unconditioned stimulus was a puff of air to the eye. By attaching a small piece of metal to the eyelid, the experimenter was able to record the number and magnitude of eyelid responses. An auditory tone formed the initially neutral event to which the infants were conditioned to respond. The tone sounded for one second before the onset of a puff of air to the infant's eye. After twenty-five trials in which tone and air puff were paired, all the infants had acquired an eyelid response to the previously neutral auditory stimulus.

Not all forms of classical conditioning fit neatly into the categories of appetitive or aversive conditioning. Connolly and Stratton (1969) carried out an experiment to determine if newborns can learn to make the Babkin response to an originally unconnected event. This response is a reflex that takes the form of opening the mouth after pressure has been applied to the palms of a supine infant. In the study by Connolly and Stratton a sound was presented while the experimenter pressed the palms of infants two to four days of age. After twenty-five pairings the sound alone was provided. Infants made an average of five Babkin responses in the fifteen succeeding test (extinction) trials. This was four times the number of responses made by infants in a control group and thus provides a further demonstration that classical conditioning can occur in newborns. However, one recent study has failed to repeat this result (Sostek *et al.*, 1972).

2.2.3 *Problems and artefacts in research on classical conditioning in young humans*

Conceptually, classical conditioning is relatively simple, but experimental research on conditioning in children does present a number of practical difficulties that add to the complexity and hence to the expense of research on child learning. A problem shared with much child research is that of obtaining experimental subjects of the appropriate age who can be observed frequently over extended periods. In addition, there are problems with observation and measurement of responses in young children. A further problem is that infant behaviour is very susceptible to changes in state, determining the degree of alertness or arousal. In young infants this can change rapidly and unpredictably. Experimental manipulations can inadvertently produce variations in arousal leading to changes in performance that may be incorrectly interpreted as indicating the relatively permanent modifications that learning brings about.

2.2.4 *Sensitisation and pseudoconditioning*

Among the experimental artefacts that can occur, that is to say the changes in performance that might mistakenly be regarded as indicating that learning has taken place, but which are in fact brought about by factors such as alteration in state and other variables that are not adequately controlled, two deserve to be mentioned. The first is 'sensitisation'. An increase in response to a neutral stimulus may be brought about by an individual's simply becoming increasingly sensitive to the (supposedly) conditioned stimulus. We previously noted that the study by Lipsitt and Kaye (1964) on conditioned sucking included a necessary control to detect the possible presence of a sensitisation effect. A second form of artefact is known as 'pseudoconditioning'. This is a general increase in the organism's sensitivity resulting from presentation of the unconditioned stimulus, and making *any* stimulus likely to evoke a response. This, too, may be mistaken for a genuine conditioned response.

In classical conditioning the rate of learning can be influenced by any of a number of procedural events. The time interval between the onset of the conditioned stimulus and the unconditioned stimulus is important, and faster conditioning is generally found with a small interval. When there is a long gap of time between the conditioned and unconditioned stimuli, conditioning is likely to occur only if both are of such a form that there is little probability of events similar to either occurring during the interval between them (Estes, 1970). It is conceivable that some findings attributed by Seligman (1970) to differences in associability between different classes of events may be at least partly due to factors of this kind. For instance, simple differences in the probability of different kinds of events might conceivably account for a finding by Garcia and Koelling (1966) that exposure to X-rays evokes the avoidance of responses to food but not to other stimuli. This research will be described in greater detail later.

There are further important considerations. First, for conditioning to take place it is important that the unconditioned stimulus occurs more often in the presence of the neutral stimulus than in its absence. In experiments by Rescorla (1968) in which shock (unconditioned stimulus) occurred as often when the neutral stimulus was not present as when it was, the neutral stimulus did not come to acquire control over the subject's responses. In other words, there was no conditioning. Secondly, if the neutral stimulus has appeared alone on several occasions prior to the experimental trials, a greater number of pairings of the neutral and unconditioned stimuli are required in order to elicit a conditioned response (Estes, 1970). For instance, a sound that was heard at frequent random intervals throughout the day would be unlikely to provide an easily conditioned stimulus when paired with an event that naturally elicited a response.

2.2.5 *Age differences in classical conditioning*

Classical conditioning provides a kind of learning through which the behaviour of infants can be modified from a very early age. The evidence is that classical appetitive conditioning can take place from the earliest days of human life, and although the occurrence of avoidance conditioning has not been firmly established in newborns, this form of learning is certainly possible by the time an infant reaches one month of age. Children's capacity for learning increases with age. We might expect that it would be useful to study the effects of changes in classical conditioning as the child gets older, and indeed, the findings from a number of studies indicate that the speed of conditioning does increase with greater age, just as the results of Papousek's study described in the previous chapter were that the number of trials to reach criteria of learning decreased as age increases. However, attempts to demonstrate age differences in learning capacities are beset with difficulties. There is no doubt that performance does change, but, as Reese and Lipsitt (1970) point out, it is difficult to determine whether some of the observed age differences in performance are due solely to learning ability or to factors such as motivation, attentiveness and sensory capacities, all of which also alter as the infant's age increases. This complication makes it difficult to put forward any statement about indvidual differences in basic learning capacity. Furthermore, some differences in speed of learning, for instance between normal and retarded children, may be due not to variations in learning capacity as such, but to motivational factors and to differences in ability to attend to appropriate aspects of the environment. This matter is discussed more fully in chapters 6 and 7.

2.3 OPERANT CONDITIONING AND THE CONCEPT OF REINFORCEMENT

Operant conditioning is sometimes known as 'instrumental' conditioning, the terms often being interchangeable. Central to operant conditioning is the concept of 'reinforcement'. A reinforcing event is one that raises the probability of a response that it regularly follows. Estes (1970) defines reinforcement as 'any consequence of a response which leads to an increase in the probability of that response upon future occurrences of the same situation'. According to Estes, for an organism to survive there must be events that have the property of reinforcing its behaviour.

Note that reinforcement is defined in a somewhat circular manner in terms of its consequences; no claim is made concerning why or how a particular event produces an increase in the probability of a response. Rather than suggesting that reinforcement leads directly to learning, it is customary to make the more innocuous statement that reinforcement simply alters the likelihood of responding, or 'response strength'.

In operant conditioning, the experimenter arranges for a response by the subject to be regularly followed by an event that is expected to reinforce the response. If the frequency of the activity does increase, it is assumed that the event is reinforcing, and operant conditioning is said to have occurred. Thus behaviour is influenced by manipulating the consequences of the learner's actions. Whereas in classical conditioning the experimenter selects a stimulus event that already elicits a response, in operant conditioning a response is selected for observation, and the nature of stimulus events is of less interest.

2.3.1 *Operant conditioning in young infants*

Studies of operant conditioning in infants and in humans of all ages have been numerous. A good illustration is provided by the research of Rheingold *et al.* (1959) into the conditioning of vocal sounds in infants at three months of age. Initially, they made a record of the infants' average number of vocal responses, to provide a baseline measure. The experimental procedure was to follow vocalisations with a combination of events designed to provide reinforcement of a social nature. These events took the form of smiling, saying 'tssk' and touching the baby. After two daily conditioning sessions of three minutes' duration, the frequency of vocalisations doubled. When the reinforcement was withdrawn, the rate of responding declined to the original level.

The findings of some experiments of this kind can have important practical implications, since by providing appropriate reinforcing events it is possible to acquire control over many forms of human behaviour. In fact, operant techniques have been used for dealing with practical problems in the behaviour of children at various ages, and in mentally retarded adults. Some of these applications will be discussed in chapter 6. A cautionary point is that procedures that are practically effective for the control of behaviour may be open to misuse.

2.3.2 *Reinforcing human behaviour*

The range of effective reinforcers for human behaviour is extensive. There are two kinds of reasons for wanting to know what events will reinforce behaviour. Firstly, this knowledge can supply practical information concerning how behaviour is effectively controlled, and make it possible to use the operant techniques mentioned in the previous section. Secondly, if we know what kinds of consequences of human actions lead to their repetition, we may gain some insight into the mechanisms underlying human behaviour. We can assume that if a given event is found to be reinforcing, then it is contributing to meeting a requirement of one of the various subsystems of processes that form the human organism. Furthermore, knowledge about the categories of events which do and which do not influence behaviour can provide information that is important for understanding of both perceptual and learning capacities. For instance, if it was found that presentation of visual patterns increased the rate of a response in infants, but auditory tones did not, we might postulate that the infant is sensitive to visual events and that their presence in some manner contributed to the child's functioning. However, if auditory tones elicited no change in response, we might suspect that either the infant is insensitive to auditory signals, or he is constructed in such a way that auditory information has no bearing on the mechanisms involved in the observed response. The results of any single experiment are usually open to a number of equally plausible interpretations, but bringing together a good deal of evidence of this kind may make it possible to build up a body of knowledge concerning the functioning of the human infant.

Broadly speaking, the conception of reinforcement implicit in much modern research is of a function or mechanism having a role in the processing of data or information required by the organism. Earlier, the tendency was to regard reinforcement as a mechanism involved in simple rewards or simple drives (Gagné, 1971). According to both of these accounts, the function of reinforcement is seen to relate to the needs of the organism. The more recent approach emphasises the fact that the organism's well-being is dependent on the supply of a variety of kinds of data inputs.

2.3.3 *Age-related changes in the nature of reinforcing events*

As the child alters, with increasing age and experience, changes are seen in the kinds of events that reinforce his behaviour. Broadly speaking, the range of effective reinforcers widens. Food can reinforce behaviour from the earliest days of life. Visual patterns soon come to take on reinforcing properties for the infant. Bruner (1970) describes an experiment whereby the rate of sucking in infants aged one month was increased by a procedure in which a picture was drawn into focus when sucking rate exceeded 1.5 responses per second. In another condition the picture would come into focus only when sucking ceased, and the infants were able to adapt their operant behaviour accordingly. Auditory events appear to become effective as reinforcers at a slightly later age. Watson (1966) found that a soft tone was effective in modifying eye-fixation responses in ten-week-old infants. By four months, the novelty of visual stimuli influences their effectiveness as reinforcers. For instance, the opportunity to see coloured slides leads to a greater increase in sucking behaviour among infants who have not previously seen the slides than amongst children who have been exposed to them on a previous occasion (Reese and Lipsitt, 1970).

The effectiveness of social reinforcers has been demonstrated by the findings of the study by Rheingold *et al.* (1959) described above. One problem in studies of this type is to identify the effective elements among the combination of events provided in social reinforcement. What is the role of each individual component, and does their combined effect differ from the sum of their individual contributions? Further evidence is required. It is clear that by the age of three months the response of smiling is reinforced when visual, auditory and touch stimuli are provided by the mother, but not if a stranger provides the same or similar physical events (Wahler, 1967). This result provides a good illustration of the infant's increasing selectivity with regard to the circumstances eliciting a response, mentioned in the previous chapter. Thus, on the one hand, the older child's behaviour can be reinforced by a wider range of events than in the newborn, and, on the other hand, increased selectivity restricts the variety of events that actually do have a reinforcing effect.

2.3.4 *The timing of reinforcement*

In addition to the research into the nature of effective reinforcers, some investigators have examined the effects of variations in the timing and frequency of reinforcing events. The important contributions of B. F. Skinner (1938) showed that among mammals the rate and stability (resistance to extinction) of responses are generally higher when the responses are reinforced intermittently than when every single response is immediately followed by a reinforcing event. The majority of human studies varying the frequency of reinforcement have used children and older infants, but it has been found by W. C. Sheppard that even in babies aged three months behaviour in the form of vocalisations and kicking was emitted at a higher level when the experimenter reinforced one response in five than when every action was reinforced (Reese and Lipsitt, 1970).

2.3.5 *Reinforcement schedules*

One needs to be very careful in interpreting the findings of experiments in which the frequency of reinforcement, or 'reinforcement schedule', is varied. For instance, consider the findings of a study by Brackbill (1958). She compared the effects of continuous reinforcement and intermittent reinforcement (only reinforcing during one quarter of the periods of time in which responses might occur) on smiling in infants aged four months. For reinforcement the experimenter smiled, talked, picked the baby up, and cuddled and patted him. After training, when reinforcement was withdrawn, it was observed that the intermittently reinforced infants smiled more often than the babies who had received continuous reinforcement throughout the experiment. These findings certainly support the point of view that intermittent reinforcement is the most effective. The reason for caution in interpreting them lies in the fact that in one respect the results appear to contradict the findings of the study by Wahler (1967) described above. He observed that the effects of touch, visual and auditory events on smiling in infants aged three months closely depend on whether the events are provided by the mother or by a stranger. The result of Brackbill's study, in which a stranger provided the stimuli designed to reinforce behaviour, are similar to those observed in the condition of Wahler's study in which the mother reinforced responses made by the infant. However, they differ from the findings of the more similar condition in Wahler's study, in which a stranger provided the reinforcing events. Thus there seems to be a discrepancy between the two sets of results, for reasons that are not clear. Perhaps Brackbill's findings would have been different if the mothers had taken the experimenter's role. What does emerge clearly from this confusingly discrepant group of results is that in order to be able to predict or understand what happens in any learning situation, it is necessary to have a good deal of information about the learner. In particular, we need to know what kinds of events reinforce his behaviour. There is no point in carefully controlling the values of events, such as visual or auditory stimuli, while neglecting other stimulus attributes that may be equally important for the child, such as whether it is the mother or a stranger who provides them.

2.3.6 *Operant techniques in research on human perception*

The main emphasis in this discussion of operant learning has been on how the infant's behaviour is modified by its consequences, but it is worth emphasising that operant techniques have also been used with a view to investigating the perceptual capacities of infants, rather than the learning abilities as such. A study by McKenzie and Day (1971) provides an instance in which operant methods formed a means of enquiry into the visual discriminative capacities of infants aged six to twelve months. McKenzie and Day wished to know whether the infants could discriminate between simple patterns, and they designed an experiment in which social reinforcement was provided whenever the infants turned their heads in appropriate directions, determined by the particular patterns that were presented. Their results showed that the infants were able to vary the direction of head-turning according to the pattern shown, indicating that they possessed the capacity to discriminate successfully.

Some forms of child behaviour may incorporate operant principles that involve other individuals. In the case of the signalling responses described in chapter 1 a response by the child may serve to evoke behaviour on the part of the mother. Infants who are crying tend to quieten when they are picked up (Korner and Grobstein, 1966), and evidence cited by Schaffer (1966) shows that crying by the infant is very likely to be followed by contact with the mother. It is likely that crying by the infant influences the mother's behaviour, the mother's interaction with the child being reinforced by the cessation of the crying.

2.4 FURTHER ASPECTS OF CLASSICAL AND OPERANT CONDITIONING

2.4.1 *Mixed forms*

Some kinds of learning contain elements of both classical and operant conditioning. The experiment by Watson and Raynor on conditioned fear responses in young Albert was an instance that appears to provide a simple example of classical conditioning. In fact, closer examination of the experimental procedures used indicates that it could equally well be described as a case of operant learning. Papousek's (1967) experiment, described in chapter 1, provides another situation that combines elements of both classical and operant conditioning. It will be recalled that Papousek sounded a bell for ten seconds, and the infant received milk if he turned his head during this period. In order to train the responses the experimenter touched the infant's face: if a head-turn followed, milk was provided immediately, and if not the experimenter turned the infant's head. Some parts of this procedure can be described as forming an instance of classical conditioning. Thus the bell forms a neutral stimulus to be associated with the unconditioned stimulus of touching the corner of the mouth, which is known to elicit reflex head-turning (rooting). But giving reinforcement in the form of milk following the head-turning response can be seen as an example of operant conditioning. In short, it would be reasonably accurate to say that Papousek's experiment includes components of both classical and operant conditioning in combination. Papousek's study illustrates the point that there are forms of learning that do not exactly fit either of the two categories of classical and operant conditioning. Real life provides many situations in which it is clear that children are modified by contact with the environment, but which do not appear to conform to the frameworks of operant or classical conditioning. Some examples will be discussed in the remainder of this chapter.

We have seen that the programmes of research carried out into classical and operant types of learning in infants provide unquestionable evidence that the human infant is an organism which from its earliest weeks onwards can and does learn. The behaviour of the young human is considerably modified by his contact with the environment. We have examined two forms that learning can take in the young child, the acquisition of associations between previously unconnected events (classical conditioning), and the association of certain consequent events with the actions that precede them (operant conditioning). Important questions remain concerning the extent to which the changes that take place in the child as he gets older are the result of learning, and concerning the extent to which learning in the child is based on the classical and operant forms that have been most extensively studied in experimental research. However, the claim that learning is important to the infant as a means of adapting to his world is not seriously questioned.

Classical and operant conditioning are generally distinguished by the different experimental procedures involved. At what level do they differ? It is very difficult to say whether they represent types of learning that are different in a fundamental sense, or whether the differences between them are simply ones of experimental procedure or of forms of behaviour change that learning is observed to take. Attempts to differentiate the two kinds of learning have not been entirely successful (Reese and Lipsitt, 1970), and consequently psychologists have relied on the distinction between them in terms of the experimental procedures that are involved.

2.5 EXTINCTION

An important concept, which forms a part of research on child learning, is 'extinction'. Experimental reports frequently contain the statement that a particular response was extinguished, and extinction rates are sometimes used in comparisons of learning under different experimental conditions. Extinction rates are most simply described as measures of the stability of responses. After operant conditioning, if a response is no longer reinforced its frequency is likely to decrease. Alternatively, if a classically conditioned stimulus is repeatedly presented in the absence of the unconditioned stimulus, it may cease to elicit a response. In both these kinds of circumstances extinction is said to have occurred. As an alternative to measuring the speed of acquisition of a learned response, experimenters sometimes record the number of responses to extinction, that is, the number of further responses made after reinforcement is withheld.

Generally speaking, learning in newborns tends to be unstable, or easily extinguished. Siqueland and Lipsitt (1966) carried out an experiment similar to the one by Papousek (1967) on conditioned head-turning. A procedure involving reinforcement in the form of dextrose solution was successful in bringing about head-turning in 80 per cent of the infants tested. However, after twelve trials in which reinforcement was not given, only 60 per cent of the infants continued to rotate their heads.

Among young infants, conditioning rates are generally slow, and extinction fast. In Papousek's study those of the newborns who conditioned slowest were the fastest to extinguish. Stevenson (1972) suggests that this finding indicates the response was less stable in the slowest learners, disintegrating rapidly when reinforcement ceased. However, there are other factors that can affect extinction rates, so we should be wary of accepting such simple interpretations. Differences in extinction rates have been attributed to a number of causes, such as deficits in inhibitory processes and differences in attention to contextual cues from changing stimulus contexts. Knowledge about the reasons for variations in extinction rates would be of great practical value as an aid to understanding the differences in learning that exist between normal and mentally retarded individuals, especially since there is evidence (Estes, 1970) that in simple forms of learning, such as classical conditioning, normals and retardates do not substantially differ in rates of acquisition, although they do differ in extinction rates.

2.6 HABITUATION

Habituation provides a third way in which experience can lead to useful modifications in the child's activities. Much learning takes the form of increases in infants' responsiveness, but it is also necessary that children acquire the ability to avoid responding repeatedly to continued or irrelevant stimuli. Sometimes it is necessary to inhibit the tendency to respond. The individual has to be able to ignore events that have no significance, and attend only to stimuli that are important. A useful strategy is to give priority to things that are novel, unfamiliar or unexpected, and to cease responding to events found not to be significant. Habituation provides a mechanism that enables the child to use this kind of strategy.

Whether habituation is strictly speaking a form of learning is largely a matter of semantics. Habituation shares with other forms of learning the fact that responses are influenced by experience. However, the word has sometimes been applied to phenomena that appear to have been caused by sensory mechanisms that are peripheral to those parts of the brain involved in most forms of learning. Habituation can be defined quite simply as a decrease in responsiveness that follows from the repeated presentation of a stimulus. This definition is elaborated by Thorpe (1956) who describes habituation as a relatively permanent reduction of a response as a result of repeated stimulation that is not followed by reinforcement. In this manner the organism is able to cease responding to insignificant repeated stimuli.

In so far as habituation involves the reduction or decrease in responses previously emitted in a given situation, habituation has something in common with extinction. Since habituation is one factor determining which events in his environment receive an individual's attention, it is also related to phenomena underlying human attention, to be discussed in chapter 6. Kessen *et al.* (1970) point out that experimental research into habituation may provide an especially useful means of enquiry into the effects of early experience in infants, since it does not require that a new response is to be observed and measured, and avoids the complicating factor that responses are easier to elicit in older than in younger infants. This complication can lead to misinterpretations of research findings, differences in responsiveness between children of varying ages being incorrectly attributed to differences in the ability to learn.

Habituation can occur to any of a variety of events. Engen and Lipsitt (1965) presented an odour to infants, and this led to an increased level of bodily activity. However, when the odour was repeatedly presented on a number of trials the activity in response to it decreased. The subsequent provision of a different odour once more produced an increased level of activity, showing that the diminished responsiveness to the original stimulus after repeated presentations cannot be attributed to simple causes such as fatigue of the sense organs. Habituation can also occur to auditory tones. It is found that an intense tone initially produces an increase in heart rate, but with repeated presentation of the same tone the acceleration is considerably reduced (Bridger, 1961). There is some evidence that visual habituation may occur in newborns (Friedman, 1972). In addition, the findings of a number of studies have demonstrated habituation in children to visual stimuli that take the form of light onset or visual movement with young infants, and the form of pictures and faces in older infants.

2.6.1 *Some uses of habituation measures*

In common with conditioning procedures, habituation has been used to provide evidence about children's discriminative abilities. For example, Stratton and Connolly's (1973) demonstration that newborn infants can make auditory discriminations along any of the time, pitch and intensity dimensions, was based on a technique that involved measurement of heart-rate habituation. The most common use of habituation techniques has been to study infants' ability to store information in memory and hence to recognise familiar stimuli. The fact that habituation occurs indicates that the repeated stimulus is perceived as being familiar. Habituation measures can provide information about children's ability to store increasingly complex representations of events, and to use the contents of memory as a basis for the increasing selectivity in responsiveness mentioned in the previous chapter. The underlying reasoning, stated simply, is that if a child makes less response to, say, a tone, on the tenth than on the first presentation, he must have previously stored some kind of representation of certain aspects of the information, in order for him to recognise it on the tenth presentation as familiar, or at least as not novel. For recognition of complex items to be possible, it is necessary that the memory store contains a representation of the important attributes of such items.

This reasoning has been elaborated by Sokolov (1963) in the form of what is called a 'neuronal model', which retains information in the learner's memory about a number of stimulus attributes. Subsequent inputs are compared with this stored model and are either recognised if they match it or not recognised if there is a mismatch between input and the expectancy induced by the model. In the latter case the organism makes an 'orienting response', by which the new input receives attention. Such a mechanism would ensure that novel stimuli gain the infant's full attention. This would tend to increase the individual's effectiveness, since unexpected events are likely to be ones to which it is important to attend and respond.

2.6.2 *Experience and habituation*

Since habituation is related to the infant's ability to store information it would be predicted that as memory capacity increases with age there would be corresponding developmental changes in the rate of habituation. There has been little systematic research on the effects of age increases on habituation (Kessen *et al.*, 1970), but the available findings do indicate faster habituation in older infants. The results of an ingenious experiment by Lewis and Goldberg (1969) suggests that habituation rates in infants may be related to the amount of stimulation they receive from their mothers. The authors observed mothers and their four-month-old children during a waiting period that took place before the learning sessions, and measured the amount of time the mother spent reading magazines, and the number of contacts between mother and child in the form of touching, holding and smiling. The infants were rated for habituation to a visual stimulus, and it was found that degree of habituation was positively related to the amount of contact provided by the mother, and negatively related to the amount of time the mother spent reading magazines.

2.6.3 *Artefacts and peripheral effects in habituation research*

Habituation experiments, in common with investigations into the classical and operant forms of learning, require controls to detect the presence of possible artefacts. Procedures have been devised to isolate phenomena that are caused by relatively simple or peripheral sensory processes, and which therefore are not closely comparable with the kinds of modifications brought about by other forms of learning. Another source of problems, unless adequate controls are included, is the state of arousal or alertness. In an infant this can change rapidly, even during the course of an experiment, and it alters the infant's responsiveness to a constant stimulus. As a check on this possibility one can present a novel stimulus just after habituation to a previous stimulus has been observed. If the second stimulus evokes a response that is comparable to the original response to the first stimulus, it would appear unlikely that the learner's state of arousal has appreciably altered. Assuming the second stimulus is in the same sensory modality as the original one, an equivalent response will also rule out the possibility that habituation is due to simple accommodatory changes at a sensory level.

A procedure that solves some of the problems associated with the presence of possible artefacts is to present familiar and novel items simultaneously. Fantz (1964) provided ten one-minute presentations of pairs of visual stimuli. One of each pair was the same on every trial, and the other was changed between each trial. Over the ten trials infants aged two months and older attended progressively less to the constant stimulus and more to the new stimuli, the difference being especially marked among the oldest infants tested in the experiment, who were four to six months of age. For the youngest infants, aged one to two months, there was no tendency for the proportion of the child's total attention directed to the new stimuli to increase over the trials. Evidence of this kind supports the viewpoint that habituation-like phenomena can require the higher (cortical) brain functions involved in other forms of learning. Further support is provided by the finding (cited by Schaffer, 1971) that children with damaged brain structures are less likely to demonstrate habituation than normal infants.

2.7 THE EQUIVALENCE OF ASSOCIABILITY ASSUMPTION

It has been suggested that learning in the forms of both classical and operant conditioning involves the formation by the learner of associations between previously unconnected events. We have observed that in operant conditioning, when a particular response is consistently rewarded, the learner acquires some kind of connection between the response and information about its consequences. In classical conditioning, following the repeated paired presentation of two events, one of which has habitually led to a response by the learner, it is observed that presentation of the originally neutral event on its own will produce the response initially elicited only by the other event.

In all species there are limitations to what can be learned. Behaviour repertoires are not infinitely plastic or malleable, a fact that has not always been appreciated. Seligman (1970) states that some experimental psychologists have wrongly inferred from demonstrations of associability between events in classical and operant conditioning that any pair of items can be associated with approximately equal facility. This has led to the assumption that it is possible to state general laws of learning, without taking into account the particular content of what is being learned. Seligman refers to the premise that associations between all pairs of items can be learned with equal ease as the 'assumption of the equivalence of associability'. He quotes statements by I. Pavlov, W. K. Estes and B. F. Skinner to support his claim that it has been widely accepted among those who have been the leaders of research on learning, and who have attempted to deduce general laws and theories about the nature of learning.

On reflection, it would seem that the 'equivalence of associability' assumption is unlikely to be correct, unless the learner initially constitutes a tabula rasa. As we made clear in the previous chapter this is by no means the case for the human learner. Even the youngest infant brings to any situation some preformed structures for receiving information and dealing with it, and these will determine what events are perceived, and influence the likelihood of associations being made between different kinds of items. Seligman suggests that organisms are more or less prepared by evolution to acquire learning in the form of associations between particular pairs of events or between particular responses and their outcomes. If this is correct, it will be difficult to devise general laws of learning that apply to all situations and circumstances. Particular laws concerning learning by association will apply only to events for whose association the learner is at a given level of preparedness. There is some evidence that Seligman's argument is substantially correct, and in that case the goal to produce simple laws of learning that predict exactly what will occur in all situations needs to be replaced by more realistic intentions.

Among the findings cited by Seligman as evidence against the 'equivalence of associability' assumption is the report of a study by Garcia and Koelling (1966). Rats, which served as the experimental subjects, were given sweetened water, and at the same time lights flashed and a noise sounded. There were thus three simultaneous events, the taste, the lights and the noise. During these sessions the rats were also exposed to X-radiation, which made them ill, the sickness setting in about one hour later. The authors wanted to find out to what extent the rats had learned to associate illness with the different events. If the 'equivalence of associability' assumption is correct, the rats would acquire equivalent aversions to the taste, sight and sound. In fact, the rats learned to avoid the sweet taste, showing they had associated the taste with their illness. However, they did not acquire an aversion to the light or the sound. Findings such as these suggest that all events are not equally associable. Seligman considers that rats are prepared by virtue of their evolutionary history to associate tastes with malaise. Such a preparedness would have clear survival value for rats in their natural habitat, ensuring that they quickly learn to avoid eating noxious substances. However, while this explanation appears to be very convincing, we need also to bear in mind the possibility, mentioned earlier in this chapter, that Garcia and Koelling's findings may have been due wholly or in part to timing factors, in relation to the time interval between the onset of conditioned and neutral stimuli.

Seligman also mentioned a finding in an experiment on child learning. We have previously mentioned the well-known early study by J. B. Watson and R. Raynor, in which a nine-month-old child named Albert came to respond fearfully to a white rabbit after presentation of it had been paired on a number of occasions with a startling noise. Albert came to associate the sight of the animal with the unpleasant noise and thus learned to respond fearfully whenever he saw the rabbit. In a second experiment innocuous items such as blocks of wood and cloth curtains were paired with the startling noise. The 'equivalence of associability' hypothesis would lead one to predict that the child would learn to associate these items with noise, as happened with the white rabbit, but this did not occur.

In short, there is evidence that what is learned depends not only on the contents of the environment, but also on the make-up of the learner. As we shall see, since the act of learning itself produces changes in the structure of the organism, the nature of the learner is progressively changing. Thus what a child acquires from a given situation depends partly on what he has learned before. Furthermore, what was learned previously depends not on the environment alone, but also on unlearned characteristics of the individual. Hence the prediction, control or understanding of human learning, for practical and scientific ends, requires not only a knowledge of what general principles or laws of learning can be discovered, but it is also important to know about the particular qualities of the learner.

2.8 LEARNING AND BEHAVIOUR: COGNITIVE AND 'S–R' APPROACHES

For reasons of this kind there has been much criticism of the 'stimulus –response' (or 'S–R') approach to human learning, associated with behaviourism, whereby much emphasis is placed on behaviour in relation to environmental events, little attention being given to structural characteristics of the individual learner. For instance, the Swiss psychologist Jean Piaget, who is representative of those who favour a structuralist or cognitive approach, considers that the stimulus–response viewpoint, which he labels 'empiricism', has exerted undue influence on experimental research on learning. He points out that the nature of the human species is such that environmental events cannot be imposed on the child in the absence of a highly active contribution by the latter (Piaget, 1970). The idea of experience is meaningless without an experiencing organism.

2.8.1 *Learning as an inference from behavioural changes*

It is usual to conceive of learning as involving some change that takes place in the learner. However, in experimental research it is not possible to make a direct record of changes in the learner, and in fact it is the *behaviour* of the learner that is observed and measured. Of course, we can infer from the changes in the learner's behaviour that some modification has taken place within the learner himself. Psychologists differ in the kinds of inferences they are willing to make. To some, the nature of the learner is the primary concern, and the reason for measuring performance at learning tasks is to provide evidence for inferences about the cognitive structures that underlie behaviour in situations involving learning. Other psychologists argue that while it is certainly possible to make inferences about the processes that underlie human behaviour, such inferences can be little more than guesses, and just as unreliable. For this reason they consider it wiser to concentrate on trying to discover lawful relationships between the environment and human performance. Such inferences about inner processes that they are willing to make tend to be restricted to simple concepts such as stimulus–response bonds which to some extent are conceived as mirroring what can be observed externally.

Schaffer (1971) points out that whereas an external stimulus may indeed initiate a sequence of behaviour, the precise nature of that behaviour may not be at all predictable from knowledge of the nature and intensity of the stimulus alone. Cognitive psychologists such as Piaget regard the human organism as a largely self-organising, self-regulating active system, in which the inputs provided by external stimuli and the outputs, or measurable responses, form part of a complex sequence of events by which the individual adapts to the circumstances in which he is placed. Whereas Piaget favours description at the level of the broad adaptive strategies by which humans maintain themselves, strict behaviourists are more likely to seek descriptions at the level of measurable responses and stimulus events.

As we have noted, psychologists such as Piaget who advocate cognitive or structural outlooks consider that the only relationships that can be predicted from knowledge about the environment are relatively trivial ones. They argue that only an approach that makes inferences about the underlying structures or processes responsible for behaviour can form the basis of a scientific understanding. This is probably the most basic of the disagreements between behaviourist and cognitive approaches to learning.

Some simplification has been introduced in order to clarify the differences between so-called behaviourist and cognitive outlooks. In reality the division is not so clear-cut, and it is by no means possible to divide all psychologists into separate camps according to their standing on this issue. However, at the extremes, there are researchers who definitely favour a straightforward behaviourist line, including A.

Bandura, J. L. Gewirtz and A. W. Staats, and psychologists who adhere fairly strictly to a structuralist or cognitive approach, such as the late Heinz Werner, and Jean Piaget and his co-workers. It is irritating to have to dwell on differences in outlook between various investigators, but it is important to appreciate the differing kinds of assumptions that have influenced the manner in which research has proceeded.

As it happens, the major initial emphasis on experimental research into learning came at a time when the behaviourist approach was dominant, and the formative early work in developing methods and procedures, and in choosing the forms and contexts for experimental research on learning, was influenced by the kinds of learning research then current, in which animals were the experimental subjects. The behaviourist traditions of research on learning, its assumptions, theories and experimental methods, have exerted an influence on the kinds of data that have been collected.

In this chapter we have described some of the forms of child learning that have been examined in experimental research. The next chapter will discuss more fully the questions that have been raised concerning the representativeness of these kinds of learning. Discussion of these questions also necessitates a fuller enquiry into the concept of reinforcement and the varying forms it can take.

REFERENCES

Brackbill, Y. (1958). Extinction of the smiling response in infants as a function of reinforcement schedule. *Child Dev.* xxix, 115–24

Bridger, W. H. (1961). Sensory habituation and discrimination in the human neonate. *Am. J. Psychiat.* cxvii, 991–6

Bruner, J. S. (1970). The growth and structure of skill. In K. Connolly (ed.), *Mechanisms of Motor Skill Development*, Academic Press, New York

Connolly, K., and Stratton, P. (1969). An exploration of some parameters affecting classical conditioning in the neonate. *Child Dev.* xl, 431–41

Engen, T., and Lipsitt, L. P. (1965). Decrement and recovery of responses to olfactory stimuli in the human neonate. *J. comp. physiol. Psychol.* lix, 312–16

Estes, W. K. (1970). *Learning Theory and Mental Development*, Academic Press, New York

Fantz, R. L. (1964). Visual experience in infants: decreased attention to familiar patterns relative to novel ones. *Science, N.Y.* cxlvi, 688–70

Friedman, S. (1972). Habituation and recovery response in the alert human newborn. *J. exp. Child Psychol.* xiii, 339–49

Gagné, R. M. (1971). Some relations of reinforcement theory to education. In R. Glaser (ed.), *The Nature of Reinforcement*, Academic Press, New York

Garcia, J., and Koelling, R. (1966). Relation of cue to consequence in avoidance learning. *Psychon. Sci.* iv, 123–4

Kaye, H. (1967). Infant sucking behavior and its modification. In L. P. Lipsitt and C. C. Spiker (eds), *Advances in Child Development and Behavior*, vol. 3, Academic Press, New York

Kessen, W., Haith, M. M., and Salapatek, P. H. (1970). Human infancy : a bibliography and guide. In P. H. Mussen (ed.), *Carmichael's Manual of Child Psychology*, 3rd edn, vol. 1, Wiley, New York

Korner, A. F., and Grobstein, R. (1966). Visual alertness as related to soothing in neonates : a failure to replicate. *Child Development* xxxvii, 867–76

Lewis, M., and Goldberg, S. (1969). Perceptual-cognitive development in infancy : a generalized expectancy model as a function of the mother –infant interaction. *Merrill-Palmer Q.* xv, 81–100

Lintz, L. M., Fitzgerald, H. E., and Brackbill, Y. (1967). Conditioning the eyeblink response to sound in infants. *Psychon. Sci.* vii, 405–6

Lipsitt, L. P., and Kaye, H. (1964). Conditioned sucking in the human newborn. *Psychon. Sci* i, 29–30

McKenzie, B., and Day, R. H. (1971). Operant learning of visual pattern discrimination in young infants. *J. exp. Child Psychol.* xi, 45–53

Papousek, H. (1967). Experimental studies of appetitional behavior in human newborns and infants. In H. W. Stevenson, E. H. Hess and H. L. Rheingold (eds), *Early Behavior: Comparative and Developmental Approaches*, Wiley, New York

Piaget, J. (1970). Piaget's theory. In P. H. Mussen (ed.), *Carmichael's Manual of Child Psychology*, 3rd edn, vol. 1 Wiley, New York

Reese, H. W., and Lipsitt, L. P. (1970). *Experimental Child Psychology*, Academic Press, New York

Rescorla, R. A. (1968). Probability of shock in the presence and absence of CS in fear conditioning. *J. comp. physiol. Psychol.* lxvi, 105

Rheingold, H. K., Gewirtz, J. L., and Ross, H. W. (1959). Social conditioning of vocalizations in the infant. *J. comp. physiol. Psychol.* lii, 68–73

Schaffer, H. R. (1966). The onset of fear of strangers and the incongruity hypothesis. *J. Child Psychol. Psychiat.* vii, 95–106

Schaffer, H. R. (1971). *The Growth of Sociability*, Penguin, New York

Seligman, M. E. P. (1970). On the generality of the laws of learning. *Psychol. Rev.* lxxvii, 406–18

Siqueland, E. R., and Lipsitt, L. P. (1966). Conditioned head-turning in human newborns. *J. exp. Child Psychol.*, iii, 356–76

Skinner, B. F. (1938). *The Behavior of Organisms: an Experimental Approach*, Appleton-Century-Crofts, New York

Sokolov, E. N. (1963). Higher nervous functions: the orienting reflex. *A. Rev. Physiol.* xxv, 545–80

Sostek, A. M., Sameroff, A. J., and Sostek, A. J. (1972). Evidence for the unconditionability of the Babkin response in newborns. *Child Dev.* xliii, 509–19

Stevenson, H. W. (1972). *Children's Learning*, Appleton-Century-Crofts, New York

Stratton, P. M., and Connolly, K. (1973). Discrimination by newborns of the intensity, frequency and temporal characteristics of auditory stimuli. *Br. J. Psychol.* lxiv, 219–32

Thorpe, W. H. (1956). *Learning and Instinct in Animals*, Methuen London

Watson, J. S. (1966). The growth and generalization of contingency awareness in early infancy: some hypotheses. *Merrill-Palmer Q.* xii, 123–36

Wahler, R. G. (1967). Infant social attachments: a reinforcement theory interpretation and investigation. *Child Dev.* xxxviii, 1079–88

3

Reinforcement and the Impact of Early Learning

The instances of human learning described in the previous chapter make it clear that classical conditioning, operant conditioning and habituation all provide means by which experience contributes to the development of abilities in the child. However, in natural living conditions human learning can take a variety of forms : just how representative of these are the kinds of learning we have described? An attempt to answer this question raises some broad issues concerning the nature of research on human learning, and leads to an extended discussion of the concept of reinforcement. In considering the problems involved in systematising and making use of knowledge about reinforcing events, we once more encounter differences between behaviourist and cognitive approaches to learning in young humans. This chapter deals mainly with conceptual and theoretical issues in psychology, and it can be omitted by readers who would prefer to concentrate on practical matters.

3.1 THE REPRESENTATIVENESS OF THE KINDS OF LEARNING OBSERVED IN EXPERIMENTAL RESEARCH

An emphasis in research on child learning on investigations of learning in the above three forms is justifiable only if these are in some respects representative of kinds of learning that make an important contribution towards the child's acquisition of necessary human abilities. There are many kinds of learning that do not appear to fall into the simple categories of classical conditioning, operant conditioning and habituation. The circumstances in which human learning occurs typically involve greater complexity than do the forms of learning investigated in laboratory studies : for purposes of clarity the latter typically use deliberately simplified conditions. In addition, many varieties of human learning involve a number of factors ignored in the studies described in the previous chapter. For instance, some forms, such as concept acquisition and rule learning, necessitate sophisticated processes requiring, among other things, an important contribution of language and symbolic processes. These make possible the more abstract forms of learning, and increase the complexity of processes involved. In addition, a high degree of organisation may be necessary. For practical purposes it may be important to understand the principles underlying organisation of the learned elements involved in whatever is to be acquired. Furthermore, since the categories of operant and classical conditioning were developed and elaborated within a context of research on animals rather than humans, it may well be that these categories do not in all respects provide the most appropriate of all possible frameworks on which to build a body of knowledge about learning in human life.

In fairness, it has never been claimed that classical conditioning, operant conditioning and habituation phenomena do account for all the factors that can be encountered in every form of human learning. However, it has been suggested that the processes underlying these simple forms can be regarded as forming 'building blocks' or elements that are present in a wide range of learning phenomena. To understand complex learning situations also necessitates knowledge of the principles involved in the organisation of learned elements.

We can rephrase our original question, asking whether the kinds of learning studied in experimental research are representative of learning in all its forms. To be more specific we need to know whether the associative and reinforcement phenomena observed in studies of simple learning form basic elements in all forms of learning, or whether there are kinds of learning for which the elements are of an entirely different nature from those encountered in classical and operant conditioning and in habituation. In attempting to answer this question we encounter evidence of some learning phenomena that do not appear to fit into the forms of learning we have previously described. Some instances of learning seem to be very different; the question is whether or not radically different basic principles are involved.

3.2 PERCEPTUAL LEARNING

Learning that involves perception, or perceptual learning, has been observed in circumstances that lack any clear reinforcing or rewarding events. For example, when animals are reared in perceptually complex environments, subsequent performance indicates that the animals have acquired perceptual abilities and capacities that are absent among individuals reared in bare cages, lacking equivalent wealth of environmental stimuli. In short, animals brought up in a perceptually rich environment seem to have learned things that the others have not. There does not seem to be any explanation of the differences in terms of the simple forms of learning described above : for instance there is no apparent reason why operant or classical conditioning should occur in one group, but not in the other.

Perceptual learning is extremely important for human life. Is it based on identical or similar principles to the ones we have discussed? If not, what other basic principles underlie perceptual learning? There is no doubt that humans learn a great deal from observing other individuals. This learning cannot be explained in terms of simple rewards or punishments, because these are not experienced by the learner (Estes, 1970). Perceptual learning also occurs in non-human species. By way of illustration, cats that have been given the opportunity to observe other cats pressing a bar for food are immediately able to carry out the bar-pressing performance themselves. Cats that have not had the opportunity to observe bar-pressing by others are quite unable to do this. Clearly those cats that are able to observe learn something from this opportunity, without receiving any apparent reinforcement at the time. They do not *demonstrate* this learning until placed in the bar-pressing situation, but their performance on that occasion provides evidence of learning that must have taken place during the earlier observation period.

Much human learning must occur through individuals observing others, and such observations are particularly crucial for learning that involves imitation. The latter has particular importance for humans in the acquisition of social responses. A large number of experimental studies undertaken by A. Bandura and his associates (see, for example, Bandura and Walters, 1963) indicate that much social learning in man occurs through the observation and subsequent imitations of other people, known as 'models' among those involved in this area of research. For instance, aggressive patterns of behaviour are commonly acquired from observing and subsequently imitating similar behaviour in other people.

Perceptual learning brings about an increase in the organism's ability to gain information from its environment. Through practice in perceiving events the learner is able to acquire stored representations of information permitting the matching and recognition of new stimuli. We have previously mentioned the importance of such learning in connection with the child's growing ability to recognise familiar items.

3.2.1 *Suggestions concerning laws of perceptual learning*

It has been suggested by some investigators of perceptual learning that the basic underlying principles are indeed different from those involved in other forms of learning. Thus Eleanor Gibson (1969, p. 471) writes that the laws underlying perceptual learning are 'laws of differentiation and filtering, not laws of association; and laws of the reduction of uncertainty, not laws of external reinforcement'. A similar point of view is expressed by Fantz (1967) who has studied perceptual learning in the young child. Fantz considers that there are two distinct kinds of learning process. The first is learning as usually studied by behaviourists and learning theorists, which he describes as changes in response tendencies through reinforcement and repetition. He claims that a second kind of learning, 'the acquisition of knowledge apart from specific changes in response', represents 'learning as it was used by prebehaviorist empiricists and as it is still generally used outside the behavioral sciences'.

A problem in Fantz's distinction lies in the significance of the presence or absence of a response as a criterion of the kind of learning. A response may provide clear evidence that learning has taken place, but the absence of a response does not necessarily indicate the absence of learning. Nor is learning when demonstrated by a response necessarily different in kind from learning that occurs in the absence of a response. The bar-pressing example illustrates this statement. It was not until the cats were placed in a cage containing a bar to press that they gave evidence of learning from observation. At this point, but not before, they acted in a manner different from that of animals that had not been able to observe other cats. However, the learning took place earlier, during the observation period, even if the evidence for it was not forthcoming until later. In short, it is important not to confuse the moment at which learning is first demonstrated with the time when learning occurs. Responses certainly provide useful evidence that learning has taken place, but the occasion on which a response is first observed may be considerably after learning has occurred. For similar reasons, learning that happens to be demonstrated by a clearly observable response need not be fundamentally different from learning that is not accompanied by such a response.

Perceptual-learning phenomena may require sets of explanatory principles that differ from those that have been put forward to describe the acquisition of new or altered forms of behaviour in the infant. However, it is conceivable that the differences between perceptual learning and other forms of learning are relatively superficial. Instances of perceptual learning differ from typical forms of operant conditioning in two easily apparent ways. First, there is usually no observable response at the moment of perceptual learning, whereas a response is customary in conventional forms of operant conditioning. However, as we have been shown, this difference is not a crucial one, since the presence or absence of a response at a particular time provides no basis for inferring differences in the kind of learning that has taken place.

The second difference between perceptual learning and other kinds of learning lies in the fact that while reinforcement is essential for all forms of operant conditioning we have described, in perceptual learning it appears not to be necessary at all. Indeed, both Piaget and Gibson explicitly state that external reinforcement is unimportant for perceptual learning. However, the claim that perceptual learning occurs in the absence of reinforcement is open to dispute. In the previous chapter a reinforcing event was simply defined as one that leads to an increase in the occurrence of a response. This definition carefully avoids the restricting denotation of 'reward', which seems to be implied by the phrase external reinforcement. If this definition of the word 'reinforcement' is accepted, it is doubtful whether a meaningful categorisation can be made into 'external' and 'internal' varieties.

3.2.2 *Reduction of uncertainty as a reinforcer*

It is suggested that reinforcement may have a role in perceptual learning. In place of Gibson's claim that reduction of uncertainty leads to learning, *rather than* reinforcement, we would argue that it is quite acceptable to state that reduction of uncertainty *is* a form of reinforcement. Although reduction of uncertainty does not fill the rewarding function associated with everyday use of the word reinforcement, it is quite admissible as a reinforcer under the operational definition that has been adopted and widely accepted in experimental psychology. In fact, a number of the reinforcing events encountered in the previous chapter are equally deficient in apparently regarding qualities. Thus, in addition to reinforcers, such as milk, which supply tissue needs, the reinforcing events that we have encountered include, for instance, tones, visual patterns and touch stimuli, none of which are rewarding in the usual sense. However, all these events can serve to reinforce human actions, and so can reduction of uncertainty. Therefore, to state that that reduction of uncertainty leads to perceptual learning is roughly equivalent to the statement that certain events are reinforcing because they reduce uncertainty.

In short, there are reasons for suggesting that perceptual learning, which on the surface seems to depend on entirely different basic elements from those involved in the kinds of learning described in chapter 2, may not be so radically different as at first appears. Earlier, we stated that the range and variety of events that can function as effective reinforcers alters as the child becomes older. With increasing age and experience, the child builds up an internal store of information in the form of representations against which newly perceived events can be matched, enabling recognition of items that are familiar. It is likely that events that contribute to the reduction of uncertainty may reinforce behaviour over a range of ages. However, the particular forms of the stimuli required to bring about such reduction of uncertainty alter considerably with age differences.

3.3 THE RANGE AND VARIETY OF REINFORCING EVENTS

The suggestion that reduction of uncertainty may function as a reinforcer raises the question of whether there are any limits at all to the kind of events that can reinforce human behaviour. If not, could it be that the concept of reinforcement is an empty one, and therefore meaningless? After all, if anything can function as a reinforcer, to say that a particular event is reinforcing cannot be very informative! The fact of the matter is that it is of practical value to know the form of events that can influence particular behaviour, in particular circumstances. Furthermore, knowledge about the events that function as reinforcers can tell us a good deal about the nature of the organism.

3.3.1 *Age-related differences in reinforcers*

The range of events seen to reinforce human behaviour is very wide. The newborn infant is initially responsive to events that take the form of simple physical stimuli. With increasing age he becomes increasingly responsive to qualities embedded in them, that is, to objects, defining the latter as abstracted qualities of the physical events. Correspondingly, the nature of the reinforcing events alter from those that can be satisfactorily described at a simple physical level, for example, foods and sounds, to those for which a higher level of analysis is appropriate. Visual patterns, tones and touch may all serve to reinforce the newborn child, yet by the age of three months the same stimuli are found to be positively reinforcing if the mother provides them, but aversive if presented by a stranger.

In order to describe the crucial components in events that reinforce behaviour in older infants and children a change in the level of description is required. Thus, in the three-month-old it would be appropriate to describe the reinforcer as 'presence of mother' whereas in the newborn child it would be more appropriate to describe the reinforcing events in the terms of their simple physical qualities. In short, the physical stimuli may be identical in the two cases, but it is necessary to adopt different levels of description in order to focus on the elements that are crucial for the child who is being reinforced.

Broadly speaking the most appropriate level for describing reinforcing events coincides with the level at which they can be perceived or understood by the developing child. However, there are *some* reinforcers for which the level of description need not alter as the child ages, food being a notable example. Reinforcing events such as reduction of uncertainty differ from simpler reinforcers, such as food, not only in being at a higher, or more abstract, conceptual level, but in the inherent statement concerning the effects of stimuli on the particular learner. Note, however, that the degree of abstraction in a statement about an event that reinforces behaviour need not coincide with the level of the learner's awareness. An infant does not have to be aware that something reduces his uncertainty about the environment in order for it to have reinforcing effect.

3.3.2 *Reinforcing properties of novel items*

Effective reinforcers include various items such as food and drink that are required for 'primary' needs. In addition, at various ages, visual, auditory and touch stimuli of one kind or another have been observed to reinforce behaviour. On the whole, stimuli that are novel to the perceiver are especially likely to be effective. For instance, Parry (1972) observed that ten-month-old babies spent more time in looking at and playing with unfamiliar than familiar objects. Furthermore, when twelve-month-olds leave their mothers and are confronted with a choice between entering familiar and unfamiliar rooms, they most often choose the latter, and when they are allowed to select one of two toys, they again choose the one that is most novel (Ross *et al*., 1972). These authors note that by selectively approaching the novel elements of his environment the young child increases the range of his opportunities for learning. In play and exploration the child seeks out things that are new to him and becomes familiar with an increasing variety and number of the objects that form his environment.

Kagan (1972) considers that items that are partly but not entirely novel are particularly effective. He suggests that there is an optimal level of discrepancy from the familiar, at which new items are sufficiently unfamiliar to require adaptation or accommodation by the individual in order to incorporate them into existing cognitive structures, but not so familiar that he is unable to see any relation between the new item and what he had previously experienced. In the latter case the items have no meaning to the perceiver, and fail to engage prolonged attention.

The behaviour of young infants can be reinforced by visual movement, for instance in the form of a spinning wheel. It has also been observed that bringing a visual pattern into focus can serve as a reinforcing event for young infants' sucking activities (Bruner, 1970).

In an experiment described by Schaffer (1971) it was found that while simply touching a young infant may reinforce behaviour, a stronger effect is obtained by picking up the child. Toys, especially ones that are new, can provide powerful reinforcement. Normally, a child aged ten months when deposited in a strange environment immediately tries to follow his mother. However, the presence of a new toy to play with can be sufficiently reinforcing for the child to delay following for three minutes, on average. In the same situation an infant left with a toy that is already familiar to him follows his mother after a period of less than one minute (Corter *et al*., 1972).

A further category of reinforcing events is indicated by Piaget (1970), who points out that infants engage in a number of separate behaviours that have in common the effect of making interesting sounds or sights last. In addition, he has observed that organised patterns of behaviour within the infant's repertoire seem to 'run themselves off', as if the opportunity for the individual to run through or practise his available behaviours is reinforcing in itself. Similarly, Kessen and Mandler (1961) have suggested that 'the running off of an organised behavioural act' may be reinforcing, having a number of functions for the infant. It would certainly be advantageous for human learning and development if it were the case that the opportunity to practise new behaviour had a reinforcing role, since practice provides a good means of improving the efficiency of human performance. In this respect, people, like violins, are improved by being played on.

Some observations by Ploog (1969) support the idea that running off organised behaviour patterns may reinforce other activites. Some of Ploog's findings were discussed in chapter 1, in connection with infant squirrel monkeys' reactions to the mother's body as a series of separate physical stimuli rather than as a single unitary object. Ploog has extensively observed various kinds of behaviour in squirrel monkeys, and his findings indicate that the infant monkeys have certain innate responses, which he calls 'behaviour fractions'. These form a kind of basis or ground-plan for behaviour, on which later responses can build as they are acquired. Ploog has found that the innate behaviour fractions serve as reinforcers for the in-between parts, which emerge gradually, through learning.

3.4 CLASSIFYING REINFORCERS

Since the number and variety of kinds of events found to be capable of reinforcing human behaviour is so large, it would be valuable to provide some kind of classification of effective reinforcers. However, although most psychologists would agree that a system for classifying events would be valuable, there are disagreements as to the preferred basis for classification. Broadly speaking, there are two approaches to the problem of classifying reinforcers, and the division is based on that between behaviourist and structuralist (cognitive) viewpoints. Again, it should be emphasised that to imply a clear distinction represents something of an oversimplification: it would be naïve to assume that all researchers adhere faithfully to one of two rival positions.

3.4.1 *Cognitive processes and behaviour*

In examining differences in approaches to organising knowledge about reinforcers, it must be remembered that there are changing fashions in the science of psychology. In the 1950s the value of a behaviourist approach to the analysis of learning was practically unquestioned. However, it is increasingly common for researchers to make fairly elaborate inferences about underlying cognitive processes from the behavioural data obtained from experimental research. As we stated earlier, a major difference between psychologists leaning towards behaviourist and structuralist approaches is in the kinds of inferences they are willing to make about the structures that enable humans to process information and that account for behaviour.

Reinforcers are defined in terms of their effects on behaviour. The relationship between behaviour and the person who produces it is a curious one. Behaviour is a product of the behaver, but it does not form an enduring part of him: a behavioural act is fleeting, gone as soon as it is completed. However, this lack of permanence does not make behaviour trivial: the sound produced by a gramophone record is equally fleeting, yet it is the sole criterion of the record's quality. The analogy is a limited one: one important difference between gramophone records and humans is that the former produce a practically identical output each time they are played. A knowledge of the relationship between the physical structure of a record and the sound produced makes it possible to use the sound emitted as a basis for producing a copy of the record. In humans, however, the output, in the form of behaviour, is far more variable, and this makes it much more difficult, if not impossible, to reconstruct the underlying structure from the data provided by the output (behaviour) alone. Since there is no simple relationship between observed behaviour and the structural characteristics of the individual who produces it, behaviourists argue that knowledge about the nature of events that reinforce behaviour cannot provide reliable information about processes underlying the behaviour. For this reason they suggest that classification of reinforcers should be based on straightforward observations of relationships between reinforcing events and human activities (Gewirtz, 1969).

Structural psychologists take a different approach to the problem of ordering and classifying the kinds of stimuli that function as reinforcers. Reinforcers are seen as providing data for making inferences about processes underlying behaviour. A first step in attempting to classify reinforcers is to assume that all reinforcing stimuli have a function that contributes to a need or requirement in the individual whose behaviour they are found to influence. Some reinforcers meet physical, or tissue, needs, whereas others, such as visual patterns and sounds, do not. Let us imagine that a particular auditory tone is found to reinforce an infant's activities. One might simply state that the infant has a need for sounds, and proceed by postulating a separate need for every event that is found to be reinforcing. Alternatively, some form of classification can be attempted, by which the various events found to reinforce the infant's activities are sorted into categories, each of which relates to a different class of need.

A strategy like this seems promising, and enables the classification of known reinforcers on the basis of the manner in which they contribute to human processes. We have seen that while some reinforcers exert their effects through contributing products such as food, which fulfil energy requirements, others are more appropriately regarded as contributing necessary kinds of information to the nervous system (Annett, 1969). Novel events appear to meet requirements of this kind. Unfortunately, there are problems in the implementation of this kind of approach. A major difficulty lies in deciding on the practical steps by which one commences classification of reinforcing events, in the absence of knowledge about their precise functions to the individual. As stated, the goal is to classify reinforcers on the basis of the requirements they meet, but often it is known only that they reinforce behaviour, this fact being the reason for the assumption that they do meet a requirement of the organism. In practice, it is possible to follow hunches about which of the learner's requirements is met by a particular reinforcing event, and to classify reinforcers into categories on the basis of these hunches. In this manner it may be possible to build up knowledge gradually, through a process of making inferences and checking them against available evidence.

3.5 THE MECHANISMS UNDERLYING REINFORCEMENT

Although we have taken care to define reinforcers solely in terms of their effects, avoiding any attempts to specify the mechanisms underlying these effects, we are entitled to ask the question, why is a reinforcer reinforcing? What kinds of processes are involved? A very broad answer is provided by the statement that events that are reinforcers are ones which contribute in some manner to the functioning of the individual whose behaviour they are found to reinforce. This answer, although vague, reminds us of the fact that an event can only be reinforcing if it bears some relation to the needs of an organism. In other words, to call an event reinforcing presupposes the existence of an organism that is influenced by that event. However, it leaves us completely ignorant about the details of the mechanisms through which certain kinds of events come to influence behaviour.

What must happen to the human infant in order for an event to be reinforcing? Psychologists who developed theories of learning in the 1930s regarded the effect of reward as providing a direct, automatic and immediate strengthening of associations between representations of stimuli and rewarded responses (Estes, 1972). Estes, however, has suggested that such an account is too simple to account for all learning phenomena, and he has advanced a theory that involves feedback mechanisms that produce varying levels of anticipated reward or punishment, following variations in the organism's behaviour. In a learning situation the organism scans the stimuli that are present, and a result of the scanning is to bring into the forefront of memory representations of events that have been associated with the current stimuli. These representations provide a basis for a feedback system guiding the learner's responses.

Questions about the precise functions underlying reinforcement continue to arouse controversy. The late E. R. Guthrie claimed that the contiguity of stimulus events and responses, that is to say, their simultaneous occurrence, provides the crucial factor in learning. It is argued by those who support views similar to or based on Guthrie's that the main role of reinforcers is to bring about situations in which such contiguity occurs. A further source of controversy, mentioned earlier in connection with perceptual learning, resides in the question of whether reinforcement is always essential for learning. It is certainly true that learning may sometimes occur in the absence of any easily identifiable reinforcing events. The question is whether reinforcement is indeed absent, or whether the observer is simply unaware of the reinforcing events in the situation. In cases where the reinforcing event meets needs for items such as food it is easy for the observing experimenter to specify the nature of the reinforcing event. However, in other situations it may be difficult to tell which of the current environmental events are serving to reinforce the learner's actions.

If we accept the assumption that an event which reinforces human behaviour is likely to have some useful function for the behaver, or to provide a favourable consequence to his actions, we are led to various questions concerning the manner in which particular events contribute to meeting particular needs. Since the human nervous system is very complex, it is likely to have numerous requirements. That is, a large number of conditions must be met in order for it to function effectively.

3.6 STRICT BEHAVIOURIST APPROACHES TO REINFORCEMENT

Psychologists who incline to cognitive explanations proceed from experimental data that demonstrate the reinforcing effects of specific events on specific activities, to infer something about the processes underlying the observed behaviour. The strict behaviourist approach to the ordering of events that reinforce behaviour is different. Rather than developing a classificatory system that attempts to reflect the processes through which particular events exert a reinforcing function, the aim is simply to provide an ordering that conveniently summarises observations of the behavioural effects of various reinforcers. Thus Gewirtz, who claims that non-behavioural theorists have used inefficient and unparsimonious constructs, proposes, instead, a study of human behaviour based on 'analysis of the events in the environment, both in the present and in the past, that *control* behaviour' (Gewirtz, 1969, p. 60). Gewirtz does not deny that there has to be a person to provide the behaviour, nor that it is possible to make inferences about processes or structures that might underlie this behaviour. However, he considers that at the present stage a cognitive approach must be largely a matter of guesswork, and is therefore unlikely to be particularly fruitful. He argues that a practical, more realistic goal is to construct a science of behaviour in which the behaviour itself, rather than any inferred underlying characteristics of the behaver, forms not only the data to be observed but the unit for scientific analysis.

Modern behaviourism in an extreme form is found in the writings of B. F. Skinner (1950), who strongly urges that the efforts of psychologists be directed to observing relationships between events and behaviour. He opposes the building of theories in which reinforcement phenomena are explained by reference to inner states or drives in the learner. Skinner argues that such theories, as soon as they depart from what can be directly observed, concern 'events taking place somewhere else, at some other level of observation, described in different terms and measured, if at all in different dimensions', and deflect attention from those variables that are directly observable and manipulable.

The main behaviourist objection to cognitive theories is that their dependence on inferences is too extreme. With little data and much guesswork, the details of a theory, and the constructs postulated as structures or underlying processes, can become largely a matter of the individual theorist's whim. There is little value in cognitive explanations if there is insufficient hard data on which to choose between a number of equally plausible theories.

3.7 COMPARING BEHAVIOURIST AND STRUCTURALIST POSITIONS

This reluctance of strict behaviourists to make inferences about the nature of cognitive structures underlying observed behaviour can appear unnecessarily timid. The search for underlying mechanisms or processes that can account for a variety of events appears so central to scientific enterprise that an approach that discourages the making of inferences about the processes underlying observed behaviour does appear restrictive, and even sterile. Newell (1967) argues that whenever there is an event that occurs with some regularity it is usually possible to find some underlying mechanism, and that when such a mechanism is found our understanding and our ability to predict the outcome of various situations is increased. He states that just as it is possible to find a mechanism for producing the light that shines from the stars, or for photosynthesis, so we can expect to be able to discover mechanisms that enable an organism to follow complex rules. Newell insists that:

> The psychological mechanisms are there, confronting us. If we were ingenious enough, they would yield up their secrets . . . to believe that we should proceed only with descriptions of regularities (in behaviour) and avoid any attempt to see in them the processing that is involved, seems to me almost a failure of nerve (Newell, 1967, p. 252).

3.7.1 *Arguments for non-inferential approaches*

To be fair, one needs to point out, first, that except for researchers who adhere strictly to the views of B. F. Skinner, few psychologists actually avoid any attempt to understand the processes underlying observed regularities of behaviour. As we have mentioned, behaviourists who propose what can broadly be described as S–R theories differ from cognitive theorists not by refusing to make any inferences at all about systems underlying behaviour, but by restricting the kinds of inferences they are willing to make. Even in the case of Skinner, his position is not so much that processes underlying observed behaviour are unimportant, but that as a matter of strategy observable behaviour provides not only the best data but the most appropriate level on which to build a body of knowledge.

Skinner's views are strongly opposed by Noam Chomsky (1972), who claims that whatever function Skinner's brand of behaviourism may have served in the past it now provides 'nothing more than a set of arbitrary restrictions' on attempts to acquire a real understanding of human behaviour. He argues that no physical scientist would accept the 'intellectual shackles' that Skinner sets up, and that there is no reason why scientists investigating man and society should be willing to tolerate such limitations (Chomsky, 1972, p. 17).

Yet it can be argued that cognitive approaches have often seemed to obscure rather than clarify the nature of reinforcement. A bewildering variety of human needs have been proposed by various researchers, and it is supposedly the function of reinforcing events to meet them. Lists of human requirements have included, for example, the need to be competent, needs for security, attachment, curiosity, a need for stimulation, needs for novelty, discrepancy and the need to explore. Among other events claimed to meet human needs is the reduction of uncertainty. In common with the lists of so-called instincts prevalent at the beginning of this century, the various items have rarely been defined in ways that make it clear exactly how particular reinforcing events are supposed to contribute to the functioning of the organism, and there is a good deal of overlapping between the various postulated human requirements.

Another reason for favouring non-inferential approaches to the tabulation of data on reinforcement is that they have produced a body of valuable findings. The research on 'behaviour modification' (see chapter 6), which has important practical applications for education and for the care and treatment of the mentally handicapped, is one instance. A further example is provided by research of Bandura and others on the acquisition in young children of aggressive forms of behaviour.

The choice between behaviourist and cognitive positions is a difficult one. Theories based on cognitive approaches are not theories about behaviour, which is fleeting and transitory, but about relatively enduring processes underlying it. However, proponents of behaviourist approaches can claim that their statements are directly based on reliable observations and measurements, whereas cognitive theories contain inferences that are often uncertain or even speculative. Both kinds of approach have much to offer, but although a single body of research can incorporate elements of each, some choice between them is inevitable. It is my opinion that, ultimately, cognitive or structural approaches will become dominant, and that accounting for human actions in all their complexity will necessitate a willingness to theorise about the mechanisms that give birth to those activities.

3.8 COGNITIVE PROCESSES AND STRUCTURES

To emphasise the learner's structural characteristics is not to deny the crucial nature of environmental events. However, a stimulus event or a reinforcing event can influence behaviour only if it has significance in relation to the requirements and capacities of the individual to whom it is made available. The associations that a learner makes between environmental events are in effect associations between the outcomes of the learner's actions in processing physical stimuli. The stimuli contribute some of the raw meat for human learning, but the learner is the chef who creates the meal! Piaget and Inhelder (1969) put forward a similar argument. They characterise the S–R or behaviourist approach as one in which progression depends on a mechanism of cumulative associations, by which the outcomes of conditioning are progressively added to basic reflexes. Piaget and Inhelder consider that this approach places too much emphasis on the role of responses to external stimuli. They argue that the mechanism underlying the progression from simple reflex actions to acquired 'intelligent' behaviour is one of *assimilation*. By a process comparable to biological assimilation, the input from external events is treated, filtered and sometimes modified in such a manner as to enable the data to be incorporated into the structure of the individual.

This view does not deny the importance of connections in external stimuli but insists that the individual's organising activities must be equally important. It is claimed that input is filtered through a structure consisting of mechanisms that can best be described in terms of schemes of action or in terms of operations of thought, depending on the individual's stage of development. In addition to this assimilative process, by which input is modified or filtered in accordance with the individual's structural characteristics, the latter simultaneously undergo some modification to widen the range of data that can be incorporated. The term *accommodation* is used to describe this adaptive strategy by which internal structures are modified so as to improve the capacity to deal with external events. Schaffer (1971) suggests that structures are modified by events that can activate existing patterns, but do not completely correspond to the expectancies induced by previous experience. He considers that behavioural growth comes about though such accommodatory activities whenever there is 'an optimal degree of discrepancy between existing skills and external situation'. It is for reasons of this kind that Kagan and others have suggested that moderately discrepant events are especially valuable for intellectual development, and that patterns moderately different from ones experienced in the past are likely to be effective reinforcers.

The emphasis on the need for external events to be subject to organisational activities on the part of the individual if they are to contribute to intellectual development is shared by Schaffer (1971), who suggests that the role of external stimuli, far from providing the basis for cumulative growth through association, is merely to initiate a sequence whose outcome may not be at all predictable from the nature and intensity of those stimuli. Change in the form of learning is brought about not only by external stimulation but by the response of the individual to environmental events. Even the youngest child is not only imposed on by events, but uses his processing and responding capacities to impose himself on the environment in which he lives.

REFERENCES

Annett, J. (1969). *Feedback and Human Behaviour*, Penguin, Harmondsworth

Bandura, A., and Walters, R. H. (1963). *Social Learning and Personality Development*, Holt, Rinehart & Winston, New York

Bruner, J. S. (1970). The growth and structure of skill. In K. Connolly (ed.), *Mechanisms of Motor Skill Development*, Academic Press, New York

Chomsky, N. (1972). Psychology and ideology. *Cognition* i, 11–46

Corter, C. M., Rheingold, H. L., and Eckerman, L. O. (1972). Toys delay the infant's following of his mother. *Dev. Psychol.* vi, 138–45

Estes, W. K. (1970). *Learning Theory and Mental Development*, Academic Press, New York

Estes, W. K. (1972). Learning. In P. C. Dodwell (ed.), *New Horizons in Psychology: Two*, Penguin, Harmondsworth

Fantz, R. L. (1967). Visual perception and experience in early infancy: a look at the hidden side of behavior development. In H. W. Stevenson, E. H. Hess and H. L. Rheingold (eds), *Early Behavior: Comparative and Developmental Approaches*, Wiley, New York

Gewirtz, J. L. (1969). Mechanisms of social learning: some roles of stimulation and behavior in early development. In D. S. Goslin (ed.), *Handbook of Socialization Theory and Research*, Rand McNally, Chicago

Gibson, E. J. (1969). *Principles of Perceptual Learning and Development*, Appleton-Century-Crofts, New York

Kagan, J. (1972). Do infants think? *Scient. Am.* lxxiv, 76–82

Kessen, W., and Mandler, G. (1961). Anxiety, pain and the inhibition of distress. *Psychol. Rev.* lxviii, 396–404

Newall, A. (1967). Thoughts on the concept of process. In J. F. Voss (ed.), *Approaches to Thought*, University Press, Pittsburgh

Parry, N. H. (1972). Infants' responses to novelty in familiar and unfamiliar settings. *Child Dev.* xliii, 233–7

Piaget, J. (1970). Piaget's Theory. In P. H. Mussen (ed.), *Carmichael's Manual of Child Psychology*, 3rd edn, vol. 1. Wiley, New York

Piaget, J., and Inhelder, B. (1969). *The Psychology of the Child*, Routledge & Kegan Paul, London

Ploog, D. (1969). Early communication processes in squirrel monkeys. In R. J. Robinson (ed.), *Brain and Early Behavior: Development in the Fetus and Infant*, Academic Press, New York

Ross, H. S., Rheingold, H. L., and Eckerman, I. O. (1972). Approach and exploration of a novel alternative by twelve-month-old infants. *J. exp. Child Psychol.* xiii, 85–93

Schaffer, H. R. (1966). The onset of fear of strangers and the incongruity hypothesis. *J. Child Psychol. Psychiat.* vii, 95–106.

Skinner, B. F. (1950). Are theories of learning necessary? *Psychol. Rev.* lix, 193–216

4

The Mother's Role in Early Social Development

We have previously noted that the infant enters the world with the capacity to cry, a response having the important function of signalling to the mother that her attention is required. A second kind of signalling behaviour, smiling, which also attracts the attention of adults, begins early in life, typically during the second month. Both crying and smiling have the effect of bringing about interaction between mother and infant. Thus, as Schaffer (1971) points out, the newborn human infant can be regarded as being pre-set to ensure contact with adult members of the human species.

Crying and smiling responses do not necessitate the infant having any awareness or intent of social actions. Indeed, as we have shown, the newborn has no conception of the mother as a person. She simply constitutes the source of important environmental events. When the infant begins to smile he is not aware of smiling at a mother as such, but is making a response that is equally likely to be evoked by a stranger's face or even by a couple of visual dots or an auditory tone. It is not until later that the infant begins to react to the mother as a unique individual, and thus demonstrates an ability to distinguish between her and other things in the environment. Only then can we begin to speak of activities that bear a non-superficial resemblance to human social behaviour as we conceive it.

4.1 RECOGNITION OF THE MOTHER

The increasing ability to recognise, and perhaps be aware of, the independent and continuous existence of external objects, including the child's own mother, involves the integration of a number of capacities that are each influenced by experience. It is especially important for the child to become increasingly aware of his mother, since she not only provides items that meet many of his physical needs, but by virtue of the continuing close relationship between mother and child, she is able to present an environment that is particularly sensitive and responsive to his individual requirements. In some circumstances other adults within the family may spend an appreciable amount of time with the young infant. However, the amount of time spent by others with the infant is usually small. For example, Rebelsky and Hanks (1971) found that middle-class fathers in an American city spent, on average, less than two minutes per day interacting with their infants during the first three months of life.

Schaffer (1971) has ably summarised part of the body of research that demonstrates the infant's growing awareness of the mother as an individual. A number of observers have examined babies' reactions to their mothers and to strangers, and it is inferred that a child is able to recognise the mother if his response to her is reliably different from the reaction evoked by other individuals. Smiling has been the response most frequently measured in these parent–stranger comparisons, and Gewirtz (1965) points out that the conditions leading to social smiling in infants form three stages. At first, smiling appears as a reflex action, produced by any of a number of environmental events. Later, the human face becomes especially effective for eliciting smiling (Watson, 1966). Later still, infants are observed to smile at their mothers but not at strangers. In fact, investigators have also observed differential effects of the mother and strangers on general attentiveness, cardiac rate and pupillary dilation.

Generally speaking, the findings of experiments that have measured smiling and other responses agree in suggesting that an infant becomes reliably able to recognise the mother as an individual from around the age of three months. This figure should be regarded as an approximate one, since in at least one study differential cardiac responses to mother and strangers have been observed at as little as six weeks of age (Schaffer, 1971). In addition, findings by Ainsworth (1969) indicate that there may be cultural differences between children from Africa and Europe in the age of onset of the ability to recognise the mother. However, these reservations aside, it is clear that somewhere in the region of three months of age the mother acquires the distinctiveness to the child that is necessary in order for her to play an important part in early social learning.

4.2 SEPARATION FROM THE MOTHER

The importance of the mother's role in the upbringing of children has long been recognised, but particular stress has been placed on the relationship between mother and child since the publication in 1951 of a report, *Maternal Care and Mental Health* (Bowlby, 1951). A shortened version has been widely distributed (Bowlby, 1953). Bowlby obtained evidence about the childhood years of adults exhibiting certain anti-social disorders of behaviour, and he expressed the view that the root cause of some important disorders lies in the lack of a warm, intimate and continuing relationship with a mother, or permanent mother-substitute. In particular, Bowlby regarded prolonged separation from the mother as the major cause of the psychopathic adult personality of individuals he described as having 'affectionless characters'. Typical cases were some delinquent adolescents guilty of stealing, violence, egotism and sexual misdemeanours 'who seemed to have no feelings for anyone and were very difficult to treat' (Bowlby, 1953, p. 33). The deviant features Bowlby listed included a tendency for relationships to be superficial, lack of real feeling and the capacity to care for people, inaccessibility, lack of concern, and absence of emotional responses in situations where they would be expected, often pointless deceit and evasion and stealing.

The findings of more recent research indicate that additional factors contribute to some at least of the adult personality disorders that Bowlby claimed were caused by maternal deprivation. Accordingly, some of Bowlby's early statements need to be qualified. For example, the suggestion that almost any environment in which the mother is present, however deficient she is in the provision of care and attention, is better for the child than institutional care, is contradicted by research findings (Rutter, 1972). Bowlby has admitted that some of the claims made in his report about the effects of maternal deprivation are too strong (Bowlby, 1969).

It is not entirely realistic to regard maternal deprivation as a single determining factor (Rutter, 1972). The circumstances in regard to which the phrase 'maternal deprivation' has been used generally involve the lack of a number of related but distinct sources of support, all of which contribute to the intellectual, emotional and physical development of the child. In normal circumstances these are provided by the mother. Thus, the absence of the mother may have unfortunate effects not because there is something about a child's own mother that cannot in any circumstances be provided by another individual, but because the mother, by virtue of the fact that she has regular and close interaction with her child over a long period, is particularly well-qualified to meet his varied needs. Some of these needs can be met only by a person who is sufficiently familiar with the child to be sensitive to small changes in his behaviour, and some kinds of learning appear to necessitate the infant and an adult being 'tuned in' to one another in ways that are possible only when there has been regular and frequent interaction over a lengthy period of time. The mother or a permanent mother-substitute is normally the person most likely to be effective in these situations. However, there is no firm evidence that the lack of a mother is so devastating as Bowlby's original study suggested, as long as the infant receives sufficient interaction to acquire secure bonds with one or more adults or older children.

Whatever the reservations to be drawn concerning Bowlby's claims, there is no doubt that his work has been valuable in drawing attention to the importance of mother–child relationships in determining a child's later capabilities and personality. On the whole, human characteristics are formed not by particular events happening at one moment of time, but by the cumulative effects of activities that take place with some regularity. There is no doubt at all that the early experiences of a child have an important bearing on the nature of the individual as an adult: in this broad sense, the child is indeed father to the man. However, it is important to avoid over-simple descriptions of the manner in which childhood experiences determine adult characteristics. The infant is exposed continuously to events of one kind or another, the effects of experience on the child being cumulative in nature. The influence of a particular event on a particular infant depends largely on what that infant has already learned, and specifically on his past experience of similar events. For reasons of this kind, a theory claiming that adult personality is largely determined by specific happenings in childhood is likely to be inadequate. Thus Freud's notion that the way in which the infant handles the feeding relationship is a major determinant of character in adulthood now appears too simple, even though it may contain a good deal of truth. As Schaffer (1971) points out, no definite evidence exists that any specific experience occurring at one point in time in human infancy or childhood leaves permanent effects on the child. On the other hand, recent studies based on close observations of repeated interactions between mother and child during the feeding periods and at other times (for example, Ainsworth and Bell, 1969; David and Appell, 1969) do appear to provide insight into the acquisition of individual patterns of adult behaviour and temperament. Similarly, the simple notion of 'critical periods', by which it is assumed that a particular experience must take place at a specific time if it is to have an effect on the child, has been found wanting. However, it is certainly true that the human is more sensitive at some periods than at others to various kinds of experience. In some instances sensitivity to particular events is related to what the child has learned in the past, and physiological maturation provides a further source of influences on sensitivity to environmental events. Previous learning influences the manner in which an individual receives information from the environment. Events that match the infant's needs by feeding his emerging abilities (White, 1971) and stimuli that are in phase with the activities of the infant (Richards, 1971) are particularly important. The mother, by virtue of the regular and lengthy interactions that take place between her and the child, and her own ability to respond to the child's actions, is very well placed to provide events that have a feeding function or that are phased in the manner just described.

4.3 INTERACTION BETWEEN MOTHER AND CHILD

Precisely what is it about interaction with the mother that is so important for the young child? Research findings have shown that the 'secondary drive hypothesis', by which the child is assumed to become attached to the mother by associating her presence with the satisfaction of food requirements, does not stand up to the empirical evidence. For instance, this 'cupboard love' theory is difficult to reconcile with findings such as Harlow's (1958) observation that infant monkeys taken away from the mother cling not to their source of food, but to surrogates having textural qualities similar to those of the real mother.

4.3.1 *Research by David and Appell*

Some interesting suggestions about the possible effects of regular close contact with an adult emerge from studies in which mother–child interactions have been closely observed over extended periods. David and Appell (1969) made an investigation that involved observation of infants aged one year for three-hour sessions. The authors noted striking consistencies in the kinds of interactions that took place between each of the mother–infant pairs observed, the activities within each pair forming a distinct and consistent general configuration. In some pairs the interactions often took the form of lengthy chains, mother and child each reacting to the actions of the other, as the following example shows.

Molly, under a table, is playing peek-a-boo with the observer and smiling at her. Her mother says to the observer, 'You see she is copying Susan', and to Molly 'Come along, let's go and fetch Susan' → Molly (forgetting her game with the observer) promptly comes out of the hiding place, responds to her mother with happy sounds, takes her hand → they both go towards the door → mother asks Molly to say 'good-bye' to the observer → Molly ignores this but tries to open the door → mother, wishing her to stop doing so, picks her up → Molly protests strongly → mother says 'Come along, it isn't time yet' and to distract her gives her Susan's doll → Molly takes hold of the doll and speaks to it → mother puts Molly down → but Molly goes back to her mother and wants to be picked up → mother says cheerfully 'Always Mummy' and gives her another doll → Molly smiles broadly at her mother → mother announces reluctantly 'I won't look any more' → Molly seems content and retires to play under the table → mother looks down at her and asks 'What are you doing there?' → Molly comes out and stands up . . ., etc. (from David and Appell, 1969, p. 174).

David and Appell also discuss what they call the 'tone' of interaction. This was a measure of the intensity and the apparent degree of happiness the observer judged to be involved. In three of the five pairs observed the tone was described as intense, and in one it was judged to be flat. In one of the pairs, David and Appell considered that the interactions generally provided evidence of mutual dissatisfaction, while in two pairs they recorded that interactions were consistently happy and pleasurable for each of the partners. However, there were differences in tone between the two pairs whose interactions were both considered to be happy. Thus, one pair's responses were described as 'happy and boisterous', while the interactions of the other pair were typically 'happy and quiet' (David and Appell, 1969, p. 176). The authors noted that there were occasional explosions of anger and conflict even in pairs whose interactions were predominantly harmonious.

Having satisfied themselves that there are reliable and consistent patterns of interaction between pairs, David and Appell went on to show that the characteristic patterns are found in the various situations of everyday life that involve interaction between a mother and her infant. Again, considerable differences between pairs were observed. Toiletting, for instance, was seen by one mother and child as a very important event, characterised by strong feelings in both participants, and by a certain amount of tension. In another pair toiletting did not appear to be taken seriously by either mother or child, and the latter was allowed to go about in wet pants, very little effort being made to train her. Among two of the couples different forms of pleasurable interaction were seen. In one case, the mother was highly efficient, keeping her child very clean, and the child submitted passively but with pleasure to the mother's able handling. In the second pair, toiletting was equally pleasurable, but the child was more active, and the toiletting provided an occasion for cheerful interchange. In a third pair, the interaction necessary for toiletting was much less harmonious. The mother seemed to act in sudden and unpredictable ways, and the child, frightened by her rough behaviour, was likely to scream. This sometimes led the mother to give up, thus avoiding what for both mother and child was clearly an unpleasant form of interaction.

There is no detailed evidence about the long-term effects, if there are any, of these consistent patterns of interaction in the feeding and toilet-training situations on the children's later behaviour and personality. Considerable further research is required. It appears likely that Freud's hypothesis that the manner in which the toilet-training situation is handled is a determinant of adult personality is partly correct. Like feeding, toiletting provides a situation in which close contact and co-operation between mother and child is necessary, and social habits acquired in toiletting contexts may contribute to a child's acquisition of characteristic ways of coping with situations that demand co-operation with others. Hence, as Freud suggests, toiletting is likely to be influential; though not for reasons bound up with Freudian theory concerning the localisation of libidinal energies, but simply because social habits that are acquired in this situation are likely to become part of the child's habitual modes of responding in a wider range of circumstances that involve social co-operation.

Observations made by David and Appell strongly indicate that the manner in which a mother–infant pair interacts does affect the infant's behaviour in situations where the mother is not directly involved. For instance, consider two of the children in their study who were observed to behave in quite different ways when confronted by a stranger. One of these children enjoyed a very close, intense relationship with her mother, characterised by lengthy chains of interaction in play situations, much physical contact, and a good deal of following behaviour, aimed at avoiding separation. When this child saw a stranger she would scream and cling to her mother, clearly frightened, but at the same time showing intense interest in the novel person. Very gradually, she would look up and leave her mother's lap, slowly approaching the stranger, but dashing back to her mother whenever the strange individual made a move to approach her. The second infant was much less disturbed by the sight of a stranger, and although showing signs of fear, adopted a cautious but fairly confident approach, observing the strange person for a long time, and eventually walking up to him and engaging in play. The regular patterns of behaviour observed in interactions between this child and the mother were different in predictable ways from those observed in the first pair. Interactions were shorter, less intense in tone, and there were none of the lengthy chains observed in the other mother–infant pair. There was less talking, kissing and cuddling, visual attention being the predominant mode of interaction. Neither mother nor child would go to the extremes of behaviour to ensure minimal separation observed in the other infant. In summary, the different ways of responding by the two infants when confronted by a strange person were in line with what one might have predicted following observation of a range of other situations involving the mother and infant together.

David and Appell claim that their observations indicate that all areas of the child's personality are deeply influenced by its interactions with the mother. Over a lengthy period the mother's reactions to her infant's activities progressively influence the growth of various kinds of behaviour, the interactions forming what David and Appell term 'dynamic organizing force' in the child's development. Some psychologists would prefer an alternative terminology for describing similar observations. Thus, one might say that the mother's actions shape the child's behaviour, by selectively reinforcing some responses, while she also serves as a model that the child can observe and imitate. Bandura and Walters (1963) have provided such an account of social learning in children, and much of the research on social learning in older infants and children to be described in chapter 6 is guided by a theoretical approach of this kind.

4.3.2 *Ainsworth's findings*

One of the strengths of the kind of research undertaken by David and Appell lies in their willingness not only to observe the more clearly apparent and easily measurable activities of the mother and child pairs, but to look for subtle and hard-to-measure constancies of mother–infant interaction. However, in the absence of measurements that are sufficiently precise and objective for one to be confident of a reasonable level of reliability, observational research, however fruitful in suggesting ideas and hypotheses, can rarely be conclusive. One would like to have some research that combines the sensitivity of observation encountered in David and Appell's work with some emphasis on quantification.

An attempt to combine these elements is found in investigations by Margaret Ainsworth. She too has examined interactions between mothers and young infants, and like David and Appell, she has proceeded on the assumption that there is continuity of development from infancy to later years, and that patterns of behaviour established in interactions during infancy may profoundly affect later development. That is to say, the cumulative effect of events that occur during the course of contact between mother and infant are likely to influence the personality of the infant in later life.

One of Ainsworth's reports (Ainsworth and Bell, 1969) describes mother–infant interaction in feeding situations during the first three months of life. The focus on feeding does not imply acceptance of Freudian views concerning the role of oral gratification, but simply reflects the fact that during these months feeding happens to provide the context for many of the activities in which mother and child are mutually involved.

The raw data of Ainsworth's observations are not unlike those of David and Appell, and consist of large numbers of detailed records of the behaviour of mother and infant. However, in Ainsworth's research there is an emphasis on classifying the observations into various basic patterns of interaction in the feeding situation. For example, Ainsworth and Bell (1969) classify interaction during feeding in terms of four chief aspects. These are, firstly, the timing of feedings, secondly, the amount of food ingested, thirdly, how feeding is ended, and, fourthly, the mother's handling of the baby's preferences in kinds of food and the pacing of the rate of intake. The authors asked a number of specific questions about each of these aspects. For instance, concerning the timing of feedings, they sought to discover when, how often and at what intervals each mother fed her baby; whether the feedings were timed in response to the baby's signals and after how much delay; whether or not the mother attempted to stave the infant off, whether there was a definite schedule, and if there was, whether it was rigid or flexible; whether the mother would wake the baby in order to feed him, and whether she advanced feeding if the baby gave signs of being hungry.

Ainsworth and Bell investigated each of the four main aspects of mother–infant interaction, and on the basis of their detailed observations they designated nine main patterns of interaction. Four of these patterns were associated with feeding on demand, four were related to feeding according to schedule, and there was one further category. The final categories chosen are shown below. They are ordered in accordance with the author's judgement of the extent to which the baby was permitted to determine the timing and the amount ingested in feedings, and the pacing of intake. Thus in the first two categories the baby was an active partner, but in the lower categories the mother was considerably more dominant. However, Ainsworth and Bell stress that this ordering, by the degree of activity in the infant's role, is only a rough approximation.

1. Demand : thoroughgoing and consistent
2. Schedule : flexible
3. Demand : overfeeding to gratify the baby
4. Schedule : overfeeding to gratify the baby
5. Schedule : too much staving off
6. Pseudo-demand : mother impatient
7. Pseudo-demand : overfeeding to make the baby sleep long
8. Schedule : rigid, by the clock
9. Arbitrary feeding

The above category descriptions are largely self-explanatory but some further details will serve to illustrate the manner in which a particular category was drawn up, and individual mother–infant pairs assigned to it. The seventh pattern, for instance, 'Pseudo-demand : overfeeding to make the baby sleep long' contained two pairs in which the mothers claimed to feed according to demand, but in fact stuffed their infants so full that they would sleep for a long period without demanding attention. The feedings were very long, and the amount consumed was well above average. In each of these instances the mother was determined that her infant should consume a large quantity, despite the fact that the baby spat, struggled and attempted to avert his head. Not surprisingly, the feedings were tense and anxious. At the end of the first three months feeding was not well regulated in either infant, and the regular feeding rhythms characteristic of the pairs falling into categories one and two were markedly absent. By contrast a mother in category one consistently fed her baby whenever she signalled a desire to go to the breast, sometimes simply for comfort. The infant did not receive too much milk, and was sometimes allowed to drowse at the breast, after which she might resume sucking. This child participated very actively in the feeding situation, and her mother reported at the end of three months that the baby usually signalled her need for milk at intervals of approximately four hours.

In categories one and two, and to a lesser extent in three and four, the mothers were reported as appearing able to see things from the infant's point of view, to take delight in his behaviour, to respond promptly to crying and to be generally sensitive to the state and needs of the child. The mothers' actions in the feeding situation were clearly related to each infant's individual needs. These mothers were also found to give their babies a relatively large amount of physical contact beyond that essential for physical care. A study by Tulkin and Cohler (1973) provides evidence for the importance of the mother's attitude. They found that mothers whose responses to an attitude test indicated that they were willing to encourage reciprocity, and who felt that they could understand and effectively communicate with their infants, spent more time than other mothers in a face-to-face position with their babies, and were more likely to respond to vocalisations, to imitate such vocalisations and to give their infants objects for play.

The potential value of distinguishing and classifying patterns of mother–infant interaction lies in the likelihood that the classifications can be used as a basis for generalisations about the characteristics of the infants during this period, and possibly also for making predictions about the child at a later stage. We might ask, for instance, whether infants whose role in the feeding situation is relatively active, and whose interaction with the mother is generally characterised by harmony and by responsiveness on the part of each partner, tend to have equally harmonious lives outside the feeding situation, either in infancy or later on. The objective evidence required to answer questions such as these is conspicuous by its absence. However, some of Ainsworth and Bell's findings indicate that there are some relationships between events within and outside the feeding situation. For example, Ainsworth and Bell found that the first two patterns of interaction in the feeding situation are those associated with the lowest amount of crying, both before and during feeding. The ninth pattern, arbitrary feeding, on the other hand, was associated with prolonged crying before feeding. Ainsworth and Bell state that the mothers who appeared able to see things from their infant's point of view generally tended to act in ways that led to harmonious interactions both within and outside the feeding situation. In addition, those babies who received gratifying feedback for their behaviour tended to cry less and learned more subtle ways of communicating their needs. They were also better at tolerating frustration, and they acquired more regular feeding rhythms than those babies whose own behaviour did not have much effect on what happened to them.

The fact that mothers' and infants' behaviour is related does not constitute proof that a causal link is involved. It is tempting to regard the mothers whose interactions with their infants were harmonious and mutually satisfactory as being 'good' mothers. However, there is no evidence that those mothers who are less successful in establishing harmonious patterns of mutual activities were any less loving or less concerned with their infant's well-being than the others. A complicating factor is the possibility that some of the babies may have been more difficult from the time of birth, for reasons having nothing to do with their mothers' behaviour.

The findings of the research by Ainsworth and Bell and by David and Appell suggest that the mother contributes in a variety of ways to the child's learning. As Schaffer (1971) observes, even if the mother is regarded solely as a stimulus object, she can be seen to provide a remarkably rich source of environmental events, incorporating constant movement and varied stimulation by complex and distinctive actions. These events, involving as they do a number of sensory modalities simultaneously, are successful in both gaining and maintaining the attention of young infants. In addition, if we continue to regard the mother simply as a source of environmental events, it is clear that the environment so provided is particularly responsive to the child's needs. It not only provides stimuli that have feedback or reinforcing qualities, but also, as the observations by David and Appell show especially clearly, it engages the infant in continuous chains of reciprocal interaction. The mother is a very important part of the child's environment, and a rich source of reinforcing events. Thinking of the mother in solely these terms, however, may lead to our failing to give sufficient emphasis to her ability to respond to her own infant as a unique individual. In the course of numerous chains of mother–child interactions the mother becomes able to pace the environmental stimulation she provides. Richards (1971) suggests that by carefully phasing her activites with those of her infant the mother is able, after making a response, to give him 'time to reply', as she carefully 'feeds' the infant's emerging abilities.

Observational research on mother–infant interactions can be expected to throw some light on the questions raised by Bowlby about maternal deprivation, discussed at the beginning of this chapter. It is little wonder that separation from the mother causes distress in infants. The mother's withdrawal constitutes withdrawal of a major source of nutriment for many of the child's varied needs. Some needs can be met perfectly well in the mother's absence, for instance the requirements for food and warmth. However, there is no simple substitute for those things that the mother is able to supply only by virture of the lengthy periods of close contact with the child. To lose the mother is, at the very least, to lose a rich source of needed environmental events that cannot easily be replaced.

4.4 THE CONCEPT OF ATTACHMENT

The developing infant is said to become 'attached' to the mother, a process that involves the acquisition of 'bonds' between mother and child. Attachment behaviour is demonstrated in a young infant who is left by his mother in an empty, unfamiliar room. The child will follow the mother out of the room with little delay. However, this behaviour can be modified fairly easily. For instance, ten-month-old infants left by their mothers in a room that is unfamiliar but contains one new toy remain in the room for over three minutes, on average, without apparent distress, before seeking their mothers (Corter *et al.*, 1972). In addition infants at around ten months of age may take considerable interest in unfamiliar adults, smiling at them and paying close visual attention (Eckerman and Rheingold, 1974; Corter, 1974), indicating that the fear of strangers in infants is less common and less powerful than has been claimed. These findings suggest the possibility that much attachment behaviour is not solely a matter of the infant retreating from the unfamiliar to the security offered by the mother. Perhaps the mother often provides what is simply the most interesting available location. Furthermore, the general level of intellectual development may be a factor influencing infants' reactions to the unfamiliar. Paradise and Curcio (1974) observed that among nine- and ten-month-old infants, those who scored high on a scale measuring their ability to conceive of persons as having a permanent identity were more likely than others to display fearful behaviour when confronted by strangers.

It is open to question whether terms such as 'attachment' and 'bonds' are simply convenient descriptions of observable behaviour, or whether they refer to specific underlying systems. Some psychologists are very critical of the notion of attachment between mother and infant. Thus

Maccoby and Masters (1970) point out that whereas Bowlby (1969) shows that non-reinforcement or punishment attachment responses get stronger, an observation that he suggests provides evidence in favour of an attachment mechanism and is contrary to the 'secondary reinforcement' hypothesis. Some behaviourist psychologists have suggested that the situation resembles an intermittent reward schedule, whereby failure to reinforce some actions simply produces a strengthening or increase in frequency of such responses in the future.

Unlearned, or instinctive, factors may well be involved in the growth of human attachment behaviour. In many species, behaviour on the part of mother or infant, or both, that maintains proximity, has survival value, providing protection from predators (Bowlby, 1969). However, to account for the distress caused by separation we do not have to assume that instinctive determinants must be involved. The young infant deprived of his mother is deprived indeed.

4.4.1 *Separation and the disruption of bonds*

We noted earlier that findings of modern research have led to the modification but not to the total contradiction of Bowlby's (1951) views on the effects of maternal deprivation. The association between deprivation and subsequent psychopathic or 'conscienceless' personality seems to be less clear than Bowlby indicated (Rutter, 1972).

The observations of interactions between mother and child suggest that there may be a number of separate causes of the effects that Bowlby and others have attributed to maternal deprivation. Some but not all of the beneficial outcomes of such interaction appear to depend on regular and close contact over a long period of time, and the necessary conditions for this to occur are much more likely to be present in the day-to-day routine of a conventional family life than in an understaffed institution.

As we have said, mother and child exhibit various responses towards each other that can be labelled 'attachment behaviour'. Mother and infant can be said to form a bond, as a result of regular and close interaction. Rutter (1972) makes a distinction between the disruption of bonds and their failure to develop. Disruption of bonds arises from separation of the child from the person (normally the mother) to whom he has regularly directed attachment behaviour. There is no doubt that such separation often causes considerable distress in infants, but there is no conclusive evidence that separation for periods of around a month or less has any permanent effects. The precise reasons for the separation, and the underlying circumstances, are likely to be important factors, and it is not possible to make a clear statement about the effects of brief separation *per se.* It is similarly difficult to make any conclusive statements about the results of prolonged separation. Certainly, as Rutter points out, delinquency in adolescence is associated with broken homes, but the precise causes of the breaks are crucial in determining the outcome. For instance, children from homes broken by divorce and separation tend to become delinquent, but children from homes broken by death do not have a significantly higher rate of delinquency than individuals from unbroken homes.

Circumstances in which bonds fail to develop between an infant and any adult may well give rise to the psychopathic adult personality, lacking in normal ties of affection and conscience, that Bowlby claimed to be a result of maternal deprivation. Rutter considers that failure to form bonds (but not necessarily with the mother) may lead to clinging and to dependent behaviour in infancy, followed by attention-seeking and indiscriminate friendliness, and finally by an adult personality characterised by lack of guilt feelings and of the normal ties that appear to be necessary for the formation of lasting human relationships. However, the evidence is by no means conclusive, and the very term 'bond formation' is in itself an inference.

It is always difficult to confirm or disprove the claim that an inferred process is responsible for an observed outcome, and this kind of difficulty has led some behaviourist psychologists to be wary of using concepts such as 'attachment', 'dependence', and 'identification', all of which are inferred processes said to be involved in relationships between individuals (see, for example, Gewirtz, 1969; Bandura, 1969). Gewirtz considers that dependence and attachment should both be considered simply as abstractions for classes of functional relationships in which stimuli provided either by people (in 'dependence') or a particular individual (in 'attachment') exert positive stimulus control over a range of an individual's responses. Gewirtz objects to the use of terms such as these as though they represented unitary processes, and he argues that to do so amplifies the imprecision of research on human development.

Increased attention is being paid by researchers in the field of child development to the mother's role in forming an individual's abilities, personality and temperament. It is clear that the detailed observational studies of mother–infant interaction represent an advance on

Bowlby's pioneering work, which drew attention to the crucial importance of maternal behaviour. Research has a long way to proceed before a complete understanding is achieved, and some of the attributes that are likely to prove important, such as the 'quality of feeling' on the part of the mother, remain unexplored because we do not yet possess adequate measuring procedures. It is safe to predict that in future years we shall see an increasing number of investigations into various kinds of mothering activites.

REFERENCES

Ainsworth, M. D. S. (1969). Object relations, dependency and attachment: a theoretical review of the infant–mother relationship. *Child Dev.* xl, 969–1025

Ainsworth, M. D., and Bell, S. M. (1969). Some contemporary patterns of mother–infant interaction in the feeding situation. In A. Ambrose (ed.), *Stimulation in Early Infancy*, Academic Press, New York

Bandura, A. (1969). *Principles of Behavior Modification*, Holt, Rinehart & Winston, New York

Bandura, A., and Walters, R. H. (1963). *Social Learning and Personality Development*, Holt, Rinehart & Winston, New York

Bowlby, J. (1951). *Maternal Care and Mental Health*, World Health Organisation, Geneva

Bowlby, J. (1953). Child Care and the Growth of Love, Peguin, Harmondsworth

Bowlby, J. (1969). *Attachment*, Hogarth Press, London

Corter, C. M. (1974). A comparison of the mother's and a stranger's control over the behaviour of infants. *Child Dev.* xliv, 705–13

Corter, C. M., Rheingold, H. L., and Eckerman, L. O. (1972). Toys delay the infant's following of his mother. *Dev. Psychol.* vi, 138–45

David, M., and Appell, G. (1969). Mother–child interaction and its impact upon the child. In A. Ambrose (ed.), *Stimulation in Early Infancy*, Academic Press, New York

Eckerman, C. O., and Rheingold, H. L. (1974). Infants' exploratory responses to toys and people. *Dev Psychol.* x, 255–9

Gewirtz, J. L. (1965). The course of infant smiling in four child-rearing environments in Israel. In B. H. Foss (ed.), *Determinants of Infant Behaviour*, vol. 3, Methuen, London

Gewirtz, J. L. (1969). Mechanisms of social learning: some roles of stimulation and behavior in early development. In D. S. Goslin (ed.),

Handbook of Socialization Theory and Research, Rand McNally, Chicago

Harlow, H. F. (1958). The nature of love. *Am. Psychol.* xiii, 673–85

Maccoby, E. E., and Masters, J. C. (1970). Attachment and Dependency. In P. H. Mussen (ed.), *Carmichael's Manual of Child Psychology*, 3rd edn, vol. 1, Wiley, New York

Paradise, E. B., and Curcio, F. (1974). Relationship of cognitive and affective behaviours to fear of strangers in male infants. *Dev. Psychol.* x, 476–83

Rebelsky, F., and Hanks, C. (1971). Fathers' verbal interaction with infants in the first three months of life. *Child Dev.* xlii, 63–8

Rheingold, H. K., Gewirtz, J. L., and Ross, H. W. (1959). Social conditioning of vocalizations in the infant. *J. comp. physiol. Psychol.* lii, 68–73

Richards, M. P. M. (1971). Social interaction in the first weeks of human life. *Psychiat. Neurol. Neurchir.* iv, 35–42

Rutter, M. (1972). *Maternal Deprivation Reassessed*, Penguin, Harmondsworth

Schaffer, H. R. (1966). The onset of fear of strangers and the incongruity hypothesis. *J. Child Psychol. Psychiat.* vii, 95–106

Tulkin, S. R., and Cohler, B. J. (1973). Childrearing attitudes and mother–child interaction in the first year of life. *Merrill–Palmer Q.* xix, 105–6

Watson, J. S. (1966). Perception of object orientation in infants. *Merrill–Palmer Q.* xii, 73–94

White, B. L. (1971). *Human Infants: Experience and Psychological Development*, Prentice-Hall, Englewood Cliffs, New Jersey

5

Language and the Young Child

Human language enables us to communicate with others, and it also provides the learner with an efficient means of internalising his own mental processes. We use language to communicate with ourselves. Of course, the internalisation of information about the environment does not always require language. In chapter 2 it was shown that even the simplest object recognition requires the learner to possess some kind of inner representation, specifying attributes of an object to be recognised. Infants are able to recognise objects long before they can use language. Nevertheless, language does enormously increase the scope of what can be accomplished and communicated internally. The symbolic system constitutes a kind of internal world, making it possible for man to reason, to reflect and to develop kinds of awareness that are inconceivable in other species.

Human language has received a great deal of attention from scholars in a variety of disciplines. Much of the research undertaken to investigate relationships between language and learning has a bearing on one of two relatively distinct questions. First, what is the role of learning in the acquisition of language, and second, what is the role of language in human learning?

The major part of this chapter is concerned with the second of these questions, as is part of chapter 7. The other question, concerning the contribution of learning to the acquisition of human language, is undoubtedly important. However, the issues that arise in this area of enquiry are numerous and complicated, and involve a number of theoretical approaches and forms of evidence that are not encountered in research on other kinds of learning. Consequently, an effort to reduce the mass of evidence and theory on language acquisition to a length appropriate for the present account would result in an unsatisfactorily superficial coverage of the subject of language acquisition.

For this reason no attempt is made in this book to provide a comprehensive survey of research on the role of learning in language acquisition. Instead, a number of examples of research are described to illustrate the kinds of investigations that have been undertaken and some of the considerations and problems that arise.

There is no doubt that learning is crucial for the child's acquisition of language. Scientists differ, however, in the degrees of relative importance they attach to the role of learning, on the one hand, and to unlearned factors of a biological nature, on the other, in contributing to every child's ability to speak and understand a language. Many researchers in the field of psycholinguistics, which has made a large contribution to knowledge about the structure and use of language, are in broad agreement with the views of Noam Chomsky (1966) who has suggested that a language user must possess certain innate devices predisposing him to acquire the rules and skills that constitute human language, and that these cannot be acquired solely through learning. Chomsky has conceived of human language as having a finite structure with an infinite potential to generate new linguistic utterances. As Brown (1973) points out, traditional learning theories cannot adequately explain how each individual acquires such a capacity, and the fact that a child extracts such a structured rule system from the language he hears during the short period before he reaches school age adds to the difficulty of explanation. In the following pages we shall consider both evidence concerning the role of learning in the acquisition of language by children, and evidence that it is not possible to explain language acquisition in terms of learning principles alone.

5.1 LEARNING IN LANGUAGE ACQUISITION

It is not possible to state a precise age at which language in the child begins. During the first six months of life most infants make a variety of noises, particulary when excited. In the course of babbling, crying and the cooing that occurs from the second month of life, the infant emits a number of the sounds that form a part of later linguistic utterances. Irwin (1947) noticed that as early as the first ten days of life some infants emit several vowels, the consonant *h*, and, occasionally, *w* and *k*. The first meaningful word appears at around one year of age, and at this time the child can probably understand more items than he can produce. Subsequent language development is noticeably rapid. By fifteen months the number of words spoken or understood is around twenty, by twenty-one months it is 120, and by twenty-four months something in the region of 300 words are available. At around this age the child begins to put words together, and the rate of acquiring new items continues to increase.

5.1.1 *Reinforcements and vocalisation*

Various kinds of evidence indicate that learning mechanisms play a part in the child's acquiring the ability to communicate by language. It has been found that operant-conditioning procedures can lead to increases in the amount of vocalisation observed in infants. Rheingold *et al.* (1959) discovered that the rate of vocalisation in infants as young as three months of age could be increased by operant procedures incorporating social reinforcement. Lewis (1959) noted that his ten-week infant normally made four sounds, on average, per three-minute period. However, if the father said 'Hello' every ten seconds, the number of the baby's vocalisations rose to eighteen. Ramey and Ourth (1971) observed infants aged three, six and nine months. During the first minute of the nine-minute recording sessions each infant's baseline level of vocalisation was measured. Subsequently there was a conditioning period during which an experimenter recorded and reinforced each vocalisation the infant made. The reinforcement contained three components, presented simultaneously. These were, a light touch on the abdomen, a smile, and the statement 'That's a good baby'. Perhaps surprisingly, the effects of reinforcement were found not to vary with the age of the infant. At each age, when reinforcement followed vocalisation with no delay, the frequency of vocalisation rose to about three times the baseline level. However, if the reinforcing events were delayed by as little as three seconds, they had no effect at all on the vocalisation rate. Thus, for the events to be reinforcing, they had to follow vocalisation immediately. The amount of vocalisation in infants increases when combined auditory and social stimulation is provided. In one experiment (Dodd, 1972) infants aged nine to twelve months were placed on the knee of the experimenter, who gave utterance to sequences of consonants and babbling sounds. This procedure had the effect of increasing the number and length of the child's vocal outputs. However, no such effect was observed when either the social or vocal components were provided alone, that is when either a recording of the sounds was provided, in the absence of an adult, or when the adult engaged in social play with the infant but without the sounds provided in the condition combining auditory and social stimulation.

These findings clearly indicate that the amount of vocalisation produced by young infants can be modified by experience. However, it is open to question whether the amount of infant vocalisation is a major factor determining later progress towards acquiring advanced language skills, despite the fact that the sounds uttered in infancy undoubtedly form the ingredients of subsequent speech sounds. An unexplained finding of experimental research into this question is that there is a sex difference in the predictive power of early infant vocalisation for later speech development (Mussen *et al.* 1969). In infant girls, considerable babbling in response to the sight of human faces is associated with high intelligence test scores and attentiveness at as late as three years of age. In boys, however, no such positive relationship between early vocalisation and later intellectual competence has been found. This sex difference has been observed in three independent studies, two of which were undertaken in the United States, and one in Britain. A number of possible explanations have been put forward. Some of these assume that there are innate sex differences in the organisation of the brain, which is conceivable but very unlikely. An alternative possibility is that there are greater individual differences between mothers in the extent to which they talk to their daughters than in the time they spend talking to their sons.

5.1.2 *Learning and the acquisition of advanced linguistic skills*

Research has also been undertaken to investigate the role of learning in the acquisition of specifically linguistic skills, as distinct from simple vocalisation. Staats (1971) has described some experiences with his six-month-old daughter. As part of a language-training exercise he would kneel a few feet away from his daughter and say 'Come to Daddy', while holding in his hand a key ring which was visible to the child and which previous experience had shown to be reinforcing to her. When the child approached her father she was given the key ring to play with. Subsequent variations in this training involved other rewarding objects and rewarding social interactions. In this manner Staats observed that the verbal stimulus became a reliable control of the child's behaviour.

It has been shown that the ability to use simple grammatical rules can be acquired through training that incorporates specific instances of the rule. Guess *et al.* (1968) taught an institutionalised girl who was mentally retarded and without speech. The girl learned to produce labels for objects, by imitating a model. Then she was taught the plurals for each word. Afterwards a test was given to ascertain whether she would be able to produce the plural form of a word she had just learned. Note that the girl was never explicitly taught a rule as such. However, she was nevertheless able to apply the appropriate rule for transforming words into their plural forms, learning each new word in a single trial and generating its plural with no prompting. Brown (1973) reiterates this point, stating that while children certainly gain rules of language, this does not necessarily mean that the rules are acquired in any explicit form. Both children and adults regularly make use of language rules that they would be quite unable to articulate. The fact that children do use rules is illustrated by many of the mistakes they make, an example given by Brown being 'hisself', which is an outcome of consistently following the usual rule for producing reflexive pronouns, by combining possessive adjectives with 'self', as in 'myself', 'yourself' and 'herself'.

A study by Weir (1962) provides a further source of evidence concerning the contribution to language acquisition of principles and processes encountered in alternative forms of learning. She tape-recorded all the sounds made by her thirty-month-old son between being put to bed in the evening and falling asleep. The child engaged in a great deal of speech, practising word sequences in a deliberate and systematic manner. The child, who clearly gained much enjoyment from this activity, indulged in a large amount of repetition or 'drilling', often correcting his errors in the course of his linguistic play. Some of the speech involved the build up of sentences, for instance, 'Block. Yellow block. Look at the yellow block', or an opposite 'breakdown' procedure, such as 'Another big bottle. Big bottle'. The practice that went on during these sessions was not restricted to passive repetition, but included the active formation of new word combinations. On some occasions new nouns would be substituted into fixed sentence frames, for example, 'What colour. What colour blanket. What colour mop. What colour glass'. Affirmation and negation rules were practised on some occasions, as in the following sample: 'Not the yellow blanket. The white. It's not black. It's yellow. Not yellow. Red'. In short, it appears that the kinds of systematic practice and drilling procedures that are commonly encountered in the learning of motor skills and in school-learning tasks such as spelling, or in the acquisition of a second language, also play a part, for some children at least, in the growth of a child's ability to use the language of his parents.

The findings of an experiment by Vincent-Smith *et al.* (1974) indicate that children at around twenty-four months of age perform strikingly well on tasks involving the kind of receptive learning necessary for vocabulary acquisition. The children saw 100 pairs of objects, in which the name of one of the items was unknown, and the name of the second item was known in some instances and not known in others. On the first presentation, subjects correctly matched the first item with its verbal label when they knew the name of the second item, but not otherwise. However, by the fifth presentation all the tested items were recognised from their names, and their performance in further tests indicated that the children really had learned the names of the items, and had not made correct choices merely by eliminating items they did know. It is clear that children at this age can rapidly learn the names for new objects.

5.1.3 *Language training in non-human primates*

An interesting source of ideas about the kinds of learning processes that may be involved in gaining a language has been provided by attempts to teach language to non-human primates. Until recently, such attempts have met with remarkably little success, but it seems likely that their failure was due in part to dependence on the use of speech, for which only humans are well-equipped. Recent studies with chimpanzees have made use both of pieces of coloured plastic for the language medium, and of sign language. Premack and Premack (1972), for instance, attempted to train a five-year-old chimpanzee, named Sarah. In an early session, Sarah was given a piece of banana which she was allowed to eat while the trainer looked on. Later a pink plastic square was placed close to Sarah, and a slice of banana was placed beyond her reach. In order to obtain the banana Sarah had to put the piece of plastic on a board that was on the side of her cage. On later occasions the same procedure was carried out with apples (signified by a blue plastic shape) and other fruits. In this manner Sarah acquired a different 'word' for each fruit. Later on, she learned to distinguish between the various words that were involved in transactions with the fruits. For example, she learned to distinguish between 'give apple', 'wash apple', and 'not apple'. To indicate a particular action Sarah would place two of the plastic shapes on the board, in a vertical sequence. The first shape denoted the verb, and the second denoted the item. Thus, in order to receive an apple, she had to produce the sequence 'give apple'. At a later stage Sarah was required to produce three-word sentences in order to obtain items of fruit. There were several trainers, and it was necessary for Sarah to learn the name of each one and to place on the board an appropriate piece of plastic, in addition to the shape representing the required action (for example, 'give') and the required item (for example, 'banana'). The authors report that Sarah had to pay for some of her mistakes. Thus when she mistakenly produced 'Give apple Gussie' the apple was given to another chimpanzee, named Gussie. In order to gain what she wanted, Sarah had to provide the correct words in the right sequence (for example, 'Mary give apple Sarah').

Similar procedures were used for teaching Sarah to use sentences of greater complexity. She successfully learned to use interrogative statements, and she acquired the concepts 'name of' and 'not name of', making it possible to introduce new words directly. She also learned to use conditional statements. A typical pair of sentences might be 'If Sarah take apple Mary give chocolate Sarah' and 'If Sarah take banana Mary no give chocolate Sarah'. In this instance it is clear that very careful 'reading' of the two sentences was necessary for Sarah to ascertain how to get the reward. Words for colours, shapes and sizes were also learned. For instance, the word 'brown' might be introduced in the sentence, 'Brown colour of chocolate'. Later, when confronted with four differently coloured objects, and the sentence 'take brown' she took the brown item. Note that no actual chocolate had been present at any time during these sessions, and Sarah must have retained some internal representation of the colour, enabling her to recognise which of the coloured objects was brown.

5.2 UNLEARNED FACTORS IN LANGUAGE ACQUISITION

The experiments described in the preceding several pages provide abundant evidence that learning is heavily involved in the acquisition of human language, and indeed no one has seriously doubted that this is the case. Nevertheless, there has been a great deal of support for the view, expressed by Chomsky and by other researchers in the field of psycholinguistics who have been influenced by his work, that language acquisition may be possible only if the child possesses, in addition to learned abilities, certain 'innate intellectual structures' (Chomsky, 1966) having the functions of a language-acquisition device that provides descriptively adequate grammar, given appropriate environmental input in the form of the language a child hears. The hypothetical language-acquisition device is so constructed that it can formulate rules from the regularities existing in speech inputs. To be universally applicable, the acquisition device must contain information about the general form of human language, and not be specific to any particular language. Thus the child is enabled to extract a set of often highly abstract rules from the speech to which he listens, although as we have previously mentioned, neither he nor his parents are likely to be able to articulate the rules.

5.2.1 *Similarities in different languages*

Observations of speech by children of various nationalities provide some support for the existence of some kind of unlearned mechanism which facilitates language acquisition in children. For instance, it is found that when children are learning to speak, the errors they make form only a small proportion of the kinds of possible errors, indicating that some structure or rule-system restricts the range of linguistic utterances emitted. Furthermore, it is noticeable that children acquiring different languages go through very similar stages of language acquisition. In addition to these findings, the fact that there are a number of characteristics uniform to all languages (and known as *language universals*) has been cited as providing further support for the existence of wholly or partly innate mechanisms that have the function of devices that enable linguisitic rules to be acquired.

Some of the arguments that have been put forward to support the view that complex unlearned systems are heavily involved in language acquisition appear to reflect somewhat naïve views about what can be achieved through learning. Thus it has been suggested that the impossibility of explaining language acquisition in terms of simple conditioning or associative learning principles is proof for the importance of innate biological mechanisms. However, this reasoning neglects the fact that in addition to learning new items according to associative principles, humans can also learn rules, a fact that is demonstrated by the experiment undertaken by Guess *et al.* (described previously) who taught a retarded girl the rule for forming the plurals of newly learned nouns. The application by the language-user of learned rules makes it possible to generate a large number of linguistic sequences that have not previously been encountered. Lenneberg (1964) has provided evidence of a more positive form to support the view that unlearned mechanisms are closely involved in language acquisition. He notes that there exist various anatomical and physiological correlates of language, and that language attributes are related to a large number of measurable physical characteristics. For example, there are certain parts of the human brain that have specialised functions associated with language and speech. Lenneberg also draws attention to the great regularity of the onset of speech. All children appear to follow a constant order, beginning with the acquisition of principles of categorisation, and the earliest words, according to Lenneberg, refer to classes rather than to single objects or events. Nelson (1973), who has conducted a number of experiments demonstrating children's ability to categorise objects before they can name them, provides further evidence for the cognitive primacy of categorisation and its functional role in language. Another fact cited by Lenneberg is the difficulty of suppressing a child's onset of language, even when apparently crippling handicaps are present, such as blindness, deafness, or gross neglect. Lenneberg describes a clinical condition, *Nanocephalic Dwarfism*, the victims of which have extremely small brains, less than half of the normal weight, with a correspondingly small number of brain cells (whose weight and density are within the normal limits). People suffering from this condition manifest gross intellectual retardation, but nevertheless acquire the ability to use language. Lenneberg points out that this evidence both contradicts the theory that the universal presence of language in humans and its absence in other species can be explained by the fact that man has a larger brain, and supports the view that 'specific modes of internal organisation of neurophysiological processes' are involved in human language.

5.2.2 *The acquisition of stable structures*

Piaget (1970) has reminded us that while language may certainly involve mechanisms and processes that are distinct in form, and exhibit a greater degree of biological specialisation than is evident in the processes underlying alternative kinds of complex human behaviour, there nevertheless exist important continuities between language and certain non-linguistic capacities. He accepts Chomsky's suggestion that language necessitates the user's possessing a language-acquisition device that has a strong inner structure, but disagrees with the assumption that the structure is genetically preprogrammed, and with the lack of any attempt to link language behaviour to the preceding sensorimotor forms of behaviour (Inhelder, 1971). Piaget notes some similarities between language and symbolic behaviour on the one hand and, on the other, capacities apparent in children who have not yet acquired language. Piaget uses the term 'semiotic' to refer to those functions, which include, in addition to language, symbolic games, mental imagery and imitation. He stresses the continuity between imitation ('a sort of representation through actual actions') and language. Imitation which is seen in an internalised and differentiated form in images, becomes the instrument of communicative exchange that makes language acquisition possible. In assessing the role of biological factors in language, Piaget accepts Chomsky's reasoning that language requires complex and stable mental structures, but he questions Chomsky's assumption that because such structures are complex and stable, they need to be governed by innate mechanisms. Piaget claims that Chomsky incorrectly sees only two alternatives, either an innate schema, or acquisition from the outside through simple learning. Having showed that the second of these explanations is inadequate, Chomsky accepts the first. However, Piaget points out that a third possibility exists, a process of 'internal equilibration', through which, put simply, self-regulatory processes involved in sensorimotor schemas that emerge early in human life progressively interact with, or use, environmental events to *form* the kinds of inner structures that Chomsky shows to be necessary for the human use of grammatical (rule-governed) language. Piaget notes that language does not emerge until the end of a long sensorimotor period, and he regards this fact as evidence that mental structures acquired during the earliest period of life are essential for subsequent linguistic competence. Language and 'the semiotic function of which it is the most obvious expression' (Inhelder, 1971) do not appear suddenly, out of the blue, but are preceded and prepared for by the elementary growth of knowledge at the sensorimotor level.

5.3 THE ROLE OF LANGUAGE IN HUMAN LEARNING: SPEECH AND BEHAVIOUR

Psychologists have carried out numerous investigations into the relationships between language and the behaviour of the young child. On the whole, the findings of recent investigations suggest that language plays a significant functional role before the child makes obvious use of it (Blank, 1974). As the child learns to speak, language initially exerts a somewhat coarse guidance over behaviour, but later the control becomes increasingly precise. For instance, the findings of a series of Russian studies, described by Luria (1961), suggest that as children become older there are changes in the extent to which motor activities are under the control of verbal signals. Understanding the meaning of a command does not necessarily guarantee that the child will be able to put into action the appropriate sequence of behaviour that an adult would carry out in following the command. Experimental results described by Luria show that a child aged eighteen months who is given a rubber bulb, and then told to squeeze it, is able to comply with this simple instruction. But if he is then instructed 'Don't squeeze', he goes on squeezing, often more vigorously than before. At this stage it is clear that although the verbal signals do have some power to control the child's behaviour, the control is rather crude. The child is not able to act discriminatively when the word 'Squeeze' appears on its own and when it is preceded by 'Don't'.

In the child of this age, verbal signals are not very effective for inhibiting or delaying his activities. For instance, he cannot respond correctly to the instruction 'When the light comes on, squeeze the bulb'. It may appear to an adult that the request to delay responding necessitates only a minor change from the original command to press the bulb, which the child had no difficulty in obeying. However, the child of eighteen months cannot follow this apparently simple new instruction.

Luria's research follows the increasing role of speech in the regulation of the growing child's behaviour. By the age of three years the child is able to follow the instructions to press the bulb, not to press, and to press only when a signal occurs. However, the control of speech over behaviour remains tenuous. Positive instructions are followed perfectly, but negative instructions are likely to give greater difficulty, and saying 'I must not press' on an appropriate occasion does not effectively inhibit pressing in the three-year-old. Language can regulate the child's actions most precisely when there exists a direct relationship between the signal and the following behaviour. After the instruction 'When the lamp comes on, press twice' he tends to persevere, and goes on pressing. However, the child of equivalent age who is instructed to say 'one, two' as he presses is likely to respond correctly in this situation.

The investigations by Luria and his colleagues have shown us that language and behaviour in the child are not always so closely related as they are in adults, and their studies have stimulated further research into the changing role of language in children. However, it must be noted that some attempts to reproduce the experiments, using American children as subjects, have produced findings that disagree with those reported by Luria. For instance, in a bulb-squeezing experiment by

Miller *et al.* (1970) similar to one described above by no means all of the children, who were three to five years of age, responded in a manner consistent with the actions of the subjects who participated in the original study. It appears that there may be considerable differences between cultures in the role of language in regulating behaviour.

On the other hand, Beiswenger (1971), who observed American children of three and four years of age at tasks requiring them to make conditional responses (for example, 'Every time the blue light comes on, get a blue marble and put it in the dish') and to respond to straightforward commands (for example, 'Get a yellow marble and put it in the dish') obtained results in line with those described by Luria. Beiswenger agrees with Luria that the process by which the child's verbal system acquires the capacity to organise and sequence his behaviour is a lengthy and complex one, involving the interaction, development and exercise of a number of mechanisms involved in language comprehension, and the maturation of various central nervous-system mechanisms underlying attentional and motor skills.

5.4 LABELLING FUNCTIONS OF LANGUAGE

One way in which language can influence learning is illustrated by the findings of experiments in which individuals are told to provide names or labels for the items to which they are attending. Jensen (1971) observed that up to the age of five children who are asked to name objects they are shown once can recall more items than children who are not instructed to name them. Children aged six years and above do not remember more items when they are told to name them, presumably because they provide names spontaneously on first seeing objects, although they do not necessarily say the names aloud. Thus specific instructions to name items might not markedly influence the strategies of the older children. Jensen points out that in this and other studies differences are found between middle-class and culturally deprived children and between normal and mentally retarded individuals in the extent to which naming takes place spontaneously, in the absence of any specific instructions. As a result, providing instructions to name items typically has the effect of reducing the inter-group differences in learning that are observed in the absence of labelling instructions. The evidence suggests that at an early age some children acquire a habit of providing verbal labels (and perhaps of using other verbal strategies as well) which may be used to good advantage in a range of circumstances that provide opportunities for learning. It is conceivable that differences in acquiring and in forming the habit of using widely applicable strategies and skills account for more of the individual differences found in learning than do learning differences in the narrower sense of the rate of acquiring new connections between previously unrelated items. We shall return to this suggestion in chapter 7.

An experiment by Norcross and Spiker (1957) provides a further illustration of the value of using words as labels. Children of preschool age were told to look at drawings of two boys' faces or two girls' faces. The faces differed in the shape of the eyes, mouth and hair. Each of seventy children was assigned to one of three training groups. One group learned names (Peg and Jean) for the two girls' faces, and the second group learned names for the boys' faces. The third group were trained to distinguish between the different faces. During their training two faces were presented, one at a time, identical on some occasions and different on others, and the children simply had to say whether they were the same or different. After the training all three groups were given a task that involved choosing one of the two female faces. A child chose one of the faces on each of a number of trials and for each correct choice he received a marble, which could later be exchanged for a prize.

It was found that children in the group whose training session had incorporated the girls' faces made the correct choice at the new task on an average of twenty-two trials out of thirty, and subjects from the other training groups obtained significantly lower scores. The group who had learned names for the female faces apparently acquired a greater ability to discriminate between those faces in the two-choice task than did the others, despite the fact that the other groups did receive specific training in discriminating between faces similar in form to those used in the final task. It appears that having to learn names or labels for the particular figures to be encountered is especially valuable for ensuring later recognition and discrimination. In this experiment there were some differences between the three training groups in the number of trials during training, a fact that could have influenced the findings. However, the original results were substantially repeated in a second experiment, carefully designed to ensure that each group received an identical amount of training. An interesting additional finding was that children performed better at tasks requiring them to make correct choices among items for which they learned names when the names were distinctive than when they were alike. Norcross (1958) in an experiment based on the one described above, found that children performed better when the names were Wag and Kos than when they formed the more similar pair Zim and Zam.

The advantageous effects of labelling can produce what Jensen (1971) calls an 'elaboration paradox', by which it is sometimes easier to learn a complex task than one that appears to be simpler. In an experiment reported in 1932 by Marjorie Honzik it was noticed that children who first learned nonsense-syllable labels for three-dimensional shapes learned to choose the correct item from a number of shapes much more quickly than children who did not learn the labels. As Jensen points out, the requirement of having to learn a name for each object appears to add difficulty by imposing an additional task. However, the fact that acquiring names considerably facilitates the choice task amply compensates for this extra requirement.

5.5 MEDIATION

5.5.1 *The second signalling system*

Language has various roles in human learning, extending in scope well beyond the function of simple labelling. In order to reason effectively and to be able to process in an efficient manner the information that humans receive about events in the environment, it is necessary to have ways of detecting equivalent attributes of physically dissimilar items. Reasoning operates on information that is organised at the level of abstracted common attributes of events. Thus a particular physical event becomes comprehensible when it is perceived not simply as a unique array of stimuli, but as being related to other events. Any such classification demands some kind of abstraction, but we should bear in mind that the adjective 'abstract' is a relative one. In order to account for human reasoning that is based on abstracted and classified information about the world, Pavlov introduced the concept of a 'second signalling system'. Distinct from a first signalling system, whereby the individual responds directly to physical stimuli detected by the receptors, the second signalling system accounts for the increasing tendency in developing children to make use of reasoning processes that demand internalisation and classification of events. Pavlov regarded speech and symbolic behaviour as being crucially important for the second signalling system, within which language is seen as mediating between events and the responses to them.

5.5.2 *Experiments on mediation*

The term 'mediation' broadly refers to processes involved in the internalisation of reasoning. Let us imagine that a bull which perceives the word 'red' written in white chalk responds in a manner that is identical to its response to a red blanket. In such a situation we would infer that the bull has been able to internalise information concerning the two distinct events, the written word and the red blanket, at a sufficiently abstract level for their attribute in common to be detected. Mediation is a word used to denote the internal processes necessary for the observer to perceive such a link between physically dissimilar items. In humans, mediation often makes use of symbolic processes that are verbal in nature. However, mediation can also involve imagery, and this may take a number of forms, although as yet only visual forms of imagery have been extensively investigated in psychological research.

Mediating processes can be demonstrated in a number of ways. One method is used in studies of a phenomenon known as 'semantic generalisation'. In a typical experiment, a subject's galvanic skin response (a measure of normally involuntary emotional reactivity, encountered, for example, in lie detectors) is classically conditioned to a blue light. Following this, it is found that the conditioned response can also be elicited by presentation of the word blue. In addition, words that are either similar or associated in meaning, such as sky, are also found to elicit the response, albeit in weaker form. Findings such as this make it clear that the mediational processes involved in a human learner's second signalling system provide some kind of internal link. This leads to individuals having equivalent reactions to events as disparate in physical form as a blue light and the printed words 'blue' and 'sky'.

5.6 CROSS-MODAL TRANSFER AND RECOGNITION

If we make an object available to a child via one sensory modality, say, touch, we may find that he is able to recognise the object when it is presented on a second occasion via a different modality, such as vision. Here again, it is apparent that the child's ability to recognise equivalence between items presented to distinct receptor systems must rest on some internal mediating mechanisms. Transfer and recognition of inputs between different sensory modalities is known as 'cross-modal transfer', and such phenomena provide further indications of the necessity for learners to possess mediational systems whereby information is internalised in an abstract form.

One way of investigating the development of mediational processes in children is by observing the extent to which children at different ages are able to make cross-modal transfers. It is known that memory increases with age. Thus Lampel (1973), who tested three- to six-year-old children for recall of a toy that was missing from a previously shown display of four items, noted that the older children were substantially more likely to be able to say which item was missing. However, this finding gives no clue concerning the reasons for the superior performance of the older children. In an attempt to disentangle the underlying processes Zaporozhets (1965) carried out an experiment in which the subjects were children aged between three and six years. They were initially encouraged to explore objects in one of four different ways. The forms of exploration were visual, tactual, both visual and tactual combined, and a fourth group of children explored the objects through practical experience that involved manipulating them into holes in a wooden board. After the exploratory sessions all the children were given a test for visual recognition. The findings showed that performance in all the experimental groups improved markedly with age, but that at all ages subjects who had had an opportunity both to see and to manipulate the objects performed better than those who had been allowed only to see or only to touch them. Among children up to four years of age the ability to recognise visual forms of items that have previously been encountered only in the tactual mode is severely limited, but it increases considerably between the ages of four and five years.

What specific kinds of mediational processes underlie cross-modal recognition? In the case of object recognition it is likely that verbal coding is used. However, Stevenson (1972) suggests that mediation may alternatively involve some form of mental image of the various objects, or of certain attributes or dimensions of them. In the latter case a possible explanation of the superior performance of the older children in the study by Zaporozhets is that with increasing age children's images acquire increasing accuracy and precision. The suggestion that some kinds of cross-modal recognition are possible in the absence of language is supported by the finding that infants as young as eight months of age have performed significantly better than would be expected by chance in a task requiring cross-modal recognition of elliptical shapes (Bryant *et al.*, 1972). There is some evidence that in recognising items young children depend more on noting particular features of objects than on using images that represent the objects as wholes. Pick *et al.* (1966) presented letter-like forms to young children. Some of the items were presented visually, and others by touch. The children who participated in the study were required to judge whether each of a number of different objects was the same or different from a standard item.

An important variable in this experiment was the manner in which the items that were not identical to the standard object differed from it. The different objects were produced by transformations in the linearity, the orientation, and the size of the standard object. The experimenters' assumption was that discovering which kinds of transformations are most easily identifiable by children, and which kinds produce the greatest number of incorrect or false recognitions, would provide some clues about what kinds of representations are involved in the children's stored memories for these objects. After the initial session the children were divided into two groups. At this point, items that had previously been presented visually were given in tactual form, and vice versa. In one group, the original standard object was used again, but with different transformations to obtain items for the comparison tests. For the other group the standard object was different, but the comparison objects were formed by the same transformations that were used in the original session. If a mental image of the standard object is crucial for cross-modal recognition we would predict greater transfer from the first to the second session in instances where the same standard was used in both sessions but with different transformations, than in instances in which the second session included a different standard form but used equivalent transformations to provide the comparisons. In fact, cross-modal transfer occurred in the latter condition only. This finding suggests that in recognising items children do not rely only on images of whole items, but make use of stored information about specific distinguishing features of particular items, as a basis for cross-modal recognition.

5.7 MEDIATION AND SENTENCE CONSTRUCTION IN VERBAL LEARNING

Many instances in which mediation is necessary involve verbal processes to a greater extent than seems to be required in cross-modal transfer situations such as those described above. Following a report of research by Jensen and Rohwer (1963), the results of a number of investigations have demonstrated that lists of unrelated word items can be learned more easily if subjects are provided with a means of forming some kind of meaningful connection between the separate items. Jensen and Rohwer (1963) asked their subjects to perform tasks that required them to learn lists containing pairs of words. Materials of this kind have frequently been used in experimental research on verbal learning, and are known as 'paired-associate' lists. In one of the two conditions, the subjects, who were retarded adults, were simply told to learn a list of word pairs. In the other condition subjects were instructed to make up simple sentences in which the two words in each pair formed the subject and object. For instance, a pair such as 'scissor and telephone' might prompt the sentence 'The scissors touched the telephone'. Each individual had to make up a simple sentence from each of a number of word pairs. Comparing learning under the two conditions, it was found that subjects who constructed sentences made only about a fifth of the number of errors that occurred in the other condition. This is a striking increase in learning efficiency, and is considerably greater than the effects typically observed after manipulating the variables that have traditionally been considered most important for verbal learning, such as word frequency, the number of associations that a person can make to word items, and distribution of practice.

The precise effects of sentence construction on learning of word-paired associates depend on a number of further factors, such as the concreteness of the word items, the kind of sentence used, and whether the sentence joining the words is provided by the experimenter or constructed by the learner. Rohwer (1971) summarises the findings of about twenty studies investigating the effects of sentence mediation on verbal learning under various conditions. Our present concern is with the use children can make of this kind of semantic mediation. One striking finding is that after the age of about seven years, the effect on performance at paired-associate learning tasks begins to decrease as age increases. It will be recalled that a similar trend was observed in the effects of providing word labels on the learning of objects by children of different ages. In the case of the sentence studies the most likely explanation is that older children are increasingly likely to provide some verbal mediation spontaneously, in the absence of specific instructions to do so, diminishing the effective differences between the conditions that do and do not specifically incorporate linking sentences. This suggestion is supported by the fact that when older children are questioned they do often report spontaneous verbal mediation.

By the age of about eight years children who are carefully instructed to form sentences as an aid to the learning of paired-associate word lists perform approximately as well as adults. It appears that beyond middle childhood there is rather little improvement in performance at tasks demanding relatively simple forms of verbal learning. This finding adds emphasis to a point made earlier, concerning the differences that exist between more and less successful learners. Many individual differences in success at situations requiring learning are not due to any basic variability in the rate at which learners can acquire new associations, but are caused by individual variations in the use of certain habits and learning strategies that can influence human efficiency in acquiring and retaining new knowledge and skills.

5.7.1 *The earliest forms of verbal mediation*

Can very young children benefit from the kinds of verbal mediation that have been found to aid learning? We can discover something about the mediating functions a child possesses by observing whether instructions to use strategies such as sentence construction do effectively improve performance. If children below a certain age are unable to benefit from such strategies, it would seem that they have not yet acquired the capacity to make use of this form of mediation.

The fact that mediating processes are time-consuming may contribute to some apparent mediational deficiencies in young children. Peterson (1973) noticed that seven-year-old children were less likely to mediate in a word-learning task when a time restriction was placed on them. It may be that the slowness that is inevitable in making use of a newly acquired mediating ability may lead some young children to make a quick response, before mediation is complete, especially when the children feel that they are expected to provide an answer quickly.

Among children aged five years, requests to construct sentences that join items, although successfully obeyed, do not reduce the number of trials taken to learn word lists, when performance is compared with that of children who are given no instructions that involve sentences (Jensen and Rohwer, 1965). However, the success of children who are two years older differs markedly between the two conditions: subjects told to form sentences need only two trials to learn a ten-item list, compared with thirteen trials for the other children, who simply name the items. It is likely that the five-year-olds find it more difficult to produce sentences than the seven-year-olds. The younger children are able to form sentences, but they are unable to use the connecting link so formed to improve their learning performance.

In short, children at five years of age appear unable to benefit from the kind of mediating process that older children receive from self-constructed sentences. Yet findings that we have previously described, from experiments in cross-modal transfer and from experiments investigating the effects on learning of providing word labels for objects, make it clear that some forms of mediation are available to children at this age. A single word provides a simpler mediating device than a whole sentence, so it is perhaps to be expected that learning to make use of sentence mediators occurs after the capacity to make effective use of single-word labels has become well established. Furthermore, it had been shown that five-year-olds are able to benefit from word-mediation in the form of previously established links between words presented in pairs (Cook and Smothergill, 1971).

5.7.2 *Categorisation*

As command over language increases, children become able to categorise and organise items they are required to remember, and this ability makes possible organisational strategies whereby performance at verbal learning tasks is improved. The ability to categorise objects does not entirely depend on the ability to name them, as Nelson (1973) discovered from an investigation in which she observed that young children were able to group objects according to conceptual principles not present in the physical attributes of the objects themselves, despite not being able to name the objects. Spontaneous organisation and mediation are absent in young children (Jablonski, 1974), but even at the age of two, related pairs of objects are better recalled than unrelated objects. In older children the relationships between words being learned are important. Thus nouns linked by a verb are more accurately recalled than nouns linked by a conjunction (Yuille, 1974) and the presentation of objects in an interacting fashion enhances subsequent recognition performance. Among children of kindergarten age, such interaction is especially helpful when it is produced by the activities of the children themselves, as they play with toys (Wolff *et al.*, 1974).

These findings would lead one to predict that the advantages of organising word items to be learned or recalled become progressively more apparent as children get older. This is indeed the case. Furth and Milgram (1973) found that free recall of a categorical array of pictures by four-year-olds was not superior to recall of an array of random items. By the age of six, contiguous grouping of objects in categories did improve performance, but only when all the items were presented simultaneously. At nine years of age grouping by categories helped, even when the items were presented successively. Moely and Jeffrey (1974) discovered that among six- and seven-year-olds only, training in the use of category organisation led to improved performance. Following the training, in which the experimenter suggested that items would be divided into groups of things that went together or were alike in some way, and provided necessary practice and assistance, the children's recall performance improved, both in the number of categories remembered and the number of items recalled per category. The categorising abilities on which such improvements depend become more complex with increasing age (Nelson, 1974), and category headings more effective as retrieval cues (Halperin, 1974). Such cues are more often used spontaneously by older learners (Kubasigowa, 1974), highly directive procedures being necessary for picture cues to help retrieval among six-year-olds.

5.8 LANGUAGE SKILLS IN EDUCATION

The acquisition of habits and strategies that involve the extensive use of language in a mediating function is of considerable importance for the growth of children's knowledge through learning. It is not at all surprising that teachers consider language skills to be crucial for the kinds of learning that take place at school. Most programmes and courses designed to provide compensatory education for individuals or for groups of children considered to be educationally retarded stress the importance of linguistic skills. An example is the curriculum devised by Bereiter and Engelmann (1966), which is described in chapter 8. Bereiter and Engelmann base their general approach and specific procedures on the assumption that learning deficiencies among so-called culturally deprived minorities are largely due to lack of verbal learning, in particular the lack of those kinds of learning that are transmitted from adults to children, and require language. Procedures to encourage the acquisition of linguistic skills have a prominent place in most programmes designed to promote learning in preschool children, a good example being the television series *Sesame Street*. However, the extreme viewpoint that cultural deprivation is synonymous with language deprivation (Bereiter and Engelmann, 1966) is difficult to defend, since there is some evidence that other factors such as attentional strategies (Estes, 1970; Staats, 1971) are equally crucial. In connection with compensatory education it has been suggested that some apparent deficiencies among members of minority cultural groups, as reported, for example, in studies by white middle-class observers of negroes in American city ghettoes, are more accurately seen as linguistic differences. Such differences are interpreted as deficiencies when performance is tested at language tasks using the language patterns of the majority culture, and they lead to effective deficiencies when instruction at school is provided only in the majority language (Baratz, 1969; Labov, 1970). In short, some apparent deficiencies can more accurately be regarded as mere differences. They function as deficiencies, however, when the individual has to operate in a language in which he is not adept.

5.9 VISUAL IMAGERY IN LEARNING

Earlier in this chapter we noted that not all internalisation of information about the environment by infants and young children involves the use of language. The acquisition of language is preceded by the ability to recognise objects, which we have seen to require extensive internalised representations of information about events. Such internalisation is evident, for instance, in the responses of the infants aged eight months observed by Bryant *et al.* (1972). The babies were able to perform successfully at a task requiring cross-modal transfer (between touch and vision) of information about solid elliptical objects, despite their lack of linguistic skills.

In addition to those specifically linguistic kinds of elaboration that facilitate language learning, children and adults can also benefit from mediational processes that do not depend solely on language. Much recent research has been concerned with mediational strategies involving alternative kinds of representations or images of items that have to be learned. In particular, the use of visual images has received considerable attention. In some circumstances it is likely that verbal mediators and visual images operate in combination (Jones, 1973), and it is not always easy to separate their effects. One problem with the experimental findings that show improved recall following sentence construction is that it is not clear whether the observed increase in learning is due to the semantic qualities of the sentences, or to concrete images evoked by the sentences. An experiment by Reese (1965) attempted to clarify matters by examining the separate and combined effects on the learning of words by young children of instructions to form images and to provide sentence contexts. The subjects, aged between three and six years, were required to learn concrete word items, such as cat and umbrella. One group of children were shown pictures that illustrated interactions between pairs of items, an example being a picture of a chicken waving a flag. The investigator considered that in this condition subjects would remember the items in the form of visual images. A second group of children listened to sentences describing the same interactions between items, a typical sentence being 'The fish is talking on the telephone', but they were not shown any pictures. It was anticipated that the sentences would fill a mediating role, by providing a verbal context for the word items. Subjects in a third group perceived both the sentences and the pictures showing interactions between the items. Hence these children had the opportunity to use both verbal items and visual images as mediators. Finally, there was a fourth, control, group in which children were simply shown the word pairs in the absence of any materials or instructions that would encourage visual or verbal elaborations.

One finding of Reese's experiment was that subjects in the control group required a greater number of trials to learn the words than did the children in any of the other three groups. Among the youngest children, averaging three years and seven months in age, performance was best in the condition that provided sentences, neither the picture condition nor the combined picture plus sentence condition being so effective. However, for the older children (averaging five years and eight months) the verbal and visual conditions produced equivalent amounts of learning. It is not entirely clear why sentences should be more effective than pictures for the younger children but not for the older ones. Since verbal recall is required, it may be that pictures are effective only when children are able to verbalise, at a later stage, the items they retain in image form. If this is the case, a possible explanation of Reese's results is that the older but not the younger children in his experiment were able to verbalise pictures.

Reese's findings appear to contradict the results obtained by Jensen and Rohwer (1965), who found that at five years of age children were unable to take advantage of verbal elaboration in the form of sentences. However, in Jensen and Rohwer's study the children were told to construct their own sentences, whereas in the experiment by Reese these were provided for them. It is conceivable that children as young as four years of age can profit from mediation provided by sentence elaboration, but only when they do not have to construct the sentences, a difficult task for young children, and when the sentences are highly concrete as are the ones used by Reese. This view is supported by the results of an experiment by Milgram (1967). He found that among children aged four years providing a sentence context was more helpful than giving picture elaborations, and that subjects given either sentences or pictures learned more words than children in a control condition similar to that of Reese's (1965) study. Milgram considers that his findings indicate that the visual (pictorial) condition facilitates performance only when the child is able to code the image or picture in a verbal form. As we have suggested above, it is likely that the young child is quite able to form satisfactory images, but is handicapped at a later stage in the task, when it becomes necessary for purposes of recall to code the visual images into verbal form. In other words, the younger subjects may not be handicapped in their ability to form images, and their poorer performance at the pictorial than at the sentence-elaboration condition may be due to a separate task requirement, at the recall stage. No direct test of this interpretation is possible, but results of experiments on picture recognition would provide valuable evidence.

The results of the experiments by Reese (1965), Jensen and Rohwer (1965) and Milgram (1967) all indicate that providing some form of meaningful verbal or visual context can improve children's performance at tasks of word learning. Presumably, the provision of either a verbal or a pictorial context that links normally unrelated words creates a relationship between them that provides some kind of meaning in a task otherwise requiring merely the rote acquisition of the word items. In order to achieve a more exact understanding of the underlying mediational processes it would be useful to know whether all contexts are equally effective and, if not, which kinds of sentences, pictures or other devices lead to the greatest improvements in learning. Reese and Lipsitt (1970) provide an extensive review of the available evidence, including an interesting study by Rohwer (1971), who examined the effects of providing various kinds of verbal contexts on the learning of words by young children. Word pairs were presented in conjunctive phrases, an example being 'The rock and the bottle', prepositional phrases, for example 'The rock behind the bottle', and sentences such as 'The rock breaks the bottle'. Presenting the items in conjunctive phrases did not bring any increase in learning, compared with performance in a control condition whereby subjects simply learned the words as pairs. However, both prepositional phrases and sentences facilitated learning, each being equally effective.

5.10 CONCLUSION

If there is one dominant theme, one broad conclusion to be drawn from the findings of these experiments, it is that the acquisition of knowledge through learning is largely determined not by any 'rate of acquisition' in a narrow sense, but by the processes and strategies that the learner adopts as he deals with incoming information. Even in the simple and restricted tasks we have described, requiring the learning of word items, it is clear that each individual's mediating processes, and his manner of dealing with items to be acquired, are major determinants of what is eventually learned. It follows that, first, in attempting to understand the individual differences between children in their degree of success at learning tasks (chapter 7), it would be wise to pay particular attention to differences in strategies for learning, and to examine precisely how different individuals respond in situations whereby they are expected to acquire knowledge. Secondly, when the aim is to put into practice what is known about the acquisition of knowledge, in order to help children learn (chapter 8), attempts to devise educationally practical methods that will help learners are most likely to be successful if they are designed to encourage individuals to bring into play those mediational strategies that experimental research has shown to be effective.

REFERENCES

Baratz, J. C. (1969). A bi-dialectical task for determining language proficiency in economically disadvantaged Negro children. *Child Dev.* xl, 889–901

Beiswenger, H. (1971). Linguistic and psychological factors in the speech regulation of behaviour in young children. *J. exp. Child Psychol.* xi, 63–75

Bereiter, C., and Engelmann, S. (1966). *Teaching Disadvantaged Children in the Preschool*, Prentice-Hall, Englewood Cliffs, New York

Blank, M. (1974). Cognitive functions of language in the preschool years. *Dev. Psychol.* x, 229–45

Brown, R. (1973). Development of the first language in the human species. *Am. Psychol.* xxviii, 97–106

Bryant, P. R., Jones, P., Claxton, V., and Perkins, G. M. (1972). Recognition of shapes across modalities by infants. *Nature, Lond.* ccxl, 303–4

Chomsky, N. (1966). *Topics in the Theory of Generative Grammar*, Mouton, The Hague

Cook, H., and Smothergill, D. (1971). Verbal mediation and satiation in young children. *Child Dev.* xlii, 1805–12

Dodd, B. J. (1972). Effects of social and vocal stimulation on infant babbling. *Dev. Psychol.* vii, 80–3

Estes, W. K. (1970). *Learning Theory and Mental Development*, Academic Press, New York

Furth, H. G., and Milgram, N. (1973). Labelling and grouping effects in the recall of pictures by children. *Child Dev.* xliv, 511–18

Guess, D., Sailor, W., Rutherford, G., and Baer, D. M. (1968). An experimental analysis of linguistic development: The productive use of the plural morpheme. *J. appl. Behav. Anal.* i, 297–306

Halperin, M. S. (1974). Development changes in the recall and recognition of categorized word lists. *Child Dev.* xlv, 144–51

Inhelder, B. (1971). The sensory-motor origins of knowledge. In D. N. Walcher and D. L. Peters (eds), *Early Childhood: the Development of Self-Regulatory Mechanisms*, Academic Press, New York

Irwin, O. C. (1947). Development of speech during infancy: curve of phonemic frequencies. *J. exp. Psychol.* xxxvii, 187–93.

Jablonski, E. M. (1974). Free recall in children. *Psychol. Bull.* lxxxi, 522–39

Jensen, A. R. (1971). The role of verbal mediation in mental development. *J. genet. Psychol.* xviii, 39–70

Jensen, A. R., and Rohwer, W. D. (1963). Verbal mediation in paired-associate and serial learning. *J. verbal Learn. verbal Behav.* i, 346–52

Jensen, A. R., and Rohwer, W. D. (1965). Syntactical mediation of serial and paired-associate learning as a function of age. *Child Dev.* xxxvi, 601–8

Jones, H. R. (1973). The use of visual and verbal memory processes by three-year-old children. *J. exp. Child Psychol.* xv, 340–51

Kubasigowa, A. (1974). Utilization of retrieval cues by children in recall. *Child Dev.* xlv, 127–34

Labov, W. (1970). *The Study of Nonstandard English,* National Council of Teachers of English, Urbana, Illinois

Lampel, A. K. (1973). Three-, four-, and six-year-olds tested for recall of a toy missing from a previously seen display of four toys. *J. exp. Child Psychol.* xv, 266–77

Lenneberg, E. S. (1964). *New Directions in the Study of Language*, M.I.T. Press, Cambridge, Massachusetts

Lewis, M. M. (1959). *How Children Learn to Speak,* Basic Books, New York

Luria, A. R. (1961). *The Role of Speech in the Regulation of Normal and Abnormal Behavior*, Liveright, New York

Milgram, N. A. (1967). Verbal context versus visual compound in paired-associate learning by children. *J. Exp. Child Psychol.* v, 597–603

Miller, S., Shelton, L. J., and Flavell, J. H. (1970). A test of Luria's hypothesis concerning the development of verbal self-regulation. *Child Dev.* xli, 651–5

Moely, B. E., and Jeffrey, W. E. (1974). The effect of organization training on children's free recall of category items. *Child Dev.* xlv, 135–43

Mussen, P. H., Conger, J. J., and Kagan, J. (1969). *Child Development and Personality*, 3rd edn, Harper & Row, New York

Nelson K. (1973). Some evidence for the cognitive primacy of categorization and its functional basis. *Merrill-Palmer Q.* xix, 21–40

Nelson, K. (1974). Variations in children's concepts by age and category. *Child Dev.* xlv, 577–84

Norcross, K. J. (1958). Effects on discrimination performance of similarity of previously acquired stimulus names. *J. exp. Psychol.* lvi, 305–9

Norcross, K. J., and Spiker, C. C. (1957). The effects of type stimulus pretraining on discrimination performance in preschool children. *Child Dev.* xxviii, 79–84

Peterson, C. C. (1973). The effect of time on mediation deficiency in children and adults. *J. exp. Child Psychol.* xv, 1–9

Piaget, J. (1970). Piaget's theory. In P. H. Mussen (ed.), *Carmichael's Manual of Child Psychology*, 3rd edn, vol. 1, Wiley, New York

Pick, A. D., Pick, H. L., and Thomas, M. L. (1966). Cross-modal transfer and improvement of form discrimination. *J. exp. Child Psychol.* iii, 279–88

Premack, A. J., and Premack, D. (1972). Teaching language to an ape. *Scient. Am.* ccxxvii, 4, 92–9

Ramey, C. T., and Ourth, R. L. (1971). Delayed reinforcement and vocalization rates of infants. *Child Dev.* xlii, 291–7

Reese, H. W. (1965). Imagery in paired-associate learning in children. *J. exp. Child Psychol.* ii, 290–6

Reese, H. W., and Lipsitt, L. P. (1970). *Experimental Child Psychology*, Academic Press, New York

Rheingold, H. K., Gewirtz, J. L., and Ross, H. W. (1959). Social conditioning of vocalizations in the infant. *J. comp. physiol. Psychol.* lii, 68–73

Rohwer, W. D. (1971). Prime time for education: early childhood or adolescence? *Harv. educ. Rev.* xli, 316–41

Staats, A. W. (1971). *Child Learning, Intelligence, and Personality*, Harper & Row, New York

Stevenson, H. W. (1972). *Children's Learning*, Appleton-Century-Crofts, New York

Vincent-Smith, L., Bricker, D., and Bricker, W. (1974). Acquisition of receptive vocabulary in the toddler-age child. *Child Dev.* xlv, 189–93

Weir, R. H. (1962). *Language in the Crib*, Mouton, The Hague

Wolff, P., Levin, J. R. and Longobardi, E. R. (1974). Activity and children's learning. *Child Dev.* xlv, 221–3

Yuille, J. C. (1974). Syntactic facilitation of children's associative learning: an instructional effect. *J. exp. Child Psychol.* xviii, 41–50

Zaporozhets, A. V. (1965). The development of perception in the preschool child. In P. H. Mussen (ed.), 'European research in cognitive development', *Monographs of the Society for Research in Child Development,* vol. 30

6

Further Steps in Social Learning

Much of what a child learns depends on the presence of other people. We have seen that the mother's role is particularly important, especially during the earliest years of life. The ways in which an individual learns to behave towards others have an influence on the kind of life he will lead, and if we are asked to describe a person's character, many of the descriptive terms that come to mind – for example warmth, gregariousness, honesty, shyness – refer explicitly or implicitly to the manner in which the individual is likely to behave in encounters with other members of the human species.

6.1 OBSERVATION AND IMITATION

The principles underlying social learning are broadly similar to those involved in learning of a non-social nature. For instance, the concept of reinforcement is equally applicable to the acquisition of aggressive activities in the typical three-year-old boy as it is to sucking responses in the young infant. One factor that is often involved in social learning, but which is not prominent in the simpler forms of learning by young infants, is the mechanism of observation. Much social learning depends on observation.

Observational learning takes place when an individual acquires a habit or skill through witnessing its performance by another person. Such learning often, but not always, involves imitation of the observed activities. Imitation may be deferred, as in the following investigation, which serves as an experimental illustration of social learning through observation. Bandura (1962) asked children to look at one of three different films. In each film a male adult 'model' (the word used by Bandura and others to describe a person whose behaviour is observed) exhibited a number of aggressive actions that were novel to the children.

In one of the films the model's aggressive behaviour was followed by punishment. In the second film the model was rewarded, reinforcement taking the form of food and social approval. In the third film the model's aggressive behaviour had no apparent consequence.

After the children had watched the films a record was made of the number of responses made in imitation of the model. Most of the children imitated the model to some extent, demonstrating learning through observation, but the children who had watched the film in which the model's aggressive actions were punished produced fewer imitative acts than children who had watched either the film in which the model was rewarded or the film in which aggressive behaviour produced no reaction. There were some differences between the sexes, boys making more aggressive acts in imitation of the model than girls.

It is clear that children in each of the three groups acquired new aggressive responses, but that the magnitude of learning appears to have been influenced by the reinforcing events following the observed model's actions. However, some further findings suggest that although the magnitude of *performance* in making imitative aggressive acts was influenced by the consequences to the model, the amount of actual *learning* may not have differed between the various conditions. The evidence for this suggestion was provided by extending the experiment one step further. Following the experimental trials described above, all the children were offered attractive rewards for reproducing the aggressive actions made by the model they had previously watched. The effect of providing these incentives was to eliminate the earlier differences in performance between the groups. This finding clearly shows that learning was equivalent in each of the three experimental groups, the previous differences being ones of performance only. Another effect of providing incentives for imitating the model's aggressive activities was to reduce, but not eliminate, the previously observed differences between the sexes. Thus, in the session prior to the one in which subjects were rewarded, boys displayed an average about 2.5 out of a possible four different imitative actions, compared with an average of about 1.1 responses for girls. With the introduction of rewards, the average for boys was around 3.5, and the average number of different aggressive acts by girls was about 3.1.

The findings of Bandura's experiment make it clear that children can learn aggressive activities from observing models. The findings have clear implications for those who are concerned about the effects on children of violence shown on television. Violence in cartoons has been shown in some investigations to be equally influential. Hapkiewicz and Roden (1971) observed no difference in the behaviour of six-year-olds who had watched violent and non-violent cartoon films. Events that reinforce the imitative aggresive behaviour either of the children themselves or of the models they observe may have more effect on learning as such than immediate measures of performance seem to indicate.

The findings of numerous experiments by Bandura and other investigators make it clear that children often imitate the aggressive actions of adults they observe on films and television. However, there is considerable disagreement concerning the possible implications of these somewhat artificial laboratory experiments for everyday exposure to television violence. An ingenious study by Drabman and Thomas (1974) sought to discover whether exposure to mass-media violence would increase children's toleration of aggression in a real-life situation. Children around nine years of age were shown a playroom for younger children, and they were led to believe that they were responsible for watching the behaviour of two younger children via closed-circuit television. Some of the older children (the subjects) watched a cowboy film which contained numerous acts of violence and aggression. Afterwards the younger children, whom the subjects had been told to watch, began to behave with increasing aggressiveness, culminating in a fight that brought about the apparent destruction of the television camera used for observing their behaviour. The older children had previously been told to report to the experimenter if the behaviour of the children they were watching got out of hand. As far as the older children knew, only they could observe the younger ones, for whom they were responsible, the experimenter being in a separate room which was not connected to the closed-circuit television system. It was found that those older children who had watched the violent film waited for considerably longer than did the children who had not seen the film before reporting the disruptive activities of the younger children to an adult. In other words, watching the film made them more tolerant of apparently real violent behaviour.

6.2 CONTRASTING APPROACHES TO SOME SOCIAL-LEARNING PHENOMENA

Bandura and his co-workers have carried out a large number of further investigations into the factors that influence socially important activities in children. An attempt is made to explain the acquisition of all forms of social behaviour in terms of 'antecedent social-stimulus events such as the behavioral characteristics of the social models to which a child has been exposed, the reinforcement contingencies of his learning history, and the methods of training that have been used to develop and modify his social behavior' (Bandura and Walters, 1963, p. 44).

In some instances such an approach leads to predictions that diverge markedly from those made on the basis of other theoretical systems, notably psychodynamic ones. For instance, it has sometimes been suggested that surplus aggression can be discharged by a process of 'catharsis', if individuals are encouraged to participate in aggressive activities. Bandura and Walters note that parents and teachers have often been advised to provide facilities that will allow aggressive children to participate in aggressive games, using dolls and punch-balls to encourage the release of aggression. Implicit in such a recommendation is belief in a 'hydraulic' view of personality, by which deviant forms of behaviour are regarded as inappropriate instances of energy discharge. Giving vent to aggressive behaviour is seen as allowing the discharge of negative feelings, to the benefit of the individual concerned. Bandura and Walters think that explanations of this kind are fallacious. They consider that the main outcome of a strategy by which children are encouraged to practise aggressive ways of behaving and to acquire new aggressive habits will be to increase rather than decrease the likelihood of their behaving aggressively in the future.

The findings of investigations by D. T. Kenny and S. Fesbach are cited by Bandura and Walters, in support of this point of view. Kenny measured aggression in young children by scoring their responses to a story-completion test. The children were then divided into two groups Verbal and physical aggression were encouraged in one of the groups, and children in the other group were required to play in a harmonious, unaggressive manner. Afterwards, all the children completed some more items of the story-completion test. The children who were not allowed to play aggressively showed a decrease in aggression. This was not found in the other group, and Bandura and Walters note that this finding gives no support at all for the claim that aggression can be discharged by a process of catharsis. In the second investigation, by S. Fesbach, some children listened to stories and records which conveyed aggressive ideas or themes, and they were given toy guns and other play materials chosen to encourage aggressive activities. Children in other groups were engaged in activities that were broadly similar, but which excluded aggressive themes or toys likely to evoke aggressive reactions. Observers measured the extent to which the different groups of children behaved aggressively before and after the play session. Once more the findings provided no support at all for the catharsis hypothesis, there being no decrease in aggressive responses among the children encouraged to act aggressively, and thus discharge their aggressive impulses.

The phenomenon of 'regression' provides a further illustration of the different predictions about social behaviour emerging from social-learning approaches and from alternative explanatory theories. Regression is said to occur when children, or sometimes adults, especially in stressful circumstances, show dependency responses, such as clinging or holding to parents, characteristic of the normal behaviour of much younger individuals. Under these circumstances a child's behaviour is said to have regressed. Psychologists favouring psychodynamic explanations, influenced to some extent by Freudian thought, consider that certain kinds of stress constitute threats to the ego. As a result, there is regression to behaviour appropriate to an earlier development stage, at which the child is said to have 'fixated', that is, to have failed to advance in the normal manner, due either to excessive gratification or to excessive frustration of needs.

The social-learning approach followed by researchers such as Bandura gives rise to a markedly different explanation. As a result of learning the child is thought to acquire a variety of alternative patterns of behaviour that can be evoked in response to certain social cues. These actions form what Bandura and Walters (1963) term a 'habit hierarchy', in which the various possible reactions differ in dominance. In the young child, parents usually reinforce the kinds of dependency behaviours that are involved in seeking proximity with adults. However, as the child's age increases, the parents give progressively greater encouragement to independent actions, and dependency behaviour is reinforced less frequently. By this time, however, habits of dependency, such as approaching or clinging to the parent, have become highly developed, through the frequent reinforcement of such behaviour in early childhood. Two alternative kinds of response patterns are thus available to the child. On the one hand are habits of independence, and on the other hand there remain the previously established dependent behaviours. It is hardly surprising that in some circumstances, particularly under conditions of stress, children and even adults revert to well-established early habits, directed towards individuals, typically the parents, who have consistently reinforced such actions in the past.

6.3 IDENTIFICATION

The close ties of attachment and the dependent behaviour that serve the young infant so well gradually give way to greater independence, although in some repects the child remains dependent for many years. Many of the child's attitudes and values are acquired through contact with other people, and the concept of identification has been put forward as an explanatory device to account for the learning that takes place. Identification refers to 'the strong human tendency to model one's "self" and one's aspirations upon some other person' (Bruner, 1966). The child who shares many of the standards and attitudes of his parents is said to be closely identified with them. In such circumstances it can be expected that the parents will be able to exact a high degree of control over the child's actions. Consistent with this statement is a finding of a well-known study by Levin and Sears (1956). They observed that the frequency of aggressive actions on the part of young children during sessions of play with dolls was related to the degree to which they identified with the parent of the same sex.

Identification is not restricted to children. Bettelheim (1943) observed that prisoners who had been incarcerated over a lengthy period in Nazi concentration camps behaved in a manner indicative of identification with the aggressors. They copied the guards' behaviour and sometimes acted even more sadistically than the guards towards other prisoners placed in their charge.

6.3.1 *Alternative explanations of identification phenomena*

There are differences in opinion concerning the explanatory value of the concept of identification. There can be no objection to the use of the term as a label for behaviour that imitates frequently observed models, such as the parents, but psychologists such as Bandura (1969) and Gewirtz (1969) have opposed the belief that identification constitutes some kind of basic mechanism. Bandura and Walters (1963) claim that Bettelheim's observations of concentration-camp prisoners can be explained quite simply by reference to knowledge about real and anticipated reinforcing events among prisoners living in concentration-camp conditions. Bandura and Walters argue that a variety of antecedent conditions may result in the kinds of imitative or matching responses in a child that indicate identification, and they do not consider it meaningful to draw a distinction between identification and simple imitation. Bandura (1969) considers that the processes underlying simple forms of what can be called matching, modelling, or imitation responses are responsible for the broader categories of behaviour to which the term identification has been applied. He argues that to make distinctions in terms of the particular kinds of behaviour that are copied merely causes confusion, unless it can be shown that different processes underlie learning of the various activities.

In any social learning that involves the imitation of models it is important to distinguish between the effects of what models do and the effects of what models say. Stein and Bryan (1972) carried out a study investigating the effects of a model's actions and the same model's statements on adherence to rules in girls around eight years of age. The rule concerned a pile of small coins that was placed in front of the subjects. Each child was told she could take the coins only if she achieved a winning score in the game she was playing as part of the experiment. An adult model who appeared on a television screen verbally encouraged the child either to obey or to violate the rule, and the model's own behaviour conformed to or violated the rule. It was found that the model's words and his deeds interacted in influencing the child's behaviour, but the child's own subsequent statements about the rule were largely determined by what the model said.

Bandura considers that social learning results either from direct experience, incorporating reinforcement of the learner's actions, or, vicariously, from observations of the behaviour of others and of its consequences for them. By observing others the child not only gains new ways of behaving, but also experiences inhibitory or disinhibitory effects, as a result of seeing the positive or negative outcomes of the model's actions. Thus, for Bandura, when a child first copies the actions of a parent, he is exhibiting behaviour acquired through observation. The fact that sex-appropriate differences begin to emerge between boys and girls can be explained by reference to differing reinforcement contingencies and opportunities to observe, and it may be unnecessary to involve a distinct mechanism of identification to explain actions that copy those of the parents and other people.

6.4 THE ROLE OF ATTENTION IN HUMAN LEARNING

Up to now we have given scant mention of one crucial component of most kinds of learning, especially those involving observation or imitation. This is the factor of attention. As we might expect, children's level of attention influences the amount they learn in observational settings (Yussen, 1974). At this point it will be useful to include some general remarks about the role of attention in human learning.

In young infants attentional skills are at a rudimentary stage of development, but learning is strongly influenced by variations in an infant's 'state', the latter term referring to a broad range of variables, some of which are related to the baby's degree of arousal, or alertness. Gottlieb and Simner (1966) observed close and complex relationships between learning and measures of arousal, such as change in heart rate. Kessen *et al.* (1970) suggest that, for the young infant, state variables are much more important than variations in stimulus characteristics in determining rate of learning. A complicating factor is that the infant's state has numerous components. Prechtl (1969) considers that as many as sixteen parameters of neurophysiological and other functions need to be assessed in measuring the infant's state, and to assess a baby's state he uses a number of recordings of respiration, heart rate and electroencephalographic and electromyographic responses. It has been suggested that among the various physiological measures used cardiac deceleration provides a particularly valuable single indication of attention to specific stimuli. However, as Ashton (1973) points out, the various factors contributing to an infant's state are relatively independent of one another, and it is therefore fruitless to search for one parameter that forms a reliable index of state.

An added complication lies in the fact that infants exhibit large fluctuations in behavioural state over periods of as little as ten minutes. This adds to the difficulty of determining the causes of any performance changes that are observed in conditioning experiments. Before one can state with any certainty that a change in an infant's activities is due to conditioning, one has to be certain that the altered performance cannot be attributed to state variables. Ruling out this possibility necessitates careful experimental control procedures. Even in carefully controlled investigations problems arise concerning the interpretation of behavioural changes. Thus, Prechtl (1969), discussing an experiment by Lipsitt (1969) in which newborns were conditioned to turn the head to one side, points out that head-turning occurs spontaneously in certain behavioural states. It is conceivable that uncontrolled variations in the infant's state were responsible for the changes in incidence of head-turning that Lipsitt assumed were due to the conditioning procedures. However, it should be noted that not all researchers accept the view that state variables have a crucial influence on behaviour in newborns. For example, Bell and Haaf (1971), who observed no correlations between order of behavioural states and measures of sucking, crying and head movements, question the necessity of using the complicated observation systems required to measure state variables in studies of infant learning.

In the older infant, attention becomes more selective. It is frequently necessary for the learner to discriminate between essential and unimportant or irrelevant environmental events. The general arousal level remains important, however, as has been shown in research on human vigilance, and in the investigations of the orienting response mentioned in chapter 2.

6.5 SELECTIVE ATTENTION AND DISCRIMINATIVE ABILITY

In any learning that involves discriminating it is essential that the learner attend to the appropriate stimulus dimensions. Estes (1970) suggests that the reason why people from Western countries tend to believe that all Asians look alike is that they really do look alike on the dimensions which Westerners habitually use as a basis for identifying people, such as hair colour and eye colour, attributes on which Europeans vary considerably. In order to discriminate equally well between Asian people, it is necessary for the Westerner to attend to dimensions of Asian faces, which differ from the ones that serve as a basis for discriminating between European faces.

Some experimental tasks used in research on learning specifically require individuals to discriminate between objects. Subjects tend to perform better at such discrimination learning tasks if they are given verbal instructions to attend to the appropriate stimuli. Procedures that facilitate attention to significant environmental events can often bring about increased learning. Thus Zeaman has found that learning a difficult discrimination was markedly faster if subjects were first trained on an easier task involving the same stimulus dimensions. He observed that training that provided reinforcement for attention to appropriate cues tended to improve learning, whereas training in which rewards were given for attending to irrelevant cues had an opposite effect, impairing subsequent performance. Similarly, Blank and Altman (1968) discovered that children aged three and four years performed better at tasks requiring them to discriminate between objects when the cues were tactual than when visual discrimination was required, largely because the tactual stimuli more effectively constrained the children to attend to relevant cues. The performance by retarded children who were tested by Zeaman *et al.* (1958) in a discrimination-learning situation was much improved by providing previous training in associating verbal labels with the relevant colour cues. Finally, M. A. Cunningham found that giving specific instructions to direct children's attention to relevant cues led to improvement both in nursery-school children and in older retarded children of similar mental age (Estes, 1970).

After emphasising the overwhelming importance of attentional variables in a variety of learning situations, Estes (1970) points out that one cannot realistically speak of a general trait of attentiveness. An individual must always be attending to some dimension or other of his environment, so that the probabilities of attending to the various dimensions sum to unity. Estes considers that individuals described as highly intelligent are likely to be more attentive than less intelligent individuals to the dimensions that are relevant to the kinds of problems used to test their ability.

6.5.1 *Individual differences in selective attention*

The suggestion that a major source of differences in learning between individuals lies in the extent to which they habitually attend to relevant dimensions of the task environment, can be tested by providing situations in which learners are very carefully instructed to ensure that they all attend to appropriate dimensions. Under such circumstances one would predict that, if Estes is correct, normal differences between learners would be reduced. In fact there is some evidence that this is so, thus supporting Estes's point of view. For example, Denny (1964) found that differences in children's performance at discrimination-learning tasks that were related to intelligence disappeared when special emphasis was placed on ensuring that all subjects attended to relevant cues. Similarly, Zeaman and House (1967) observed that when elaborate precautions were taken to ensure that retarded children attended to relevant task dimensions they learned much faster than usual.

In conclusion, attentional factors are especially important in forms of social learning that necessitate imitation or observation. The kinds of attentional strategies that an individual uses have considerable influence on what is learned, and thus constitute a source of individual differences in human performance. Part of the importance for individual differences of variations in attentional strategies lies in the cumulative manner in which they contribute to progress, and this point will be expanded in the next chapter.

6.6 REINFORCEMENT AND SOCIAL LEARNING: THE USE OF BEHAVIOUR-MODIFICATION TECHNIQUES

The role of reinforcing events in social learning by older infants and children can be illustrated by describing some procedures that made use of knowledge about reinforcement in order to devise practical solutions to social-learning problems. Such procedures are known as 'behaviour modification'. Their success depends on psychologists' ability to isolate and manipulate reinforcing events in order to change behaviour in socially desirable ways.

A study by Harris *et al.* (1964) provides a good illustration of the practical application of behaviour-modification techniques. A little girl, aged three years and five months, who had just been admitted to a nursery school, served as the subject in the investigation. She was the oldest child in a middle-class family, and had two younger brothers. The nursery group consisted of six boys and six girls, all around three years of age, who attended five mornings per week and were supervised by two teachers. On her first day in the nursery group the little girl showed unusually strong withdrawal tendencies. She crouched on the floor for most of the time, and when she was approached either by an adult or by another child she would turn away her face or hide it in her arms. However, the child made no attempt to stay close to her mother, who remained seated in another corner of the room.

The girl occasionally crawled from place to place, as the various playschool activities shifted, but she did not walk at all. She did not speak to anyone, staying silent and unresponsive, while the other children laughed and behaved in a noisy and active manner. By the end of her third week at school the child still avoided all contact with children and adults, and her behaviour prevented her from playing with the toys and educational equipment provided by the nursery. Observational records showed that during an average half hour she was only on her feet 7 per cent of the time, the remaining 93 per cent being spent sitting or crouched on the floor. During the first few weeks the only words she said were the occasional 'yes' or 'no' spoken very softly in response to a teacher's question, at snack time.

It was decided to apply reinforcement principles in an effort to help this child acquire habits permitting her to benefit more fully from the nursery situation. The investigators concentrated on trying to modify the child's tendency to remain off her feet, since this was the aspect of her behaviour that most clearly prevented her from participating in the range of available nursery activities. An added advantage of attending to the modification of behaviour such as sitting and crawling was that it was easily observable and measurable. The chosen procedure was for the teacher to attempt to weaken off-feet behaviour by not providing any reinforcement except at times when the child was on her feet. Since a teacher's attention appeared to be a powerful reinforcer of the child's actions, the strategy adopted was for teachers to withdraw their attention from the child whenever she was not on her feet. This was done in a relaxed way, the teachers carefully avoiding any actions that might suggest anger or dislike. No punitive measure was used at any time.

In addition to withholding attention when the child was off her feet, the teachers took the more positive action of providing immediate reinforcement, in the form of their attention and praise, for any on-feet behaviour that occurred. The broad strategy was to reinforce those kinds of activities that it was thought desirable to increase, and not to reinforce activities such as crawling or sitting that it was considered the child ought to restrict if she was to make full use of the nursery-school facilities.

At first, since the little girl stood on her feet very infrequently the teachers attended to any actions that approximated standing. To reinforce desirable behaviours the teachers would immediately approach the child and talk to her in a friendly and encouraging manner. It is known that for an event to be maximally reinforcing it must immediately follow the behaviour that is to be strengthened, and to make immediate reinforcement possible one of the teachers stayed close to the child at all times.

The effect of the behaviour-modification procedures adopted was to produce a very marked improvement, right from the outset. Within a week of the teachers' commencing to reinforce the child's being on her feet, and ignoring her off-feet activities, the original proportions of her time spent on and off the feet were reversed. After two weeks her behaviour was indistinguishable from that of the other children at the nursery. She talked and smiled frequently, made use of all the toys and equipment provided by the nursery, and communicated freely. As a check on the potency of the reinforcement procedures, the teacher later agreed, reluctantly, to make a brief reversal in the procedures. For a few days the child received no attention from the teachers while she was standing or walking and continuous attention when she was sitting or crawling. On the first morning of this new schedule the child reverted to spending 76 per cent of the time off her feet. That is, under the reversed reinforcement pattern she almost immediately reverted to her original behaviour. When the teachers returned once more to giving attention as a reinforcer for being on the feet, the proportion of time spent on her feet immediately went back to 62 per cent, and adequate behaviour was maintained thereafter.

Findings such as these make it clear that reinforcement is a very potent factor in human social learning. As was shown in chapter 3, the precise nature of effective reinforcers depends on the individual concerned. Thus the attention of adults might well be a less powerful reinforcing event in the case of older children than in the three-year-old observed in the study we have described. However, there can be no doubting the validity of the general principle that the behaviour of all children can to a large extent be controlled by someone who knows what events effectively reinforce that individual, and is able to manipulate those events at will. In the case of activities that can be described as abnormal, antisocial, or deviant it is often possible to discern the reinforcing events that have maintained them. For example, in the above study the child's original crouching or sitting behaviour was being maintained by the teachers' worried attention and concern.

A further illustration (Williams, 1959) demonstrates the maintenance of socially disruptive behaviour by reinforcement, and its subsequent modification by alterations to the reinforcement schedule. The child observed was a boy aged twenty-one months who had been ill for much of the first eighteen months of his life and had consequently received very close care and attention from adults. Understandably, he continued to demand almost continuous attention, although his physical health was now perfect. The child was especially demanding at bedtime, when he unleashed violent and lengthy tantrums. These were successful in closely controlling the activities of the parents, since if a parent left the child's room at bedtime the child would scream loudly and fuss until the parent returned. As a result, the parents were unable to leave the room until the child was asleep, and this often necessitated their staying in the room for periods of over an hour. If a parent merely picked up a book while he was waiting for the child to go to sleep, the child would scream and scream until the book was replaced.

The parents considered that the child was exerting too much control over them. To alter this state of affairs an experimental change was introduced, by which the child's crying and tantrum behaviour was no longer to be reinforced. Quite simply, the chosen procedure was that after ensuring that the child was comfortable and safe, the parent would bid him goodnight, leave the room and not return. A record was made of the duration of crying each night, and on the first occasion the child cried for about forty-five minutes. However, on the subsequent four nights he only cried for an average of about five minutes, the duration never exceeding ten minutes. By the seventh night there was no crying at all. Clearly, in this case, once the effective reinforcement was removed, crying behaviour quickly disappeared.

In some instances behaviour-modification procedures that attempt to increase a desired activity by reinforcing a related response may be more successful than direct procedures that attempt to modify behaviour by reinforcing the desired actions, especially when the initial frequency of the latter is low. Thus Nordquist and Bradley (1973), who designed a programme to increase the amount of speech in a non-verbal five-year-old girl, point out that directly reinforcing speech presents a number of problems, one being the need for constant close observation. What they did was to reinforce the child, using verbal approval, for play that involved interaction of any kind with her peers. As a result, she began to speak with greatly increased frequency.

There have been numerous applications of behaviour-modification techniques. In many cases the object has been to alter undesirable or anti-social forms of behaviour. The practical success of behaviour-modification procedures demonstrates the crucial nature of reinforcement for social learning and for the maintenance of social behaviour. There is nothing particularly novel about the statement that a child's behaviour is influenced by the expected consequences, but systematic applications of behaviour modification have emphasised the power of this generalisation, and the rigorous manner in which it applies to social learning.

6.7 SOCIAL LEARNING AND AGGRESSION

Some of the experiments described this chapter to illustrate various aspects and principles of social learning in children have been concerned with the acquisition of aggressive kinds of behaviour. The topic of aggression is one of great importance, not only for the welfare of the individual but also for the ordering and survival of human societies. In the words of one authority, 'The range and persistence of human aggression present a major problem to clinicians who deal with individual psychopathology, and are a central concern, if not the central concern, of social reformers' (Fesbach, 1970, p. 159). The remainder of this chapter will be devoted to a brief discussion of the determinants of aggression in children.

6.7.1 *The contribution of unlearned mechanisms*

Learning is not the only factor determining whether an individual will respond aggressively in a given situation. Biological research has demonstrated the importance of hormones, as indicated by the finding (mentioned by Hamburg, 1969) that female infants exposed *in utero* (that is, before birth) to androgen compounds similar in form to male sex hormones, in later life exhibit 'tomboy' behaviour, more commonly observed in males. Aggressive and violent forms of behaviour may be the outcome of interactions between biological predispositions to the learning of aggressive activities and the particular conditions in which social learning takes place.

6.7.2 *Is man inherently aggressive?*

A number of writers have expressed the view that aggressive behaviour in humans is due primarily to innate biological factors. Man is regarded as inherently aggressive, and learning is seen as unessential for the emergence of aggression, serving simply to channel and direct the precise forms that aggressive actions take. It is suggested that man shares with other species certain innate predispositions, which are expressed in 'territorial' or 'imperial' behaviours. Learning and cultural conditions are said to provide the stimuli that trigger innately determined responses. Thus Lorenz (1966) suggests that all forms of human war and conflict are broadly subject to the laws of phylogenetically developed instinctive behaviour, and Tinbergen (1951) states that both animals and man have a fighting drive which has survival value, enhancing reproduction through redistributing sexual objects, and serving to ward off predators. Ardrey (1966) uses generalisations derived from animal behaviour to support his opinion that man is instinctively a killer, possessing an 'aggressive imperative' that frequently leads to warlike and violent acts. He points out that national and tribal rivalry among humans shares features with the behaviour of animals that manifest strong territorial attachments, and are likely to fight when the territory they occupy is violated by an intruder.

Plausible though such ideas may appear, there is no really valid evidence for the claim that man is instinctively or innately aggressive. Certainly there are numerous instances of human aggression that in some respects parallel instinctive aggressive acts in other species. However, there is no reason to suppose that instinctive factors necessarily underlie acts of violence and aggression in humans. The sheer range of differences in the extent to which various human societies exhibit violent behaviour provides one powerful counter-argument for the claims that have been made about instinctive determinants of aggression.

An objection to the viewpoint that violence is inherent in man is that it is not only wrong but positively harmful. If widely accepted, such a view could act as a self-fulfilling prophecy. As Eisenberg (1972) has emphasised, what we choose to believe about the nature of man has important social consequences. If we assume that man is by nature an aggressive territorial species, despite the absence of evidence for such an assertion, we are likely to feel that the more destructive and violent actions of mankind are inevitable offshoots of human nature. This leads to an unjustifiably pessimistic attitude towards attempts to ameliorate the human condition by trying to reduce the incidence of violence and destruction in man.

Eisenberg acknowledges that violence in man is extremely common. However, he points out that the observation in man and in other species of superficially similar behaviours that can all be labelled as 'aggression' or 'attack' does not justify any conclusion about an underlying aggressive instinct, even when instinctive mechanisms are found to be the cause of such behaviour in some non-human species. To assume that human aggression must be due to the kinds of instinctive mechanisms that control certain aggressive behaviours in some animal species is to 'reify a descriptive label that has been indiscriminatively applied to markedly different levels of behavioural organisation, as though naming were the same as explaining' (Eisenberg, 1972, p. 125). Supporting

Eisenberg's point of view is the fact (noted by Fesbach, 1970) that writers such as Ardrey and Lorenz, who postulate an aggressive instinct in man, have tended to neglect the important role of learning as a determinant of violent and aggressive behaviour in *non*-human species. Fesbach mentions the work of J. P. Scott that provided evidence that animals such as mice and dogs can be trained to be fighters or to be more passive in their reactions.

Eisenberg further argues that the ubiquity of violence in Western countries guarantees that children receive ample opportunities to learn aggressive modes of behaviour. Violence is seen to pay off. After listing some of the more horrible recent examples of human violence, Eisenberg drily observes that 'television pales before real life', and he points out that if we do choose to hypothesise an aggressive instinct to explain violence in Western society, or the murderous raids of Brazilian Indians, then we are forced to invent a complicated explanation that involves repression or reaction formation, or sublimation, in order to account for, say, the comparative peacefulness of the Eskimo people.

When we find that two cultures whose members appear to draw on common or similar gene pools manifest extreme differences in the extent to which they perform acts of violence, as is found for example in comparing contemporary Britain and the United States, or the neighbouring New Guinea tribes investigated by anthropologists such as Margaret Mead and Ruth Benedict in the early part of this century, one is almost forced to conclude that the differences must be largely due to learning. In addition, as Eron *et al.* (1971) make clear, no firm evidence exists for the supposition that the nervous system is innately set to respond to particular signs or releasing mechanisms, as would be necesary if aggressive behaviour patterns were determined by instinctive mechanisms.

6.7.3 *Learning aggressive acts*

There is considerable evidence that many if not most children receive abundant opportunities to learn to act aggressively, and that the amount of violent behaviour in children is closely related to the extent to which aggression occurs in the home (Cohen, 1971). Patterson *et al.* (1967) contend that reinforced actions in children as young as seven months of age may form the basis for subsequent aggressive habits. They cite their observation of an infant whose attempts to reach for a glass of milk were ignored until the child proceeded to pummel his mother's arm. This led immediately to provision of the milk. Interviews with parents, recorded by Bandura and Walters (1959), make it clear that in many families love and reward, especially from the father, are contingent on a boy's acting aggressively.

Furthermore, other children may react in ways that reinforce aggression. Patterson *et al.*, for instance, found that among three- and four-year-olds observed over a twenty-six week period, more than 70 per cent of aggressive actions towards other children resulted in the latter acting in a manner that could be regarded as rewarding the attacker, such as by crying or by giving up a toy. We can infer from this finding that nursery-school settings may function to maintain or enhance aggressive actions in young children. The probability of a child acting aggressively is to some extent determined by the immediate anteceding events. Children and adults are particularly prone to aggressive actions after they have been frustrated in some way (Dollard *et al.*, 1939). Even so, the response of an individual child to frustration is greatly influenced by that child's experience, in regard to the models that the child has been able to observe, the consequences of aggression to those models and the consequence of the child's own aggressive reactions in the past.

REFERENCES

Ardrey, R. (1966). *The Territorial Imperative*, Dell, London

Ashton, R. (1973). The state variable in neonatal research. *Merrill–Palmer Q.* xix, 3–20

Bandura, A. (1962). Social learning through imitation. In M. R. Jones (ed.), *Nebraska Symposium on Motivation*, University of Nebraska Press, Lincoln, Nebraska

Bandura, A. (1969). *Principles of Behavior Modification*, Holt, Rinehart & Winston, New York

Bandura, A., and Walters, R. H. (1959). *Adolescent Aggression*, Ronald Press, New York

Bandura, A., and Walters, R. H. (1963). *Social Learning and Personality Development*, Holt, Rinehart & Winston, New York

Bell, R. Q., and Haaf, R. A. (1971). Irrelevance of newborn waking states to some motor and appetitive responses. *Child Dev.* xlii, 69–77

Bettelheim, B. (1943). Individual and mass behaviour in extreme situations. *J. abnorm, soc. Psychol.* xxxviii, 417–52

Blank, M., and Altman, L. D. (1968). Effects of stimulus modality and task complexity on discrimination and reversal learning in preschool children. *J. exp. Child Psychol.* x, 598–606

Bruner, J. S. (1966). *Toward a Theory of Instruction*, Harvard University Press, Cambridge, Massachusetts

Cohen, S. (1971). The development of aggression. *Rev. Educ. Res.* xli, 71–85

Cunningham, M. (1972). *Intelligence: its Organization and Development*, Academic Press, New York

Denny, M. R. (1964). Research in learning performance. In H. Stevens and R. Heber (eds), *Mental Retardation*, University Press, Chicago

Dollard, J., Doob, L. W., Miller, N. E., Mowrer, O. H., and Sears, R. R. (1939). *Frustration and Aggression*, Yale University Press, New Haven, Connecticut

Drabman, R. S., and Thomas, M. H. (1974). Does media violence increase children's toleration of real-life aggressiveness? *Dev. Psychol.* x, 418–21

Eisenberg, L. (1972). The human nature of human nature. *Science, N.Y.* clxxvi, 123–28

Eron, L. D., Walder, L. O., and Lefkowitz, M. M. (1971). *Learning of Aggression in Children*, Little, Brown, Boston

Estes, W K. (1970). *Learning Theory and Mental Development* Academic Press, New York

Fesbach, S. (1970). Aggression. In P. H. Mussen (ed.), *Carmichael's Manual of Child Psychology*, 3rd edn, vol. 2, Wiley, New York

Gewirtz, J. L. (1969). Mechanisms of social learning: some roles of stimulation and behavior in early development. In D. S. Goslin (ed.), *Handbook of Socialization Theory and Research*, Rand McNally, Chicago

Gottlieb, G., and Simner, M. L., (1966). Relationship between cardiac rate and non-nutritive sucking in human infants. *J. comp. physiol. Psychol.* lxvi, 128–31

Hamburg, D. A. (1969). A combined biological and psychosocial approach to the study of behavioral development. In A. Ambrose (ed.), *Stimulation in Early Infancy*, Academic Press, New York

Hapkiewicz, W. G., and Roden, A. H. (1971). The effect of aggressive cartoons on children's interpersonal play. *Child Dev.* xlii, 1583–5

Harris, F. R., Johnston, M. K., Kelley, C. S., and Wolf, M. M. (1964). Effects of positive social reinforcement on regressive crawling of a nursery school child. *J. educ. Psychol.* lv, 35–41

Kessen, W., Haith, M. M., and Salapatek, P. H. (1970). Human infancy: a bibliography and guide. In P. H. Mussen (ed.), *Carmichael's Manual of Child Psychology*, 3rd edn, vol. 1, Wiley, New York

Levin, H., and Sears, R. R. (1956). Identification with parents as a determinant of doll play aggression. *Child Dev.* xxvii, 135–53

Lipsitt, L. P. (1969). Learning capacities of the human infant. In R. J. Robinson (ed.), *Brain and Early Behavior: Development in the Fetus and Infant*, Academic Press, New York

Lorenz, K. (1966). *On Aggression*. Harcourt, Brace & World, New York

Nordquist, V. M., and Bradley, B. (1973). Speech acquisition in a nonverbal isolate child. *J. exp. Child Psychol.* xv, 149–60

Patterson, G. R., Littman, R. A., and Bricker, W. (1967). Assertive behavior in children: a step toward a theory of aggression. *Monographs of Society for Research in Child Development,* vol. 32

Prechtl, H. F. R. (1969). Brain and behavioral mechanisms in the human newborn infant. In R. J. Robinson (ed.), *Brain and Early Behavior: Development in the Fetus and Infant*, Academic Press, New York

Stein, G. M., and Bryan, J. H. (1972). The effect of a television model upon rule adoption behaviour in children. *Child Dev.* xliii, 268–73

Tinbergen, N. (1951). *The Study of Instinct*, The Clarendon Press, Oxford

Williams, C. D. (1959). The elimination of tantrum behavior by extinction procedures. *J. abnorm. soc. Psychol.* lix, 269

Yussen, S. (1974). Determinants of visual attention and recall in observational learning by preschoolers and second graders. *Dev. Psychol.* x, 93–100

Zeaman, D., and House, B. J. (1967). The relation of IQ and learning. In R. M. Gagné (ed.), *Learning and Individual Differences*, Merrill, Columbus, Ohio

Zeaman, D., House, B. J., and Orlando, R. (1958). Use of special training conditions in visual discrimination training with imbeciles. *Am. J. ment. Defic.* lxiii, 453–9

7
Individual Differences

No two people are completely alike, and the differences between individuals undoubtedly extend to learning. The active nature of learning processes guarantees that each individual will have an important role in determining the knowledge and skills he is to acquire. We have previously encountered the suggestion that the learner's role is a highly active one. Such a notion is implicit in the work of Piaget, for instance, by whom the child is said to 'construct' his world through the impact of experience on existing cognitive structures. Particular effects of active processing by the individual can be noted in many of the experiments described in chapter 5. For example, learners who were told to construct sentences linking word pairs vastly increased the rate at which new items of learning were acquired.

7.1 CUMULATIVE INFLUENCES

Differences in learning between individuals are compounded by the fact that the impact of learning is cumulative. This implies a kind of snowballing effect, one small initial difference leading to another, which produces another, and so on. Thus in the previous chapter it was noted that originally small differences between children in the manner in which they divide attention between various environmental events may lead to differences in learning. Eventually individual differences may emerge in a number of the habits and skills that influence learning in situations encountered later in life.

An account by Staats (1971) illustrates and adds detail to the statement that individual differences are compounded by the cumulative nature of learning. Staats considers the hypothetical case of a child who does poorly at school and who has very low scores in tests of academic achievement, but who does not show evidence of emotional or perceptual deficiencies, or of generalised retardation. He suggests that in such a case detailed reports of the child's behaviour might show that he has not gained the habit of paying attention at school, in the manner of children who are more successful. Staats suggests that perhaps, from this child's first days at school, when the teacher began to present materials for learning, the child would not look at the various stimuli provided, nor make the appropriate responses, and that he would attend to other things that were less relevant to his performing well at tasks contributing to his education at school. In addition, the same child might have had the experience of disrupting learning sessions by his hyperactive or inappropriate behaviour, and consequently evading school activities that were boring or unpleasant for him. Staats continues this hypothetical case study by suggesting that at a later stage the boy might suffer from various forms of social punishment, as a consequence of his failure to learn at the normal rate. For example, when addressed by the teacher he might act in ways that lead to other children laughing at him, or to their remarking on his backwardness and ignorance. Accordingly, various classroom situations that would be quite pleasant to a child who is advancing at the normal rate may become aversive to the child whose school achievement is low, and sooner or later he may deliberately attempt to avoid such unpleasant situations by various strategies, such as behaving in an unusual or bizarre manner, which would lead to the teacher removing him from the classroom. Staats concludes by suggesting that under circumstances of this kind the child might be expected to acquire negative attitudes towards various individuals associated with the school, and develop as avoidance strategies ways of behaving that both impede his learning and result in his being described as emotionally disturbed by adults in the school environment.

In general, Staats feels that a child who for one reason or another fails to acquire as rapidly as other children certain basic skills and habits that are necessary for future learning becomes trapped in 'a downward spiral of relative progress' (Staats, 1971, p. 314). The individual who learns basic skills more slowly than others is not ready so soon to be successful in learning slightly more advanced tasks. In addition, he fails to receive the reinforcement obtained by successful individuals for school activities, and this in turn negatively influences his attentional and working behaviours, so that he learns less quickly than a more highly motivated child. The poorer the performance, the less rewarding the outcome. The smaller the reward, the less will be the incentive to maintain effective attentional habits. Thus Staats' downward spiral continues.

The desire to understand differences between individuals in human achievement and performance has led to a good deal of research, and much of this has directly or indirectly been concerned with learning. In part, the research has been undertaken in response to demands for evidence on questions of a practical nature. Some of these questions have concerned the welfare of individuals. For example, to what extent can the progress of children whose learning has been retarded for one reason or another, benefit from sessions of remedial training? Broader questions may be asked relating to the nature of societies. For instance, what are the effects on individual achievement of social stratification within an organised culture? We can note in passing that many of the issues that have been raised about individual differences centre around the problem of comparing the contributions of hereditary and environmental influences on human capacities. This issue has been highlighted recently by suggestions that have been put forward concerning the possibility that racial factors have a place among the determinants of achievement (Jensen, 1969). However, our attention will be confined to examining the role of experience in leading to differences between individuals.

Much of the research that has examined individual differences has been undertaken by psychologists working from each of three relatively distinct perspectives; that is, three identifiably separate areas of concern have led to investigations into human differences along dimensions that have importance for learning. The first of the areas of concern that have led to research into individual differences in human learning is that of *mental retardation*. Much of this research has taken the form of attempts to discover some of the precise ways in which so-called normal children differ from individuals designated as being mentally retarded. The second broad area of concern has to do with *social class* factors, and *differences between people from various cultures* form the object of the third area of concern. We shall introduce the contributions of research from each of these three perspectives to our understanding of differences in learning between individuals. For convenience, we shall consider them one at a time.

7.2 EVIDENCE FROM RESEARCH INTO MENTAL RETARDATION

Research into differences between normal and mentally retarded individuals has shown that mental retardation can be caused by any combination of a number of factors. Some are biological in nature, others are due to abnormalities or deficiencies in a child's experience. More often than not retardation can be seen as the outcome of interactions between biological and environmental influences, rather than being the result of either of these two kinds of factors acting alone. Thus a particular child may be unusually excitable or impulsive for largely biological reasons. His excitability prevents the child from attending selectively to important environmental stimuli, and therefore he is effectively exposed to an impoverished environment, compared to a normal child. In short, biological and environmental factors do not act separately, but each influences the other, forming part of a system of interlocking processes.

7.2.1 *Broad and narrow conceptions of learning*

In order to come to grips with some of the differences in learning between normal and retarded individuals, it is useful to make a distinction between two ways in which the word learning may be used. We can use it in a broad sense, to refer to a child's performance or score on a task that necessitates learning. Thus most of the measures and scores obtained in learning experiments can be said to reflect learning in this broad sense. Alternatively, we can conceive of learning in a narrower sense, as being some form of connection between events that, for the individual concerned, were previously unrelated. The implication is that some kind of change has occurred in the learner, so that on future occurrences a perceived event will be processed differently. Learning in this narrow sense is similar in some respects to the learning that takes place in classical conditioning, except that the main concern is not with the overt changes in responses to stimuli but with changes in the internal mechanisms that give rise to these responses.

Learning in the broader sense depends on learning in the narrower sense taking place, but it also requires a number of other things. For instance, as we have observed in chapter 6, what is learned is influenced by the manner in which an individual attends to events, and this in turn depends both on motivational factors and on past experience, which determines the familiarity of events to the individual, that is to say, their meaning and significance to him.

It is suggested that many of the observed differences in learning between normal and retarded individuals do not involve learning differences in the narrower sense, that is to say in the ease with which any new connections or associations are formed, but are due to the cumulative effects of the various indirect influences on learning that are included in the broader use of the term. That is to say, many differences between normal and retarded learners are the result of differences in the strategies by which different individuals go about dealing with the task before them, and not of differences in the number of novel associations they are capable of forming.

What is the evidence to support such a suggestion? And, if it is broadly correct, what are some of the more important factors underlying differences in achievement in tasks that measure learning? One kind of evidence is the fact that attempts to observe differences between individuals in learning in the narrower sense of the word have met with failure. Such differences are either non-existent or yet to be detected. However, matters are complicated by the fact that learning in the narrower sense, as we have defined it, cannot be directly observed. Tasks used to measure learning almost invariably involve processes such as attending, which are peripheral to learning in the narrower sense. The classical-conditioning situation comes as close as is possible to learning in the narrower sense, and individual differences in ease of conditioning would thus provide some indication of differences in this kind of learning. As was noted in chapter 2, very young infants condition more slowly than older children, and the conditioning is less stable, being relatively easily extinguished. However, the slower conditioning in young infants may well be due to gross physiological factors, such as incomplete myelinisation, which do not limit learning later in life. After reviewing classical-conditioning studies on older infants and children, Estes (1970) summarises the findings by his statement that observed differences in rate of classical conditioning are remarkable mainly by their absence. Except for the earliest months, there does not appear to be any straightforward relationship between rate of classical conditioning and age, intelligence, or any other measure of success or achievement in tasks that assess ability to learn.

7.2.2 *Evidence from discriminative-learning tasks*

A second body of evidence supporting the view that ease of establishing new connections or associations is not the major factor involved in observed differences between fast and slow learners is provided by the results of experiments using discrimination-learning tasks. In a typical session the learner watches a succession of pairs of objects, and he has to choose the 'correct' item from each pair. The objects may vary along any of a number of dimensions, such as shape, colour and size, and in order to be able to make consistently correct choices the individual has to discover which of the dimensions is crucial and which are irrelevant. When an individual's performance on a task of this kind is plotted in graph form there is typically a first stage in which hardly any change in performance over trials occurs, shown by a near horizontal slope on the graph. This is followed by a stage of rapid learning, indicated by a steep positive final slope. It is suggested that the flat initial part of the graph represents a period during which the learner is discovering which are the relevant dimensions that merit attention. The final, much steeper curve represents the final learning to associate correct performance with a particular response, chosen on the basis of the appropriate dimension.

There are marked differences between individuals at performance on tasks of this kind. On the graph, a high level of performance might conceivably be represented by a short first (near-horizontal) stage, or by a steep final slope, or by both. In fact, it is usually found that good and poor performers at this task do not markedly differ in the magnitude of the slope measuring the final, learning, stage of the task. They do differ, however, in the length of the stage designated by the near-zero slope. This indicates that where the good performers gain is in the time required to discover which of the available dimensions is a relevant one to use as a basis of choice. That is to say, the good learners are marked by their superiority in being able to discover and attend to the appropriate dimension; they have more efficient attentional skills than the other slower learners. In other words, the faster learners are the individuals who are quickest at zeroing in on the relevant cues in the situation.

In summary, there is evidence that at least some of the differences to be found between individuals at tasks requiring learning are due not to differences in underlying central processing mechanisms that determine ease of learning in the narrower sense of forming new connections or associations, but to differences in other processes that determine what events will gain the learner's attention. High achievement at learning tasks is characteristically accompanied by efficient attentional habits, ensuring that items the learner associates are appropriate to a high level of performance. In one respect, we might say that the 'fast learner' actually learns *less* than the 'slow learner', in so far as his more efficient strategies of attending to and encoding perceptual input may have the effect of reducing the number of new associations that have to be made in order to achieve a given level of performance on a learning task.

Before looking into some of the detailed factors underlying individual differences in learning, it needs to be emphasised, at the risk of some repetition, that deficiencies labelled as mental retardation can be due not only to learning deficits but to biological determinants as well. Even when specific deficiencies in a child's experience can be identified as a cause of retardation, it is likely that additional factors are also involved. Generally, biological causes and those events that bring about impoverished environments for learning interact and act on each other in a complex manner that prohibits their disentanglement into separate causes of retardation. However, it is possible to identify a number of relatively clear-cut biological determinants of abnormally low intellectual achievement. One such anomaly is *cretinism*, which is caused by a congenital malfunction of the thyroid gland, associated with iodine deficiency. Cretinism leads to gross physical and mental deficiencies, cretins normally dying in childhood, but early identification followed by the administration of thyroid hormone can halve the ill-effects. A second disorder, *phenylketonuria*, is transmitted by a gene whose manifestation is recessive, and involves an error in metabolism. Some children lack an enzyme that is necessary for converting the amino acid phenylalanine, occurring in many foods, into a harmless by-product. When this fails to happen the phenylalanine is changed into phenylpyruvic acid, which damages the nerve cells, resulting in mental retardation. Phenylketonuria is now fortunately rare in young children, since the effects of this deficiency can be minimised by ensuring that the children follow a special diet, consisting of foods that contain very little phenylalanine. The condition can be detected by a urine test. A third deficiency, *mongolism* (Down's Syndrome), is more common than the others, around 18 per cent of all moderately and severely retarded children being mongoloid. In most cases it is associated with the presence of an extra chromosome. Among mothers over forty-five years in age the risk of having a mongoloid child is greater than one in sixty.

7.2.3 *Specific factors in mental-retardation – impulsivity*

The findings of research into mental retardation indicate that a number of relatively specific circumstances can contribute to observed differences between individuals in ability to learn. One fact that hinders learning in some children is *extreme impulsivity*. Estes (1970) has pointed out that in many tasks there are points at which individuals need to slow down before making a new response. In learning situations that require the ability to discriminate between a number of items or events, it may be necessary to inspect all the elements in a display before choosing and making an active response. Human learners often carry out a covert scanning process (sometimes termed 'vicarious trial and error', or 'V.T.E.'), in which various possible actions are considered. Children who are unusually impulsive or distractable are at a disadvantage in situations of this kind, owing to their inability to inhibit premature responses, or to resist the distractions that irrelevant stimulus events provide. Estes suggests that excessive impulsiveness may be due to simple failure to learn effective scanning habits. Normal children tend to become less impulsive as age increases, and acquire an increased ability to delay their actions in a variety of circumstances (Kagan, 1965). It has been shown that among children in their first year at school the more impulsive individuals make a greater number of errors in word recognition and are thus at a disadvantage in learning to read.

7.2.4 *Deficits in inhibitory processes*

These may in some instances be responsible for learning deficiencies. Support for this possibility is given by results obtained by Ellis (1970). It was found that when learning by normal and mentally defective individuals was compared under conditions whereby blocks of massed learning trials were separated by a rest period, the performance of normal subjects, but not that of the retardates, was positively related to the length of the rest periods between trials. Ellis's suggestion is that the normals built up greater amounts of inhibition during the massed trial sessions, and that they consequently profited to a greater extent than did the retardates from the opportunity that the rest periods provided for inhibition to dissipate. Consistent with the suggestion that deficits in inhibitory processes may underlie some learning disabilities is the observation in studies of classical conditioning that although mental retardates condition as quickly as normal subjects, they extinguish more slowly.

7.2.5 *Short-term memory*

A further possibility is that differences in *rate of short-term forgetting* may underlie some individual differences in learning. It is known that performance at tests of recall is strongly influenced by the kind of rehearsal strategy a learner adopts (Howe, 1967), and it seems likely that the longer an individual is able to retain remembered items, such as words, in his short-term memory system, the greater the probability of his making or detecting some kind of relationship between the new items and a permanently stored item, and hence the higher the probability of the new item being retained in a form that is relatively immune to decay. To support this suggestion Ellis (1970), who considers that retardates may have deficient rehearsal strategies, cites findings that variations in presentation-rate of word lists produce large differences in the recall of early items by normal subjects, but not by retardates. Slow rates of presentation provide increased opportunities for recall of early items, and it appears that normal individuals are able to profit from such rehearsal, but retardate subjects are not. In short, retarded individuals do not seem to benefit from opportunities to rehearse items that they are attempting to remember. It is possible either that the retarded individual fails to rehearse, or that he does rehearse but without this having the effect on memory storage that rehearsal brings about in individuals of normal ability. Ellis has also suggested that retardates suffer from reduced 'stimulus trace', which he describes as a reverberatory neuronal mechanism persisting only for a very brief period of a few seconds. Howe (1970) provides a broader discussion of the role of memory in human learning.

7.2.6 *Motivational factors*

A number of the factors that appear to contribute to degree of success in learning reflect *motivational differences* of one kind or another. For instance, in a learning task whereby correct responses are always rewarded, a child who is accustomed to failure may consider that being rewarded on 50 per cent of occasions is satisfactory, and feel no pressure to adapt or modify his behaviour in order to achieve a higher level of reward. An individual accustomed to success would be more likely to alter his responses, until a higher level of reward is obtained, thus striving harder to produce a high level of achievement. In addition, the effects of a failure in one situation are likely to depend on the individual's past history of experiences in similar situations. As a result of repeated failures, a new problem may be seen by some individuals as a cue for avoidance. A child who has most often been successful in the past is likely to follow one experience of failure by continued efforts to be successful. Estes (1970) notes that careful management of a child's environment by parents and teachers can have beneficial practical effects. If the child is customarily faced with problems that are appropriately geared to his experience of success he will be likely to acquire the habit of welcoming and seeking for new problems that are similar to those at which he has been successful in the past, and he may thus come to demonstrate 'motivation for achievement' (Estes, 1970) in a wide range of situations.

There are numerous further ways in which motivational factors can contribute to retardation. For instance, one child's exploratory actions might be severely restricted, due perhaps to chronic illness or to anxiety on the part of his parents. The child is not reinforced for engaging in any inquiring or exploratory activities, and consequently he does not acquire the habit of exploring his surroundings or demonstrating curiosity. As a result, this child is denied certain valuable experiences that exploratory behaviour would bring about in normal children. As a second illustration, consider a child whose parents punish him much more frequently than is normal. If the child comes to feel that most of his spontaneous activities are likely to be punished he will probably fail to acquire the highly discriminative body of knowledge that most individuals possess about the differing consequences of various actions, or a normal understanding of the reasons for punishment on a given occasion. If such a child is punished on one occasion for socially undesirable verbal behaviour he is more likely than most children to desist from all forms of speech in the future, reducing the extent to which he engages in communication with others.

Motivational factors are prominent in the concept of the downward spiral (Staats, 1971) that was mentioned at the beginning of this chapter. Staats notes that under normal circumstances children in school will be rewarded both by the teacher's approval and by the intrinsic value of acquiring new skills. If these do not become customary sources of reward for the child he will be less inclined than others to undertake the kinds of work necessary for learning. As a result he will learn less, leading to a further deficit in reinforcement and a further deterioration in attention and other habits necessary for learning.

To illustrate the strong influence that motivational factors may exert on intellectual performance, Staats (1971) describes a study in which backward children were first given an intelligence test, administered to the group in the usual manner, with no extrinsic rewards. Later the same children received an alternative form of the test, but on this occasion the children were rewarded financially for each correct item. Under these conditions the children actually attempted a smaller number of the test items. However, they obtained higher scores, owing to the fact that they were responding more carefully, and were more often correct, and thus, according to the test scores, more 'intelligent'. Staats suggested that if factors that affect motivation can have such a marked effect in any one situation, the effects of continuous lack of attention and lack of efficient study behaviours 'multiplied by countless hours' spent by the children at school throw some pupils further and further behind children who give careful attention to the school tasks they encounter.

7.2.7 *Transfer of learned skills*

When normal and retarded individuals learn equivalent tasks, there may exist differences between them in the extent to which what has been learned can be generalised or transferred to similar but non-identical situations. O'Connor and Hermelin (1963) describe subnormals as being 'specific' in their responses, tending to be poor at recognising similarities and essential differences. When retarded subjects were trained to respond to an auditory tone, they were less likely than normals to make an identical response if a very similar tone was subsequently presented. However, although this result is consistent with the suggestion that retarded individuals are restricted in ability to generalise from what has been learned, it is conceivable that this finding could have been due to the response to the initial tone being more strongly reinforced in retarded subjects than in normal individuals, since the latter needed a smaller number of trials to learn the original discrimination.

7.2.8 *Motivation, skills, strategies and cognitive style*

As the child becomes increasingly capable of learning more complex skills and varieties of knowledge, the role of the individual's active coding processes, whereby new material is related to existing cognitive structures, becomes increasingly more important. The influence of such coding and integrating processes in relatively simple forms is seen in experiments on cross-model memory (see chapter 5). Relatively elaborate integrative activities on the part of learners can be detected in some investigations of learning. For example, when subjects are required to provide sentences to join words that are presented, the learning of word pairs is found to improve. When older children and adults need to acquire knowledge it is necessary for the individual to be able to relate the newly available information to what he already knows. Otherwise, meaning and structure are absent, greatly reducing the probability that the individual will retain novel information.

An intelligent person's large and more highly organised body of knowledge makes him well-equipped for dealing with new information. He has at his disposal a large number of 'codes' (Biggs, 1968), that is, schemes or programmes for categorising and organising new information in a manner that securely relates it to a foundation of existing knowledge, so that the new input may resist forgetting through decay. Rehearsal strategies provide opportunities for increased exposure of newly perceived data, making it possible to organise and structure such data or to connect it to existing knowledge. It goes without saying that the contents of cognitive structure, which are seen to play an important active role in human learning, are to some extent unique to each individual; hence differences in previous experience between individuals considerably influence what they learn in the future.

Motivational factors, and the ways in which each individual's knowledge and skills are organised, jointly contribute to the formation of a learner's characteristic 'cognitive style'. Thus some individuals adopt more flexible strategies than others in reasoning and in learning, and mental retardates tend to be unusually rigid, manifesting various inappropriate perseverative and stereotyped forms of behaviour. The importance of differences in cognitive style between individuals for their efficiency as learners extends to the differences between normal adults. Harvey *et al.* (1961) found that individuals who tend to think abstractly rather than concretely, and in relatives rather than absolutes, are likely to show independence and originality of thought, to be more resourceful than others and to show a greater ability to understand and sympathise with other individuals. Children instructed by teachers who possess abstract characteristic reasoning styles tend to achieve more highly than children taught by teachers whose reasoning is more concrete in nature, and the former children are seen as being more highly involved and more co-operative in undertaking classroom activities (Harvey *et al.*, 1968).

7.3 RESEARCH INTO SOCIAL-CLASS DIFFERENCES

7.3.1 *The concept of social class*

Social class is not, in itself, a unitary causal factor in human learning. The term refers to a wide and complex range of circumstances. As Hess (1970) makes clear, it is more realistic to regard social class as an indication of probable circumstances than as a single factor. By making a statement about the social status of a person, we are, in a very broad and approximate manner, identifying the social and economic context in which he is likely to function; and providing a starting-off point for further analysis in the form of useful but very imprecise information about the kinds of situations and experiences he is likely to have encountered. In large countries, such as the United States, matters are further confounded by various regional and racial differences, and by cultural factors that reflect the nationality or place of origin of an individual's family.

It is worth emphasising that information about an individual's social-class status provides only the broadest indication of the kinds of experiences and influences that impinge on him. In giving social-class labels for a group of people taken at random, which involves composite measures based on assessment of factors such as education, occupational status and living standards, one does arrive at measures that positively correlate with alternative indicators of learning and achievement, yet the guide provided by social-class descriptions is a very crude one. This fact has sometimes been insufficiently appreciated. In many investigations, social-class measures, or indicators closely related to them, such as the occupational status of an individual's parents, have been used in ways implying the erronous belief that they give a direct measure of an individual's environment. For instance, measures of social class have been used as indexes of a child's environment in studies designed to compare the contributions of heredity and environmental determinants of measured intelligence. In fact, as Miller (1970) has shown, the correlations between measures of social class and direct measures of environmental quality, although positive, are rather low, demonstrating that social-class data provide only the roughest guide to the quality of the environment encountered by individual children. Furthermore, Majoribanks (1972), who compared the effectiveness of direct measures of environmental forces with social-class measures and related factors as predictors of children's scores on tests of mental ability, found that while the correlations between parents' educational and occupational status and various dimensions of intellectual ability were around +0.3, on average, correlations between environmental forces and mental ability were typically considerably higher, especially in the case of numerical and verbal abilities.

Naturally, some of the factors underlying observed social-class differences are related to those already encountered in the above discussion of differences between normal and retarded children. Furthermore, the class-related differences in opportunities for learning certain skills exert an influence on each of the basic learning processes described in the early chapters of this book. Thus, for instance, social-class factors are reflected in a child's environment, influencing the stimuli to which he is exposed, and making for differences in the behaviour of the available human models in whom the child observes the actions that he subsequently incorporates in his own habitual behaviours. Patterns of reinforcement may also differ: Kagan (1970) remarks that instrumental control of the environment is a pleasant experience, and that a child who persistently grapples with difficult problems is likely to enjoy the excitement that comes with success. This helps him develop an expectancy that his efforts will be successful, and, consequently, a sense of his own effectiveness. If class-related differences are important in this context, they are likely to enter into chains of circumstances not dissimilar to those we have described as part of Staats's account. As it happens, some class-related differences have indeed been observed in the kinds of phenomena that can form the elements of such chains of events. For instance, it has been noted that middle-class children as young as two years of age play with toys in a sustained manner for longer periods than children from lower-class families, and the former are consequently more likely to complete their intended activities (Kagan, 1970).

Differences related to social class are found in a large number of variables that affect learning, and it will be useful to adopt some categorisation of the various factors involved. There are a number of possibilities. One is to divide social-class influences into those that stem directly from economic factors, that is, the outcomes of wealth and poverty; those that stem from the intellectual standards and interests of the parents, a category that might include measures of the books in a child's home and the complexity of spoken language he encounters; and, finally, those influences that stem from an individual's position in society. We shall adopt an alternative scheme, classifying phenomena into, first, those that can be described as forming *causes* for the differences in learning that are related to social class, and, second, those that form *effects* of such differences. This cause–effect distinction is an imperfect one: causes and effects actually function in chains and even circles of interdependent processes. One important broad class of events that resist simple classification into these categories of class-related phenomena is language. Accordingly, we shall consider some linguistic implications of social-class differences as a separate third category.

7.4 SOME SOCIAL-CLASS PHENOMENA

7.4.1 *Causes*

The beginnings of social learning take place within the family. Members of the child's immediate family, particularly the mother, make available to the child experiences and stimuli that they think are worthy of attention, and the family provides the child with symbols or constructs enabling him to organise and communicate his experiences (Hess, 1970). In so far as the environment and social practices of a family contain elements that are exclusive to a particular social class, social-class factors contribute to the early experience of the child.

The findings of research into social-class differences in child-rearing need to be interpreted with some caution, since child-rearing practices tend to change slightly from one decade to the next, and because there are some differences between practices in Britain and the U.S.A., where much relevant data have been obtained. Hess (1970) finds that American middle-class parents tend to have greater tolerance of impulsive actions in young children than working-class parents, and less frequently punish lapses in self-control. Middle-class parents expect greater independence of their children in skills such as feeding and dressing, and tend to discipline their children by disapproval and withdrawal of affection, whereas lower-class parents more often use physical punishment. A number of investigators have observed that working-class parents tend to stress virtues such as neatness, cleanliness and obedience to a greater extent than middle-class parents, while the latter are more likely to emphasise curiosity, independence and consideration for others, and, in older children, educational achievement. However, there are large overlaps between social classes in all of the above areas of concern.

In an observational study of interactions between mothers and infants, Zunich (1961) found that middle-class mothers had more physical contact with their children than did mothers from lower-class backgrounds, and were more likely to give directions, to help, to interfere with the child's activities, to observe attentively and to interact with the child in play. Lower-class mothers, on the other hand, interfered less and were less often rated as being unco-operative with their children. Similarly, in his own research, Hess (1970) reports that middle-class mothers were found to be more prone than lower-class mothers to communicate verbally to their children, to provide specific task instructions, to require verbal feedback rather than physical compliance, to make use of rewards, and to give their child information that was useful for completing current activities and improving performance in the future. An investigation by N. Radin and C. K. Kamin (summarised by Hess, 1970) produced similar findings. Middle-class mothers were observed to be much more responsive than lower-class mothers to requests by their children, to give fewer orders without explanation, and they were more likely to reward desirable behaviour. Middle-class children sought the attention of their mothers more frequently than children from lower-class families, perhaps partly as a result of the greater likelihood of such attempts being reinforced by the (more responsive) middle-class mothers. However, it should be noted that in none of the investigations we have described were social-class differences observed in all of the behavioural categories that were selected for observation. Social-class differences have been found in only a small number of the activities that were observed.

The findings of most American studies agree in showing that middle-class mothers tend to be more responsive and attentive to the needs of their children, to communicate more frequently with their children, to exhibit a greater degree of interest, and, as a result, to be more aware of their children's needs and feelings. Middle-class parents are also more likely to explain the reason for making a request, and are less likely to use punishment and other control techniques based on the use of power. British investigations have produced very similar results. Newson and Newson (1968) observed that there was more interaction between middle-class parents and their children, greater encouragement to talk at mealtimes and more emphasis on story-telling. They found that middle-class parents were less likely to use threats based on distortion of the truth (for example, 'Don't do that or the policeman will come and take you away') and more likely to reason with their children and to explain things to them. The social-class differences appear to lie in the form of control that is exerted rather than in the total amount of control. Hess considers that class differences reflect the needs of parents to adapt successfully to the differing social situations in which they live, rather than to any unwillingness on the part of the lower-class mothers to function adequately as parents, or to any preference for punishment as a means of control. Social-class differences in the manner in which children are controlled do not seem to be caused by differences in intelligence, since the modes of behaviour in which middle- and lower-class mothers differ are not ones for which the intellectual abilities of the latter are insufficient. In arguing that the lower-class parents' actions provide a realistic adaptation to their conditions of life, Hess suggests that:

> Early orientation toward authority transmits and reinforces the orientation of adults to the economic and social system of which they are a part. They lack alternatives of action in their own exchanges with the institutions of the community and with other members of their communities, and are poorly motivated to seek other techniques because there is little reason to expect reward (Hess, 1970, p. 480).

7.4.2 *Effects*

In what ways are children influenced by these social-class differences? Although it appears reasonable to expect that the observed class-related differences in the manner in which parents act towards their children will lead to observable differences in the children's behaviour, there is little firm evidence on this point. In one study Hess and his co-workers found that the performance of young children at tests of intelligence and concept development was related to the mother's behaviour towards her child. Children's achievement was positively related to the extent to which mothers were observed to be successful at anticipating the child's needs, at providing information and appropriate feedback, and, when controlling the child's activities, communicating in a manner that explained the situation and took the child's feelings into account. There is also some evidence of early differences in habits of attention, which we have seen to be crucially important for learning. As early as thirteen months of age middle-class children have been shown to exhibit the foundations of superior attentional skills, in the form of longer fixation times to visual patterns (Kagan, 1970).

By the age of about ten years, social-class differences emerge in a range of non-school activities outside the home, thus compounding the range of situations in which the class-related differences exist in children's experience. In addition, social groupings and choice of friends within school appear to be related to social class. Children's vocational and educational aspirations are related to social class, although there do not appear to be straightforward differences in occupational interests and choices, all children being equally likely to prefer prestigious or glamorous vocations. However, middle-class children tend to have greater knowledge about occupations, and are thus in a position to make more realistic decisions and to take the necessary steps towards achieving their goals (DeFleur and DeFleur, 1967).

Partly as a result of the kinds of factors we have mentioned, children from lower-class homes tend to be, or to see themselves as being, disadvantaged or certainly different from those individuals who come from middle-class backgrounds. Hess (1970) suggested that a number of considerations are involved. First, the extent to which an individual is able to exercise power in society is related to social class. One effect of the belief in relative powerlessness among poor people is shown in a decreased readiness among working-class parents to demand that their views be considered by the school authorities or to insist on being kept informed about their children's education (Jackson and Marsden, 1962). As a consumer of goods or services the lower-class individual has less information available for making appropriate choices, and for placing complaints or demanding his rights. Movements such as Trade Unionism have helped give workers some power, through membership of large influential organisations. The rise of the Co-operative associations in the nineteenth century had some similar effects. Hess suggests that a feeling of relative powerlessness hinders the growth of capacity for effective individual action, and constitutes an important element underlying class differences in achievement. Poor people are also more vulnerable to various kinds of disaster. Despite recent government actions, manual workers are still more likely to be made redundant than salaried employees, and their relative poverty deprives them of a cushion available to middle-class families confronted by unemployment or loss of income for other reasons such as illness. Furthermore, the circumstances of the manual worker combine to restrict the range of alternatives in life style. The ability to make choices about housing, education and employment is restricted by lack of power, education and prestige. In addition, in some countries, such as the United States, the availability of adequate medical services may be restricted by financial hardship.

One implication of these facts is that if practical attempts at compensatory education that incorporate assisting the mother to teach her child are to have any chance of success, it is essential that the mother comes to believe that her actions will have some effect. Before she can wholeheartedly undertake some innovation or change in the kinds of activities whereby she interacts with her child, for example by spending more time and care in explanation and instruction, the mother needs to believe that her altered activities will have an effect. If she reluctantly allows various interventions to be imposed on her, without believing that they may help, it is unlikely that they will have much success (Kagan, 1970).

Social class and measured intelligence. By an early age class-related differences in intelligence-test scores begin to emerge. Eels *et al.* (1951) gave I.Q. tests to children aged between nine and fourteen years. They found mean differences ranging from eight to twenty-three I.Q. points between the average scores obtained by children from high and low social classes. There was considerable overlap, however, both very high and very low scores being obtained by children from all socio-economic groups, and there was no overall tendency for the magnitude of differences to increase with age. Items testing verbal performance produced the largest of the class-related differences in test scores and the authors suggest that 'linguistic or scholastic' test items are the one in which marked differences are most likely to be present. On the tests measuring performance in perceptual tasks, incorporating pictures or geometric designs, social-class differences were generally small or non-existent.

The problems encountered in trying to demonstrate causal links between class-related differences in experience and individual differences in achievement are increased by uncertainty concerning the relative importance of hereditary and environmental determinants of human capacities. When intelligence-test scores are used the possibility of a further complication is suggested by the claim that intelligence tests are in some respects biased in favour of a culturally dominant middle-class subsection of society. The issue is a complicated one, and it is clear that if the items used in a test are chosen to predict success in the kinds of activities valued among the 'successful' members of the culture, the tests are bound to be biased so long as the society is not perfectly homogeneous (Howe, 1972). Thus the concept of intelligence is a culture-bound one, and intelligent behaviour can be broadly defined as behaviour that has a value in tasks having a function within the culture. As Vernon (1969) points out, the kind of intelligence measured in the I.Q. tests used in Western countries is a 'kind of intelligence which is especially well adapted for scientific analysis, for control and exploitation of the physical world, for large-scale and long-term planning and carrying out of materialistic objectives'. (Vernon, 1969, p. 89). In so far as some social-class groups do not share the values in whose context the above are important, the tests are inevitably biased against them.

The question of bias can be approached in a more practical manner by developing procedures designed to familiarise children with test instructions, by ensuring that attitudes towards taking tests are equivalent for different social groups, and by giving children experience in attempting problems similar in form to the ones used in the test. In some instances, but not in others, procedures such as this have led to decreases in class-related differences in intelligence-test scores.

Social class, achievement and personality. Although intelligence-test scores do not by any means provide direct measures of learning ability, a point emphasised by Guildford (1967) and Estes (1970), such scores typically have a fairly high correlation with school achievement (which the earliest intelligence tests were specifically designed to predict). The fact that social class and achievement at school are related has been documented in a number of studies (for example, by Havighurst, 1964, in the U.S.A., and in Britain by Jackson, 1964), which indicate that class-related ability streaming may take place among children as young as seven years of age. As one might predict from the pattern of differences in intelligence-test scores, school-achievement measures of abilities closely dependent on language skills are affected by social class to a greater degree than other capacities (Curry, 1962). Consequently, as Kellmer Pringle *et al.* (1966) observed, by the age of seven there were marked class differences in reading performance among British children, and significant but somewhat smaller differences in arithmetic ability. Douglas (1964) observed an increase in the differences between the school achievement of manual and non-manual workers between the ages of seven and eleven. Douglas *et al.* (1968) found that among children at secondary modern schools the trend towards increasing class-related differences as children become older continued between the ages of eleven and fifteen.

Numerous investigations have looked for relationships between social class and various manifestations of personality and adjustment, factors that might reasonably be expected to exert an indirect influence on some kinds of learning. Sewell and Haller (1956), for instance, found that the lower the social-class background of children in a large sample aged ten to fourteen years, the higher their scores on measures of concern over status, concern over achievement, and repertoire of family 'nervous symptoms'. However, none of the correlations was higher than +0.3, and thus the magnitude of the relationship is not sufficient to provide much assistance in making predictions about individuals. A number of studies have sought to discover relationships between aggressive behaviour in children and social class, but the results are conflicting, and no clear pattern of findings emerges. There appears to be somewhat sharper differentiation into sex roles among lower-class families, and it has been found that the extent to which girls become involved in 'masculine' activities is positively related to the parents' educational level.

7.4.3 *Language differences*

Various linguistic differences are also related to social class. The fact that language and speech are given prominence in almost all the compensatory learning programmes that have been devised to aid children who have failed to acquire skills necessary for success at school is indicative of the widespread belief that the language an individual uses is of considerable importance for a range of learned abilities.

Bernstein's approach. Bernstein (1961) suggested that spoken language is the main agency through which class differences in educational achievement occur, and through which there may emerge a clash of values between those of the school and those of individuals whose background does not lead to easy acceptance of the customs and values implicit in school environment. Forms of spoken language, Bernstein suggests, 'induce in their learning, orientations to particular orders of learning and condition different dimensions of relevance'. He points out that the mode and content of communication is strongly influenced by the form of social relationships between people. Thus the language that a child uses when he is in a group of other children differs in content and structure from the language he uses when addressing an adult. When two people share considerable interest in and knowledge about a topic under discussion, meaning can often be conveyed without the words being fully explicit. A complex meaning may be conveyed by a small gesture, and by slight variations in pitch or stress. In these circumstances it is likely that speech will be abbreviated, with individuals communicating with one another 'against a backcloth of closely shared identifications and effective empathy which removes the need for elaborate verbal expression' (Bernstein, 1961).

To an outsider lacking the close 'communion of the spirit' that is shared by individuals possessing common backgrounds and interests, the actual words that are spoken may be misleading or incomprehensible. The dialogue may appear illogical, disjunctive and highly concrete, and the outsider will be struck by his own exclusion, effective communication being restricted to a relatively small number of individuals. Bernstein suggests that for many working-class individuals this informal language is the only one at their disposal. In other words, he suggests that some people are unused to communicating except against such a background of common knowledge, attitudes and beliefs. Bernstein considers that children in lower-class homes are likely to acquire the ability to make use of language as a form of communication only in circumstances in which complex and very precise language forms are redundant, owing to the system of shared identifications common to all the individuals to whom the child customarily speaks. In the absence of pressure to speak in a manner that is comprehensible to individuals who do not share the experiences of the relatively small and homogeneous group of individuals among whom a child resides and interacts, he fails to acquire some of the skills required for communicating meaning through language to an audience with wide-ranging background experiences.

The kind of speech that is adequate for communicating only in situations where there is considerable identification in aims and backgrounds among group members, is termed 'restricted code speech' by Bernstein. He emphasises that it is found in all social classes. However, there is a tendency for working-class children to learn to use this kind of communication exclusively, whereas middle-class children are in addition more likely to learn to use a more formal kind of language, in which meaning is conveyed in a precise and explicit manner by highly organised linguistic utterances. Bernstein uses the term 'elaborated code' to refer to this more formal language, whereby detailed messages are conveyed by the specific content of speech, without requiring the listener and the speaker to share the commonality of world view necessary for adequate communication when a restricted code is used.

It is claimed by Bernstein that differences between social classes in the means of language available both reflect and tend to solidify a number of class-related differences in the way that life is perceived. Bernstein writes, for instance, of the 'affective inclusiveness' characteristic of tightly knit working-class communities, and he contrasts this with the greater stress laid on the role of the individual as a decision-maker among middle-class families. Furthermore, he suggests that the working-class mother may be less experienced in using speech as a way of proclaiming her individuality. Bernstein claims that the working-class parent is unlikely to perceive spoken language as a major vehicle for presenting to others one's inner status, and he suggests that the 'I' of the working-class mother is not to a marked extent a verbally differentiated 'I'. Among middle-class families, however, Bernstein considers that there is some pressure to verbalise one's feelings in an individual manner, and this is possible when an elaborated speech code is available, providing the formal means for such communication.

Bernstein considers that these and other factors contribute to an inability among individuals limited to a restricted code to organise their experience. Thus an emphasis on planning for the future, accuracy of time perspective, expertise in decision-making, concern with self-control rather than conformity to external authority, are all seen as necessitating a precise, finely differentiated means of thought and communication, and therefore Bernstein considers that language and speech are at the heart of the factors involved in observed social-class differences. How are class-related differences in language codes acquired? For Bernstein the answer is simple. The child learns the language that is spoken to him and in his presence by his parents and family and by the other children he encounters in daily life.

Evidence for Bernstein's views. Bernstein's theory undoubtedly provides a bold and ingenious attempt to link together a number of apparently diverse phenomena associated with class differences in achievement. Is the theory basically correct? Does the available empirical evidence tend to confirm or contradict Bernstein's position? Broadly speaking, there is much evidence that social classes do differ in the language they use. In Britain, Lawton (1968) observed that, by adolescence, individuals from relatively wealthy homes use more complex syntactic structures, with greater use of verbs in the passive mood, a wider variety of adjectives and a greater number of subordinate clauses. Dale (1972) cites a number of American studies, most of which indicate some differences in language acquisition between children of higher and lower socio-economic groups. However, Dale finds that there are no particularly clear-cut differences in syntactic development (that is, in the structural aspects of language, as distinct from size of vocabulary) and he considers that this lack of evidence of syntactic differences gives some support to the position that emphasises the common biological endowment underlying the development of linguistic skills, and by which specific experiences and exposure to particular speech patterns are seen as a relatively small influence on language development.

Supporting Bernstein's position is a body of evidence showing that the manner in which the mother speaks to her children has a powerful influence on their speech and behaviour. For instance, Hess and Shipman (1968) observed mothers and their four-year-old children from four socio-economic levels, in sessions that contained a number of tasks requiring interaction between mother and child. There was a high positive correlation between observed scores for each child's performance and the specificity with which the mother gave directions, and there was also a high negative correlation between performance in children and the mother's tendency to use negative statements. The importance of the mother's speech is further indicated by the fact that both the above measures were more highly correlated with the child's performance than was a combined index of social class and the mother's I.Q. One year later these same children were given a test for verbal vocabulary, and correlations were calculated between their scores and a number of measures of maternal variables that had been made in the previous year. It was found that the best single predictor of a child's score on the vocabulary test was the mother's own earlier vocabulary score. Middle-class mothers are also able to vary the redundancy and simplicity of their own speech, in accordance with the age of the child they are addressing (Snow, 1972), and it is possible that lower-class mothers, who rely to a greater extent on restricted codes, are less well-equipped to adapt their speech to the needs of young children.

In general, there clearly are differences associated with social class in the use of language. The findings indicate that a parent's language is associated with various measurements of her child's development. Bernstein and his colleagues have been involved in a body of research designed to examine the more detailed aspects of his theory. Thus Brandis and Henderson (1970) found that the measured ability of children at five and six years of age on tasks requiring verbal skills was related to the manner in which their mothers responded to a child's questions. The children scoring most highly were those whose mothers tended to give explanations in reply to questions, showing a concern with what the authors term the 'relevance' of language. Brandis and Henderson obtained various measures of maternal communication, such as a 'communication index', rating the extent to which a mother responded to her child in a manner that encouraged conversation and questions. Scores on this index of mothers' behaviour correlated more highly than did a broad social-class measure with estimates of the child's own language and mental abilities. Kagan and Tulkin (1971) noted that even during the first year of an infant's life middle-class mothers spoke more often to their children than did lower-class mothers. These authors found that many working-class mothers believed that only after the children began to talk did it become important for the mother to speak back. Kagan and Tulkin consider that reluctance to stimulate the child's verbalisation is also indicative of a mother's belief that she can have little influence on the child's development, a feeling related to a broader fatalism based on an awareness of powerlessness to change one's way of life. We have previously suggested that poverty may tend to promote such feelings of powerlessness.

E. R. Heider discovered that, by the age of ten years, differences related to social class can be seen in the manner in which children code novel abstract figures that are presented to them (Dale, 1972). Descriptions produced by children were classified along two dimensions. The first indicated whether the description referred to the whole item or only to part of it. The second dimension indicated whether the child provided a straightforward description of what he saw, or whether he made an inference going beyond the appearance of the figure. Middle-class children produced responses that were categorised as 'part descriptive' much more often than did the working-class children. An example is, 'It has an opening at the top'. The working-class children were more likely to attempt to describe the stimulus as a whole, for example, 'He looks like someone hit him'. Ability to give precise descriptions of details is implicit in communications that make use of an elaborated code, as defined by Bernstein, and hence it is more likely to be encountered among children able to communicate via an elaborated code than among those who are not. In this experiment middle-class children were more successful, on the whole, at providing descriptions, and they also performed better at a task of 'decoding', in which they listened to descriptions provided by other children, and then attempted to state which one of a number of figures the speaker was describing.

As further evidence for the reality of the class-related language differences postulated by Bernstein, he draws attention to the finding (Bernstein, 1962) that, when conversing, working-class boys have a tendency to finish remarks with phrases like 'Didn't I', 'Wouldn't it', or 'You know what I mean', all of which have the effect of assuming agreement and of discouraging any further discussion that does not tacitly imply acceptance of the first speaker's point of view. This tends to restrict communication, preventing its development except within the narrowly prescribed direction encompassing the respondent's agreement. Middle-class children, on the other hand, even in their earliest years at school, were found to use many more expressions that indicated tentativeness, such as 'I think', or 'I am not exactly sure', providing greater freedom for the individual who is addressed to develop conversation on his own terms.

The demonstration that working-class children habitually make use of restricted codes does not by itself constitute proof that such children are unable to use elaborated codes. Robinson (1965) required boys from middle- and working-class families to write both a formal and an informal letter. The working-class boys did not have any particular difficulties in preparing the formal letter, although when they were asked to guess at words that had been deleted from a prose passage, the working-class boys did make more predictable responses, using a smaller vocabulary.

The mass of evidence on the role of variations in language content and style among different social classes resists straightforward summary. The evidence indicates that Bernstein is certainly correct up to a point, and that considerable differences do exist in the use of language and speech among different social-class groups. It is open to question whether the differences are so consistent or so marked as Bernstein suggests, whether the differences in language style really do indicate an inability among working-class respondents to use elaborated codes, rather than a simple preference for restricted codes, and whether the differences are as closely bound to individuals' thought processes relating to planning, decision-making, conceptions of oneself, and philosophy of life as Bernstein considers them to be. Linguistic factors defy categorisation into roles of cause and effect, and form part of an untidy confusion of data from which they emerge as being related to many if not most of the numerous differences between individuals that have been found to be related to social class.

7.5 CROSS-CULTURAL RESEARCH

Historically, an interest in the manner in which infants and children are influenced by experience and an interest in cross-cultural differences between individuals have often gone hand in hand. In the nineteenth century, two popular notions were, first, Haeckel's 'ontogeny recapitulates phylogeny', a statement implying that individual organisms repeat the anatomical history of their species in embryological development, and, second, that human society tends to evolve in a continuum from the primitive to the civilised. This is implicit in Darwin's suggestion that the evolution of the intellect can be inferred from the evolution of culture. Putting these ideas together gives rise to the following three assumptions: first, that primitive adults are an early form of adults of advanced societies, second, that the European child is an early form of the European adult, and, third, that the primitive adult is, in some respects, equivalent to the civilised child.

Following the work of later anthropologists such as Franz Boas, who raised a number of objections to these assumptions about the close relationship between culture and thought, the nineteenth-century viewpoint has long been discarded. It rests on the fallacious belief that certain observed similarities in thought between European children and primitive men inevitably imply close similarity in culture, and that differences in culture imply basic differences in thought processes. As we shall see, culture and thought are undoubtedly related, but this relationship is neither inevitable nor invariable, since it is based on environmental causes rather than on the genetically transmitted mechanisms that were at one time thought to be involved.

Some of the cultural factors that investigators have suggested may influence what is learned by children in different societies, and the postulated underlying mechanisms, parallel those brought forward in research on social-class differences. Thus Cole *et al.* (1971) mention the possibility that certain cultural traits, such as strict directive upbringing, will lead to modes of cognitive functioning that are relatively undifferentiated, in being inexplicitly analysed and articulated. This suggestion is clearly similar to statements made by Bernstein (1961), to which we have previously referred, concerning social-class differences in the mother's conception and articulation of feelings about herself as an individual. Whorf (1956) emphasised the role of language in giving both form and direction to human thought. He stressed that language does not merely serve as a reproducing instrument for communicating ready-formed thoughts, but also functions as a 'shaper of ideas', and guides the mental activity of the individual. Language thus provides a framework or filter through which we conceive nature and environmental events. The manner in which stimuli are categorised and organised by each person is, Whorf claimed, largely determined by the linguistic system he has available. Human conceptualisation reflects the fact that individuals are 'party to an agreement' to organise experience in a way which occurs in the pattern of language. Thus Whorf regarded the structure of language as largely determining the structure of thought.

The nineteenth-century tradition, by which thought and culture are seen as being closely intertwined, is extended in the works of Levi-Bruhl (Cole *et al.*, 1971), who considered that the primitive nature of beliefs and technological developments among non-Western peoples is evidence that their thought processes are fundamentally more primitive than those of Western man. Cole *et al.* cite the work of Robin Horton in refutation of this view. Horton contends that all human groups develop theories as part of an attempt to make sense out of the world they inhabit, and he notes that the manner in which Western people do this, by scientific taxonomies and systems of logic, has much in common with those of African belief systems. In both there is a quest for unity underlying apparent diversity, and both attempt to show that diverse events can be accounted for by reference to a relatively small number of forces. Both go beyond the surface of things, that is beyond common sense, in the explanatory concepts they put forward. Thus the African witch-doctor postulates the malevolent feelings of enemies, in order to account for diseases, while Western man appeals to the machinations of germs. (Even in the West, however, tumours are still described as malevolent, to denote their demonic origin!)

In *The Savage Mind*, Lévi-Strauss (1966) is equally committed to the view that the differences between so-called primitive and modern thought are relatively superficial in nature. All human groups use complex forms of categorisation, or taxonomies, in order to discover some order in the world. The differences in thought between human groups, according to Lévi-Strauss, lie mainly in the detailed forms of the categorical systems that are developed, and are thus comparatively minor. Among primitive tribes, taxonomies are sometimes formed on the basis of the appearance of objects, or, sometimes, according to their function or to their supposed origins. Western scientific communities are more prone to categorise on the basis of abstractions of items or of their components, or of their properties : things that are not apparent to the non-scientific observer. Lévi-Strauss notes that the categorical systems of so-called primitive people can be extremely elaborate. For example, one tribe he describes has over 5000 item terms for various species of flora and fauna. The items encompassed in systems of classification used by primitive people are by no means restricted to those having a practical function. In this respect the manner in which primitive groups may conceive and classify reality is at least as 'intellectual' or even 'academic', in being detached from purely pragmatic considerations, as are the thought-systems of Western man. Lévi-Strauss denies that people who manifest a low level of material and technological development are necessarily restricted in their thought processes, and he cites the Australian aborigines as an instance of a human group simultaneously manifesting extreme primitiveness of material development and extraordinary sophistication in development of social customs, beliefs and fashions.

Cross-cultural differences are reflected in a variety of ways in children's learning. However, as Levine (1970) points out, various differences between investigators in their theoretical approaches and in their methods make it difficult to compare data on thinking and learning in different cultures. Another problem is that relatively few studies have directly investigated learning. There have been a number of cross-cultural comparisons of intelligence-test scores, and, generally, children from technologically advanced cultures score higher. Such differences probably reflect the fact that the tests tend to emphasise particular kinds of achievements valued by the kind of society in which the test was constructed, and do not necessarily indicate any fundamental differences in the mechanisms or cognitive processes underlying human learning. As in the case of differences between social classes within a society, some cross-cultural differences in performance are caused by motivational and attitudinal factors. Thus Gay and Cole (1967) found that among the children of the Kpelle tribe in north Africa limited school achievement reflected the fact that unquestioning acceptance of authority is seen as socially desirable, active enquiring and questioning being very strongly discouraged by the elders of the tribe. The child who deviates from the customary manner of doing something is likely to be punished. Similarly, it has been observed among children in Guatemala that obedience and passivity are so much the rule that a test situation in which children were expected to find the answer to questions represented an entirely new experience for them. Ordinarily, answers to questions were given to the school pupils, and it was expected that they would memorise them.

Evidence from cross-cultural studies indicates that not only the precise content of learning but also the broad cognitive strategies that learners adopt may be influenced by the kind of culture and environment to which a child is exposed. Thus Cole *et al.* found that among the Kpelle, for whom linguistic communication is largely confined to social and ritual functions and is little used for everyday practical purposes such as in agriculture or in house construction, children were very poor at giving reasons or explaining how they arrived at the answer to problems. On the other hand, Kpelle individuals performed much better than Americans at a task requiring leaves to be sorted into piles that distinguished between vines and trees, objects that form a familiar part of the Kpelle environment. In so far as learning depends on the ability to make distinctions, what is learned is likely to depend on the manner in which an individual discriminates between items. This, in turn, is largely determined by the kinds of classification and categorical systems used in the culture to which an individual is exposed in childhood.

7.5.1 *Do non-literate people have superior memorising ability?*

Many observers have drawn attention to the existence of excellent memorising or rote-learning abilities in non-literate people, and Cole *et al.* quote Bartlett's conclusion that high achievement at tasks of pure memorisation is associated with 'a mental life having relatively few interests, all somewhat concrete in character, and no one of which is dominant' (Bartlett, 1932, p. 264). Bartlett considered that 'this state of affairs in mental organisation', making extremely accurate and detailed memory possible, is related to the social organisation of an individual's culture.

To test the ability of non-literate Kpelle children on rote-learning tasks Cole *et al.* devised a procedure in which subjects were shown a series of objects, one at a time, and then tested for recall. It was found that children at the age of six performed almost as well as ten-year-olds, that their initial performance was roughly equivalent to that of American children of similar age, but did not improve so much as a function of repeated trials. Kpelle children who had received some years of formal education performed better than those with no education. Generally, the view that non-literate children have better rote-learning abilities than educated individuals, implicit in Bartlett's statement, received no support from the results obtained by Cole and his colleagues. However, it is conceivable that the unfamiliar testing situation may have contributed to the relatively poor performance by individuals from the primitive society.

Cole and his colleagues also carried out a number of experiments designed to investigate differences between children from literate and non-literate cultures in some aspects of transfer of training among learned skills. They were interested in the extent to which learning one kind of skill or problem makes it easier to learn a related skill. Generally speaking, American children were more likely to impose various kinds of organisation on the materials to be learned, and this led to bigger practice effects. On the whole American children were more likely than the others to be able to form strategies based on linguistic mediation. This produced larger amounts of transfer in a number of learning tasks. Correspondingly, non-literate children showed less 'learning to learn' than children who had attended school at a task requiring the ability to discriminate between objects on the basis of colour, ignoring irrelevant dimensions. In a discrimination task situation requiring a reversal shift (see chapter 5), performance of older Kpelle children and adults matched that of younger American children, indicating an absence of the verbal mediating processes that improve performance in a variety of problem-solving situations.

7.5.2 *Cultural differences in aggressive behaviour*

Some research has been undertaken to investigate cultural differences in opportunities for learning aggressive patterns of behaviour. Minturn and Lambert (1964), who measured the extent to which parents allow or encourage aggressive actions in their children, found that Mexican parents placed considerably greater restrictions on aggressive activities and fighting in their children than did the American parents living in a New England community. The American parents actively encouraged their children to behave aggressively when attacked, and were more permissive of aggression than parents from any of the Indian, Japanese, Philippine, Kenyan and Mexican samples that were observed. Levine (1970) describes a number of findings that are consistent with the view that in developing countries the more modern or progressive parents tend to be more permissive of their children's aggressive acts against other children. These findings are consistent with the earlier observation (Whiting and Child, 1953) that parents who are careful to keep strictly to the mores and conventions of their culture tend to be more severe than others in child-upbringing. On the whole, however, although there have been numerous studies of cross-cultural differences in child-rearing, it is very difficult to tease out clear cause–effect relationships between observed differences in child behaviour and achievement and in the numerous ways along which styles of life vary between different cultures.

REFERENCES

Bartlett, F. C. (1932). *Remembering*, University Press, Cambridge

Bernstein, B. (1961). Social structure, language, and learning. *Educ. Res.* iii, 163–76

Bernstein, B. (1962). Social class, linguistic codes and grammatical elements. *Lang. Speach* v, 221–40

Biggs, J. B. (1968. *Information and Human Learning*, Cassell Australia, Melbourne

Brandis, W., and Henderson, D. (1970). *Social Class, Language and Communication*, Routledge & Kegan Paul, London

Cole, M., Gay, J., Glick, J. A., and Sharp, D. W. (1971). *The Cultural Context of Learning and Thinking*, Basic Books, New York

Curry, R. L. (1962). The effect of socio-economic status on the scholastic achievement of sixth-grade children. *Br. J. educ. Psychol.* xxxii, 46–9

Dale, P. S. (1972). *Language Development: Structure and Function*, Dryden Press, Hinsdale, Illinois

DeFleur, M. L., and DeFleur, L. B. (1967). The relative contribution of television as a learning source for children's occupational knowledge. Am. soc. *Rev.* xxxii, 777–89

Douglas, J. W. B. (1964). *The Home and the School*, MacGibbon & Kee, St Albans

Douglas, J. W. B., Ross, J. M., and Simpson, H. R. (1968). *All Our Future*, Peter Davies, London

Eels, K. W., Davis, A., Havighurst, R., Herrick, V., and Tyler, R. (1951). *Intelligence and Cultural Differences*, University Press, Chicago

Ellis, N. R. (1970). Memory processes in retardates and normals: theoretical and empirical considerations. In N. R. Ellis (ed.), *International Review of Research in Mental Retardation*, vol. 4

Estes, W. K. (1970). *Learning Theory and Mental Development*, Academic Press, New York

Gay, J., and Cole, M. (1967). *The New Mathematics and an Old Culture*. Holt, Rinehart & Winston, New York

Guildford, J. P. (1967). *The Nature of Human Intelligence*, McGraw-Hill, New York

Harvey, O. J., Hunt, D. E., and Schroder, H. M. (1961). *Conceptual Systems and Personality Organization*, Wiley, New York

Harvey, O. J., Prather, M., White, B. J., and Hoffmeister, J. K. (1968). Teacher's beliefs, classroom atmosphere and student behavior. *Am. educ. Res. J.* lvi, 264–9

Havighurst, R. J. (1964). *The Public Schools of Chicago*, The Board of Education of the City of Chicago

Hess, R. D. (1970). Social class and ethnic influences on socialization. In P. H. Mussen (ed.), *Carmichael's Manual of Child Psychology*, 3rd edn, vol. 2, Wiley, New York

Hess, R. D., and Shipman, V. C. (1968). Maternal attitudes towards the school and the role of the pupil: some social class comparisons. In A. H. Passow (ed.), *Developing Programs for the Educationally Disadvantaged*, Teachers College Press, New York

Howe, M. J. A. (1967). Consolidation in short-term memory as a function of rehearsal. *Psychon. Sci.* vii, 355–6

Howe, M. J. A. (1970). *An Introduction to Human Memory*, Harper & Row, New York

Howe, M. J. A. (1972). *Understanding School Learning: a New Look at Educational Psychology*, Harper & Row, New York

Jackson, B. (1964). *Streaming: an Educational System in Miniature*, Routledge & Kegan Paul, London

Jackson, B., and Marsden, D. (1962). *Education and the Working Class*, Routledge & Kegan Paul, London

Jensen, A. R. (1969). How much can we boost I.Q.'s and scholastic achievement? *Harv. educ. Rev.* xxxix, 1–123

Kagan, J. (1965). Reflection-impulsivity: the generality and dynamics of conceptual tempo. In J. D. Krumboltz (ed.), *Learning and the Educational Process*, Rand McNally, Chicago

Kagan, J. (1970). On class differences in early development. In V. H. Denenberg (ed.), *Education of the Infant and Young Child*, Academic Press, New York

Kagan, J. (1973). Cross-cultural perspectives on early development. Mimeographed article, Harvard University

Kagan, J., and Tulkin, R. R. (1971). Social class differences in child rearing during the first year. In H. R. Schaffer (ed.), *The Origin of Human Social Relations*, Academic Press, New York

Kellmer Pringle, M. L., Butler, N. R., and Davis, R. (1966). *Eleven Thousand Seven-year-olds*, Longmans, Harlow

Lawton, D. (1968). *Social Class, Language and Education*, Routledge & Kegan Paul

Levine, R. A. (1970). Cross-cultural study in child psychology. In P. H. Mussen (ed.), *Carmichael's Manual of Child Psychology*, 3rd edn, vol. 2, Wiley, New York

Lévi-Strauss, C. (1966). *The Savage Mind*, University Press, Chicago.

Marjoribanks, K. (1972). Environment, social class, and mental abilities. *J. educ. Psychol.* lxiii, 103–9

Miller, G. W. (1970). Factors in school achievement and social class. *J. educ. Psychol.* lxi, 260–9

Minturn, L., and Lambert, W. W. (1964). *Mothers of Six Cultures: Antecedents of Child Rearing*, Wiley, New York

Newson, J., and Newson, E. (1968). Some social differences in the process of childrearing. In J. Gould (ed.), *Penguin Social Sciences Survey 1968*, Penguin, Harmondsworth

O'Connor, N., and Hermelin, B. (1963). *Speech and Thought in Severe Subnormality*, Pergamon, Oxford

Robinson, W. P. (1965). The elaborated code in working-class language. *Lang. Speech* viii, 243–52

Sewell, W. H., and Haller, A. O. (1956). Social class and the personality adjustment of the child. *Sociometry* xix, 114–25

Snow, C. E. (1972). Mothers' speech to children learning language. *Child Dev.* xliii, 549–63

Staats, A. W. (1971). *Child Learning, Intelligence, and Personality*, Harper & Row, New York

Vernon, P. E. (1969). *Intelligence and Cultural Endowment*, Methuen, London

Whiting, J. W. M., and Child, I. (1953). *Child Training and Personality*, Yale University Press, New Haven, Connecticut

Whorf, B. L. (1956). *Language*, Wiley, New York

Zunich, M. A. (1961). A study of relationships between child-rearing attitudes and maternal behaviour. *J. exp. Educ.* xxx, 231–41

8

Accelerating Learning: Enrichment and Compensatory Education

The preceding chapters have illustrated some of the ways in which each child gains a progressively widening repertoire of the habits and skills that help determine the kind of individual he will become as an adult. While a broad concern with the factors that influence learning is clearly widespread among parents and teachers, there has also been interest in more specific and highly focused expressions of this concern. In particular, considerable attention has been paid to attempts to bring about modifications in the course of learning that are larger and more sweeping than those encountered where the customary patterns of upbringing and education are in force. Most of the concern is related to one of two questions. Firstly, is it possible to accelerate learning in children of normal or above normal ability, in order to give them what the authors of one book on the subject term 'a superior mind'? Secondly, is it possible to devise educational schemes that will adequately compensate individuals who for one reason or another have failed to learn some of the abilities that are generally regarded as essential for coping with the tasks required for leading a relatively independent and well-regulated life in the existing world?

Each of these problems raises a number of further issues. Some are of a scientific or practical nature, concerning, for instance, the feasibility of certain behavioural changes or the effectiveness of programmes designed to induce the acquisition of particular skills. Other issues raise broader psychological and social questions. For instance, what are the effects on a child's personality of concentrating upon the acquisition of a narrowly restricted range of capabilities?

Attempts to accelerate or enrich learning have not produced any simple universal prescriptions, and they are unlikely to do so. From time to time one hears of various 'discoveries' that are supposed to revolutionise learning. For example, a doctor in South Africa claimed to have found that providing oxygen enrichment to embryonic human infants produces substantial increases in subsequent intelligence. Others have claimed that people can acquire foreign-language abilities and academic knowledge by learning from a tape-recorder played during sleep. Suffice it to say there is no solid evidence at all to back claims of this nature. It has also been suggested that some drugs can influence learning. It is certainly true that any of a number of drugs can affect a person's alertness or state of arousal, and since these influence the individual's ability to concentrate on what he is attempting to learn, such drugs will affect performance at learning tasks. However, it seems unlikely that it will be possible in the immediate future to produce a drug that has a specific and direct positive influence on learning as such, and that can be administered on a frequent and regular basis with no unwanted side effects.

8.1 EXTRAORDINARY LEARNERS

If we look into the lives of individuals who are extraordinary in the degree to which they have profited from learning, we find no single factors that are quite so dramatic in their effects as the phenomena described above have been claimed to be. What we do observe in the lives of many such people are home backgrounds providing a relatively rich store of the kinds of experience that we have noted in earlier chapters to bring about the acquisition of skills, knowledge and the habitual activities required for the prolonged attention and practice that underlie many learned abilities. Biographical information shows that the early backgrounds of so-called geniuses have often contained a variety of features that give enriched opportunities for learning. Typically, not only are there numerous books in the home, but other members of the family can be observed to be in the habit of reading them and deriving pleasure thereby, and to show attentive interest and give capable help or encouragement when the child attempts to imitate the adult models by using books himself. Furthermore, the child typically spends time in the presence of adults who are capable of using language to communicate in an abstract and precise manner, are willing to spend time communicating to the child, and are able to do so in a way that matches the child's growing linguistic capacities.

These qualities of the home environment are, as we have noticed, largely those previously mentioned as contributing to the more favourable circumstances for certain kinds of learning that tend to be more often encountered in middle-class than in working-class homes. As in the case of statements about class differences, however, certain qualifications are necessary. By no means all individuals who are apparently exposed to the enriched circumstances we have described grow up to be noticeably adept at learning, and, conversely, by no means all geniuses are found to have had childhoods abundant in apparent enrichment. On the whole, however, it does appear that most individuals who have been extraordinarily successful at some learned activites were exposed early in life to circumstances containing rich opportunities for learning. Such differences between the backgrounds of normal and extraordinary individuals need not be qualitative; rather, we find quantitative differences in, say, the amount of verbal communication between parent and child, at an early age, or in the sensitivity with which adult models are able to act in ways that match the child's existing capacities.

Studies of the childhood of talented men do not support the notion that the first few years of life are invariably critical, and some great thinkers appear to have spent their early years in environments that have been remarkably barren of intellectual stimulation. However, talented adults who were prodigies as infants are almost always found to have been exposed to unusually intensive tuition, often by a parent, during their earliest years. Jeremy Bentham, for instance, received careful and regular instruction from his father in Latin, from the age of three. Macaulay, who produced a world history at the age of six, received similar intensive early training, and Pascal's father devoted all his time to the education of his son from the time when the child reached the age of three. Goethe, Grotius and Leibnitz all experienced devoted attention to their education from earliest childhood. Like Pascal, John Stuart Mill was educated at home by his father, and at three years he began to learn Greek. Engelmann and Engelmann (1971), who are at pains to emphasise the role of environmental factors in contributing to achievement, write that in Mill's case:

> Granted his performance is good, but notice the characteristics of (his) environment.... The environment works throughout the child's waking hours; it takes pains to ensure that the child has learned his lessons; it carefully reduces the possibility of mistakes; it establishes a clear pattern for using what is learned; it forces the child when necessary; it establishes firm models for him to follow. This is an environment that will succeed with *any* healthy infant (Engelmann and Engelmann, 1971, pp. 35–6).

We can appreciate the force of these statements even if we hesitate to accept the inevitability of the conclusion.

8.2 ENRICHMENT OR PRESSURE?

These intensive regimes can certainly inflict damage on a vulnerable young child. Norbert Wiener, the inventor of the science of cybernetics, suffered great misery as a result of his father's successful attempts to impart him with intellectual gifts, and Wiener has described the case of a contemporary child prodigy, William Sidis, whose family's efforts to provide intensive early educational experiences led him not only to total rejection of his family but to a denial of his own intellectual abilities (Engelmann and Engelmann, 1971).

There is little doubt that intensive early childhood education can have adverse effects, if it faces the child with burdensome pressures, or if concentration on the acquisition of specialised kinds of abilities results in the child being denied the kinds of experiences necessary for normal emotional and social development. However, not all forms of accelerated learning need have adverse effects. Durkin (1966), who studied children who learned to read unusually early, did not observe psychological abnormalities in such children, and she found that children who learned to read at an early age maintained their lead in achievement over children of the same measured intelligence who did not commence learning to read until they went to school. Durkin did not find that those children who learned to read early were unusually bored or confused at school. She insists, however, that if a child is to profit from reading skills at an early age, he must first be conscious of a desire to read. Young children are much more responsive to assistance with learning to read that results from their own expressed interest than from their parents' ambitions for them.

The possibility of accelerated learning in young children raises a number of separate problems for which there are no straightforward answers. On the one hand (Howe, 1972) there are people who argue that even if acceleration of intellectual growth through enriched opportunities for early learning is possible, it is none the less undesirable. They would claim that childhood is best filled with play, in which the stress and pressures imposed by efforts towards early education are absent; that precocious intellectual development in the absence of parallel attention to social and emotional learning may be harmful, that Western societies already suffer from an overvaluation of intellectual skills at the expence of tenderness, warmth and other affective components of human personality, and that the child whose intellectual abilities are far ahead of those possessed by other children of his own age may find it difficult to interact socially with others. On the other hand, advocates of measures to provide enriched opportunities for early learning can state with some confidence that there is no clear evidence for the inevitability of any of these dire consequences. It is certainly true that a parent's desire for a child to be successful *can* result in actions leading to the child's feeling pushed or pressured, but there is no reason why this has always to be the case whenever enrichment and unusual degrees of encouragement are provided. Indeed many children suffer considerably from the boredom of unfilled time, and would not only appreciate increased opportunities for interesting activities, but would gain by the greater resourcefulness that comes with the acquisition of skills such as reading.

8.3 LEARNING AND HUMAN PLASTICITY

Some of the problems that are involved in attempts to accelerate the course of learning are also encountered in enterprises that involve the introduction of enriched experiences in order to provide compensatory education. Basic to both concerns are some broad questions about the plasticity or modifiability of human behaviour. In addition to the various enquiries that were raised in the Introduction, concerning the extent to which different kinds of behaviour are governed by learning, there are further problems relating to variations in the timing of necessary experiences. For instance, are there critical periods during which certain abilities must be learned if they are to be acquired at all?

Throughout this book we have stressed the fact that the outcomes of experience are cumulative. That is, what is learned on one occasion builds on previously learned capacities. One finds an explicit emphasis on the cumulative nature of learned acquisitions in the writings of A. W. Staats, which we have surveyed in previous chapters. Bloom (1964), who reviewed a great deal of evidence on the predictability for adult scores of various childhood measures of intelligence, personality and physical characteristics, concluded that environmental variations have their greatest effects on human characteristics at the period of most rapid change, that is to say, in the case of intelligence, the earliest years of life. The data collected by Bloom have been interpreted as indicating that 50 per cent of adult intelligence is achieved by the age of four, and that if a child lives in a culturally impoverished environment for the first four years of his life, the loss in intellectual achievement may be irreversible. However, these conclusions are largely based on observed correlations between scores obtained at different ages, and there is no conclusive evidence that early deprivation must always lead to low adult achievement.

The timing of certain kinds of learning does seem to be important. In chapter 4, for instance, we noted that some findings by H. R. Schaffer and others about the social learning that occurs when mother and child interact are consistent with the suggestion that bonds of attachment need to be formed during early childhood, if normal emotional development is to take place. It was also pointed out in the Introduction that providing visual enrichment can accelerate the acquisition of visually guided reaching in the infant, but, if the visual stimuli are provided at a period in development during which the child normally spends time in gazing at his hands, such stimuli can actually impede the acquisition of co-ordinated eye–hand skills. We noted that in the research undertaken by B. L. White and his colleagues at Harvard University, the practical problem raised by this finding was solved by placing attractively patterned coloured mittens on the infants' hands.

These considerations would appear to indicate that we ought to be pessimistic about attempts to provide compensatory education for children who lack the learned skills that have been acquired by most individuals of equivalent age. If all forms of human learning are highly dependent on appropriate timing and the exact sequencing of experiences, it would appear that once an individual becomes retarded in any way, for whatever reason, he is likely to stay that way. Happily, however, there is evidence that even though the impact of learned experiences may be cumulative, not all forms of learning suffer irreversibly from disruption of normal timing and sequencing. Certainly, the child who by the age of three has not learned a particular skill is at a disadvantage compared with the child who has gained the skill, particularly if it is a necessary prerequisite for further important learned abilities. Yet some findings indicate that the vast majority of learned abilities *can* be learned at a much later age than is normal.

8.3.1 *Evidence for plasticity*

Let us consider two kinds of evidence that lend support to the above statement. First are some findings reported by Skeels (1966), who studied

American children committed as infants to an orphanage in the mid 1930s. As we previously explained, children reared in orphanage environments that provide neither the care and adult attention mothers normally give to their children, nor, perhaps less importantly, the opportunities for play and for a variety of experiences that are available in most families, are found by the age of a year or so to be extremely retarded in many respects. For instance they first smile at a later age than is normal, they vocalise less, they show retarded motor development and fail to exhibit normal attachment behaviour and fear of strangers. Skeels removed from the orphanage thirteen children, aged around eighteen months, and placed them in a ward containing mentally retarded women who lived in a state school for the mentally handicapped. The children placed there received a great deal of affection and attention from these women. The children's intelligence was tested before admission to the new environment, and again about eighteen months later. By this time they were around three years of age. These children showed average gains of thirty I.Q. points over the eighteen-month period after being removed from the orphanage. A control group selected for comparison purposes, whose I.Q. scores had previously been roughly equivalent, and who remained in the orphanage, had an average loss of twenty-six I.Q. points. A follow-up test was subsequently carried out when the children were six years old, by which time most of the group previously transferred to the ward for mentally retarded women had either returned to the orphanage or had been placed in adoptive homes. The results of the follow-up test showed that these children had maintained their advantage over the others. About twenty years later a further follow-up study was undertaken. It was discovered that the thirteen individuals who as children had been taken from the orphanage and placed in the care of retarded women had achieved occupational and educational status that was representative of the American population as a whole. Thus, each of the thirteen was either self-supporting or married, nine had children, and on average they had completed twelve years of formal schooling. In contrast, of the group of initially comparable children who had remained in the orphanage, only seven were self-supporting or married, only one had children, and, on average, they had completed less than three years of schooling. Their median income was less than half that of the individuals in the other group.

Skeels's findings demonstrate that the adverse effects of deprivation during the first eighteen months of life can be reversed, if the child is transferred to a warmer and more stimulating environment at a relatively low age. An alternative possibility is to bring in more adults. For instance, Saltz (1973) found that a 'foster-grandparent programme' whereby young children in an orphanage received part-time 'mothering' from elderly institutional aides over periods of up to four years led to appreciable increases in I.Q. As Jensen (1969) points out, there may be limits to what can be achieved by changing a child's environment, but nevertheless Skeels's results do make it clear that although the course of learning involves cumulative and sequential factors, the provision of a reasonably enriched environment can adequately compensate for early deprivation, and enable children whose progress has been retarded to catch up to what is normal.

A second body of evidence indicating that apparent retardation related to impoverished early environments need not be permanent has been obtained by Jerome Kagan, from research among Indian children in Guatemala. Kagan (1972) observed the infants living in a very isolated village and noticed that they spent most of their time in the dark interior of their family's thatched-abode hut. The infant usually remained close to the mother, but was rarely played with or spoken to, and had very few objects for play, apart from the occasional orange or ear of corn. The infants were seen to be extremely passive, fearful, very quiet and they smiled little, showing few reactions to visual or auditory stimuli. Observations indicated that the infants were played with or spoken to only 6 per cent of the time, compared with an average 25 per cent for infants in middle-class American homes.

In short, these infants manifested the symptoms of passivity and retardation that are normally associated with extreme deprivation occurring in orphanages where normal attention, affection and environmental stimulation are absent. And yet, by middle childhood, the achievement of children from this village in a variety of activities that depend on learning was by no means poor. Among ten- and eleven-year-olds, litle difference was observed between the Guatemalan children and American children in performance at a task of recognition memory for pictures, although there were very large differences among five- and eight-year-olds (Kagan *et al.*, 1973). Similarly, by the age of eleven, the scores obtained by children from this isolated Guatemalan village at a variety of perception and memory tests were, on the whole, only slightly lower than those of similarly aged American children. Kagan concludes that the intellectual retardation observed during the first year does not have any serious predictive validity for the cognitive functioning of the children later in life.

Both Skeels's and Kagan's findings provide good illustrations of the fact that quite serious forms of retardation occuring early in life are not always irreversible. Perhaps, in the long run, disruptions in the phasing and timing of experiences are less serious than might be expected from the short-term consequences observed by researchers such as White (1971). One writer (Rohwer, 1971) has gone so far as to suggest that many of our implicit assumptions about the appropriate sequencing of educational experiences are misplaced, and he argues that we should judge the effectiveness of schooling practices by the degree to which they assist the child in tasks outside the school. Rohwer notes that reading instruction usually commences when the child starts school, and that success in reading is normally regarded as a major desideratum for judging educational achievement. Yet, he claims, there is no compelling evidence that delaying the teaching of reading by several years would make it harder to learn to read, in the long run. He also states that there is no strong evidence that reading is the principal means of acquiring useful information during the first five years at school. This is certainly a controversial point of view. Many young children derive great pleasure from reading, and it is difficult to believe that they derive no benefit from what they read. To be fair to Rohwer, his intention is not to suggest that no young children be allowed to learn to read, but that we should be willing to question the assumption that it is necessary or valuable for *every* child to read at an early stage in life. To support his case Rohwer presents some interesting findings from a cross-cultural study of achievement in mathematics, in which a mathematics test was administered to thirteen-year-old children from twelve different nations. They were also given a test measuring their attitudes towards school, and data were obtained concerning the children's age of entry to school. It emerged that there was no significant correlation between age of entry to school and mathematics achievement; that is to say, children who had attended school for seven years did no better than children who had started school considerably later. In addition, there was a large negative correlation (rho$= -0.72$) between attitudes to school and the number of years over which a child had attended. It appears likely that spending many early years at school may have some adverse effects on a child's motivation to learn. Findings such as this lead Rohwer to suggest that it is conceivable that formal schooling for children aged less than eleven or twelve might do more harm than good. He thinks that prior to this age such formal education may result in decreased plasticity, and in a lower final level of intellectual capacity. However, even Rohwer baulks at the possibility of entirely abandoning formal schooling prior to adolescence, and he finally suggests that the need is for changes in the direction of giving the child 'repeated experiences of gratification resulting from intellectual activity' (Rohwer, 1971, p. 338).

8.4 ISSUES IN COMPENSATORY EDUCATION

The past few years have seen the development and evaluation of a number of attempts to provide compensatory experiences for educationally deprived children, mostly in the U.S.A. Concern with profound social problems, together with the availability of evidence that young children can gain appreciably from intensive pre-school experiences, led to the well-known 'Head Start' programmes, under which title there were a large number of endeavours, common to all of which was an effort to provide children from culturally deprived environments with extra stimulation in order to counteract their lack of the experiences which a middle-class child has as a matter of course and which are necessary if a child is to profit from school education.

Although it has been suggested that compensatory education in the U.S.A. has failed to achieve what was expected of it, it is by no means true that all compensatory programmes have been ineffective. Generally speaking, intensive pre-school experiences have led to gains across a wide range of abilities, providing ample evidence that pre-school compensatory education can be effective. Critics have been quick to point out that not all of the gains have been permanent, but it is clearly naïve to expect that they should be. It is hardly surprising that an individual living in a culturally impoverished environment should continue to require enrichment over a period of years, if the initial advantage gained by a short Head Start programme lasting, say, one summer, is to be maintained. A deprived child may certainly benefit considerably from such a brief 'shot in the arm' but if he then returns to the identical environmental conditions that led to retardation in the first place, he is unlikely to maintain the benefit unless further 'shots' are subsequently administered, at least throughout the early years of school.

What are the specific goals and contents of the more successful of the pre-school programmes designed to compensate for environmental deprivation? Broadly speaking, their aim has been to teach skills and habits required for a child to benefit as fully as possible from school education. Some children start school without having acquired the habit of giving sustained attention to the sound of the adult voice. Consequently they cannot understand the information or instructions that are conveyed. Others have not learned to discriminate between small visual patterns, and this is necessary for deciphering letters and reading. Children who start school with the basic skills underlying these activities not only have an initial advantage in performance at school, but consequently receive to a greater extent than others the various kinds of reinforcement that are contingent on competence.

Basic to many of the differences between young children in readiness for school learning are variations in the ability to use language as a means of communication. In previous chapters we have noted that there are differences associated with social class in the effectiveness with which individuals can communicate explicit and finely differentiated meanings to people outside the family. In the United States the problems of communication are complicated by the existence of minority dialects, one outcome being that even when the language a minority-group child uses is not impoverished as such, compared with the language spoken at school the mere fact that it is different may create major obstacles to effective communication. In these circumstances a child will receive the full benefit of formal schooling only if he first learns to communicate in the language that is used in the school environment, or if the teachers learn to communicate in a language that is familiar to the child. A disadvantage to the latter solution is that it may cease to be effective when the child leaves the school in order to seek employment or more advanced forms of education or training, for which standard English is essential.

8.5 RECENT COMPENSATORY PROGRAMMES

8.5.1 *The Bereiter and Engelmann curriculum*

Most of the compensatory programmes that have been developed give considerable emphasis to the acquisition of linguistic skills. A good example, and one that is perhaps more extreme than most in its emphasis on linguistic factors as the major ingredients of success at school, is the programme developed by Bereiter and Engelmann (1966). They argue that cultural deprivation can be treated as being practically synonymous with language deprivation, and they consider that the lack of verbal learning, and in particular the lack of the kinds of learning that have to be transmitted through language, is mainly responsible for most deficits in learned achievements. The programme they developed is highly structured and designed to correct specifically defined deficiencies. Among the linguisitic deficits common among culturally deprived children Bereiter and Engelmann draw attention to the omission of articles, prepositions, conjunctions and short verbs, failure to understand the function of the word 'not', inability to produce or understand the implications of plural forms of words, inability to differentiate between tenses, failure to use 'he', 'she', and 'it' in appropriate contexts, non-comprehension of many common prepositions and conjunctions, for example 'Next to' and 'between', inability to describe one's own actions in words, and failure to appreciate that two or more different words can both describe one object. Not all of these factors are necessarily indicative of impoverished kinds of language, but even when they merely reflect deviations from standard English the user who is not *au fait* with the latter is clearly at a disadvantage in a conventional school environment.

Bereiter and Engelmann make five major assumptions about disadvantaged children. These are: first, that by the age of four years some children are seriously behind others in the acquisition of capacities required for school success; second, that if they do not catch up in the acquisition of the necessary capacities they will meet continued failure at school; third, that they need to progress at a faster than normal rate in order to match normal progress; fourth, that a pre-school compensatory programme that attempts to provide a broad spectrum of experiences cannot be expected to lead to abnormally high rates of learning; and fifth, that selectivity is therefore essential in the objectives of an enrichment programme. Since it is unrealistic to expect that a short-term course will produce above-normal gains in all areas of competence at once, a broad, well-rounded programme is ruled out.

The language-training system developed by Bereiter and Engelmann contains considerable drill and repetition. It is assumed that only by systematic and lengthy practice can linguistic habits be acquired, and accordingly use is made of intensive periods of drill, during which the children continuously practice using specific language forms. There is no emphasis on free expression as such; the purpose is simply to acquire usable skills through repetitious practice, in which children are carefully trained to make use of language.

Bereiter and Engelmann's pre-school programme is based on a large number of explicitly specified behavioural objectives. These include: ability to use the following prepositions correctly in statements describing arrangements of objects: on, under, over, between – for example, 'where is the pencil?' 'The pencil is under the book'; ability to use 'not' in deductions, for example 'If the square is little, what else do you know about it?' 'It is not red'; ability to count objects correctly up to ten, and ability to distinguish printed words from pictures (Bereiter and Engelmann, 1966, pp. 48–9). To achieve these objectives the teachers are instructed to use a number of specific strategies. Once more, the requirements are made explicit. Teachers are told to adhere to a rigid and repetitive pattern of presentation, to require children to speak loudly and clearly, to accent basic language patterns and conventions by clapping, to phrase statements rhythmically, to use plenty of repetition and numerous different examples, and to dramatise the value of learning wherever possible.

Some of the measured outcomes of Bereiter and Engelmann's curriculum have been extremely favourable. Bereiter (1968) reports above average scores in reading and in arithmetic by children from disadvantaged homes who were exposed to the programme, and favourable results of the Bereiter and Engelmann programme have also been reported by D. P. Weikart who observed I.Q. gains of around thirty points over a one-year period Farnham-Diggory (1972) discusses a report concerning three groups of children who had been in the programme for two years. Over the two years each group made gains, averaging ten, twenty-five and twelve I.Q. points, and all three groups were achieving above average levels of reading and spelling.

8.5.2. *Alternative compensatory programmes*

Some critics have argued that the highly intensive and rigid features of the system may place unnecessary pressure on young children. An alternative pre-school compensatory programme, which like that of Bereiter and Engelmann emphasises language skills, but which is much less highly structured and less likely to exert pressure on children has been developed by Blank and Solomon (1968). Their goal is to help children use language to communicate effectively, and they are less concerned than Bereiter and Engelmann with correct grammar and articulation, and more concerned that children be helped to think, reflect and make inferences. Blank and Solomon, whose ideas display the clear influence of Bernstein, emphasise the child's acquisition of the ability to use language in organising his environment. They consider it important to encourage the child to question, to probe and to investigate. In Blank and Solomon's programme children are asked to imagine what would happen in a variety of hypothetical situations. For instance, the following question is asked: 'Where would this doll be if it fell from the table?' The child is thus confronted with situations in which he has to use language, and the teacher deliberately avoids using gestures and other non-verbal cues that might have the effect of making speech partially redundant.

To test the effectiveness of the Blank and Solomon curriculum an experiment was designed in which the experimental group received individual sessions for about twenty minutes per day, over a period of four months. Members of a control group spent an equivalent amount of time in individual sessions at which an adult was present, but they played at will and did not receive any formal training. It was found that the experimental group made an average gain of fourteen I.Q. points (from 98 to 112) compared with a two-point gain for the control group. Other positive changes were observed among children in the experimental group. For example, some who were previously withdrawn and never talked at school became more lively, and began to communicate clearly and coherently. It appears that the Blank and Solomon programme, in common with the one devised by Bereiter and Engelmann, can successfully accelerate the acquisition in young children of abilities that are necessary (although possibly not sufficient) if they are to gain the full benefit of attending school.

Alternative programmes have also met with some success in helping disadvantaged children. For instance, the Ypsilanti Preschool Curriculum Demonstration Project, which is based partly on 'verbal bombardment', has been evaluated by Weikart and Lambie (1969), who found it produced I.Q. gains comparable to those obtained from the Bereiter and Engelmann Language Training Curriculum. Weikart and Lambie describe a course developed by D. M. Gagahan and G. A. Gagahan which is in one respect very similar to that of Blank and Solomon, in that it puts into practice the suggestion that children need to gain practice in talking in 'low-context' situations, wherein the speaker has little or no shared background with his audience, so that the elaborated-code style of speech described by Bernstein becomes the sole effective means of communication. Typical of the techniques used in this curriculum is one called 'telephone', in which children who cannot see each other work in pairs, and are given a box containing pieces of material that vary in texture, colour and pattern. Each child selects a piece of material and then describes it to the other child, who attempts to choose the equivalent piece from his own box.

Intensive forms of pre-school education are undoubtedly expensive and there may be alternative means of providing some of their functions. Some encouraging findings have been obtained from measuring the effects of watching the *Sesame Street* TV productions. Other promising ventures include attempts to help mothers to provide more effective experiences or tuition at home (see, for example, Weikart and Lambie, 1969).

8.6 TEACHING MACHINES

A decade ago, most answers to queries about the possibility of devising ways of accelerating learning either in normal and above-normal children or in deprived individuals would have included references to Teaching Machines or 'programmed learning'. B. F. Skinner (1954) had strongly advocated the use of such systems, whereby what is to be learned is divided into very small steps (usually known as frames), each of which is followed by a question. The learner attempts to answer each question, and thus frequent active responses are ensured. Subsequently, the correct answer is provided, giving feedback to the student about his progress, and providing the encouragement engendered by being most often correct, so long as the programme is designed to proceed at a rate ensuring that the student makes few errors. Various kinds of mechanical devices, for which teaching machine is a generic name, have been used to present materials organised in this manner. It needs to be emphasised that the role of the machine as such is limited to that of making available the instructional material as conveniently as possible. The machine does not have any magical qualities. Nevertheless Skinner suggested that programmed-learning methods of presenting material would bring about great improvements over the results of conventional methods of teacher instruction, which he considered to be remarkably inefficient.

We have now had time to realise that teaching machines can perform no miracles, and that their function is, at best, to transmit carefully structured instructional sequences that contain provision for active responses and for immediate feedback. In many circumstances such devices can be very useful (for further reading see Annett, 1966; Howe,

1972; Kay *et al.*, 1968). However, some of the advantages brought about by dividing the content of instruction into small steps may be offset by the resulting inflexibility of format compared with materials presented in book form. Developments such as 'branching', whereby alternative sequences of frames are provided, so that rather than each individual having to work through an identical sequence of instructional frames, he can be directed either to miss out frames covering knowledge he already possesses or to enter 'branch' sequences, which repeat more thoroughly any items that give trouble in the basic programme, do something to bring about greater accomodation to the varying requirements of different individuals than is available in the simple kinds of sequences originally advocated by Skinner. Even so, it should be emphasised that by no means all kinds of knowledge can be acquired by a learner more efficiently when they are made available in a programmed-learning format than when they are presented in conventional prose form. Pressey and Kinzer (1964) carried out an experiment that involved reproducing the content of a programmed sequence devised to teach introductory psychology to adult students, in the form of a much shorter typed summary. It was found that students who merely read the summary achieved equally high scores on a subsequently administered test as those students who learned from the programme, despite the fact that, on average, the latter group took five times as long as the former. It is conceivable that students who used programmed learning gained in ways not measured by the test. Nevertheless, a finding such as this illustrates the fact that one cannot decide on the effectiveness of any instructional method or procedure without taking into account its appropriateness for the particular children who are expected to learn from it.

8.7 COMPUTER-ASSISTED INSTRUCTION

The development of computer-assisted instruction (C.A.I.) offers the eventual possibility of providing curricula that are extremely flexible in form and adaptive to the particular requirements of individual learners. Patrick Suppes predicts that 'in a few more years millions of schoolchildren will have access to what Philip of Macedon's son Alexander enjoyed as a royal prerogative: the personal services of a tutor as well-informed and responsive as Aristotle' (Suppes, 1971, p. 257).

Individual instruction becomes possible when computers are used because they can be programmed to store information about a child's previous learning, his failures and successes, and to make use of this knowledge about performance in the past as a basis for selecting the information, concepts or problems that should next be made available to the learner. In a typical system using C.A.I., young children sit at terminals on which there are screens displaying information transmitted from the computer. Next to the screen, which is a cathode-ray tube, there is a typewriter keyboard, to be used by the child for making his responses. In addition, each child is given a light pen, enabling him to make simple responses by touching items presented on the screen. This is especially useful with very young children, although even at pre-school ages individuals can quite easily learn to make use of the key-board (Suppes, 1971). In addition to the visual-display apparatus there is equipment for presenting information by ear. Suppes considers that the capacity to present spoken messages is extremely important in the education of young children, especially at points where a child may experience difficulties, and that such auditory provision is a crucial element in C.A.I. that is missing from teaching machines or alternative instruction techniques that do not have access to computers. Atkinson (1968) notes that C.A.I.-using methods developed at Stanford University have been successfully applied to the teaching of reading to children from culturally disadvantaged homes in their first year at school. By the end of one year a group of children who had received computer-assisted reading instruction gained higher scores on a number of reading-achievement tests than did a control group who learned from conventional methods. It is unlikely that this finding was due solely to a 'Hawthorne Effect' (that is, that the C.A.I. group felt that they were receiving special treatment) since the control group also had regular instruction from the computer, but in mathematics.

The strengths of C.A.I. methods lie in their effectiveness in meeting learners' individual requirements. Our present understanding of the processes involved in human learning is far from perfect, but we undoubtedly possess a more accurate body of knowledge about learning than was available to our grandfathers, and the great improvements that have taken place in the effectiveness of educational institutions bear witness to this. Appreciation of the fact that learning is largely dictated by characteristics of the individual is central both to our improved understanding of human learning and to the success of attempts to facilitate learning in infants, children and adults.

REFERENCES

Annett, J. (1966). Programmed learning. In B. M. Foss (ed.), *New Horizons in Psychology*, Penguin, Harmondsworth

Atkinson, R. C. (1968). Computerized instruction and the learning process. *Am. Psychol.* xxiii, 225–31, 235–9

Bereiter, C. (1968). A nonpsychological approach to early compensatory education. In M. Deutch, I. Katz and A. Jensen (eds), *Social Class, Race and Psychological Development*, Holt, Rinehart & Winston, New York

Bereiter, C., and Engelmann, S. (1966). *Teaching Disadvantaged Children in the Preschool*, Prentice-Hall, Englewood Cliffs, New Jersey

Blank, M., and Solomon, F. (1968). A tutorial language program to develop abstract thinking in socially disadvantaged preschool children. *Child Dev.* xxxix, 379–90

Bloom, B. S. (1964). *Stability and Change in Human Characteristics*, Wiley, New York

Durkin, D. (1966). *Children who Read Early*, Teachers College Press, New York

Engelmann S., and Englemann, T. (1971). *Give your Child a Superior Mind*, Simon & Schuster, New York

Farnham-Diggory, S. (1972). *Cognitive Processes in Education: a Psychological Preparation or Teaching and Curriculum Development*, Harper & Row, New York

Howe, M. J. A. (1972). *Understanding School Learning: a New Look at Educational Psychology*, Harper & Row, New York

Jensen, A. R. (1969). How much can we boost I.Q.'s and scholastic achievement? *Harv. educ. Rev.* xxxix, 1–123

Kagan, J. (1972). Do infants think? *Scient. Am.* lxxiv, 76–82

Kagan, J., Klein, R. E., Haith, M. M., and Morrison, F. J. (1973). Memory and meaning in two cultures. *Child Dev.* xliv, 221–3

Kay, H., Dodd, B., and Sime, M. (1968). *Teaching Machines and Programmed Instruction*, Penguin, Harmondsworth

Pressey, S. L., and Kinzer, J. R. (1964). Auto-elucidation without programming. *Psychol. Schools* i, 359–65

Rohwer, W. D. (1971) Prime time for education: early childhood or adolescence? *Harv. educ. Rev.* xli, 316–41

Saltz, R. (1973). Effects of part-time mothering on I.Q. and S.Q. of young institutionalized children. *Child Dev.* xliv, 166–70

Skeels, H. M. (1966). Adult status of children with contrasting early life experiences: a follow-up study. *Monographs of the Society for Research in Child Development*, No. 105

Skinner, B. F. (1954). The science of learning and the art of teaching. *Harv. educ. Rev.*, xxiv, 86–97

Skinner, B. F. (1971). *Beyond Freedom and Dignity*, Knopf, New York

Suppes, P. (1971). The uses of computers in education. In R. C. Atkinson (ed.), *Contemporary Psychology*, Freeman, San Francisco

Weikart, D. P., and Lambie, D. Z. (1969). Early enrichment in infants. In V. H. Denenberg (ed.), *Education of the Infant and Young Child*, Academic Press, New York

White, B. L. (1971), *Human Infants: Experience and Psychological Development*, Prentice-Hall, Englewood Cliffs, New Jersey

Author Index

Subject Index